#MYPRIVACY
#MYRIGHT

PROTECT IT
WHILE YOU CAN

ROBIN M SINGH

PARTRIDGE

Library of Congress Control Number:		2021918332
ISBN:	Hardcover	978-1-5437-6195-5
	Softcover	978-1-5437-6196-2
	eBook	978-1-5437-6194-8

Print information available on the last page.

To order additional copies of this book, contact
Toll Free +65 3165 7531 (Singapore)
Toll Free +60 3 3099 4412 (Malaysia)
orders.singapore@partridgepublishing.com

www.partridgepublishing.com/singapore

CONTENTS

FOREWORD

Living in today's increasingly digital world means constant trade-offs between privacy and convenience when it comes to protecting our personal information. As a prosecutor with the Department of Justice for eleven years, much of it leading a unit dedicated to fighting healthcare and government fraud, I saw firsthand the harm that can result when personal information falls into the wrong hands. Yet it is neither possible nor, for most, desirable in today's society to live a truly private life. A wide range of laws, regulations, and policies attempt to provide a level of protection. But a countless and growing number of examples make clear that they can only do so much – the trade-offs are real and unavoidable. Ultimately, individuals and companies have a responsibility for respecting and protecting privacy.

First, as a prosecutor and now as a professor, I have been fortunate to get to know Robin through his work as well-respected regulatory compliance, privacy, and risk expert. He is a person with a firm understanding of people – what drives them, what they value, and when organizations must act to protect against those who wish to violate the social trust. The perspective he shares throughout this book, *#MyPrivacy*

#MyRight, is one of a person's who not only values business efficiency but also recognizes the importance of people's privileged information as a fundamental human right directly connected to freedom. He is a person who knows not only what organizations can and should do to protect the privacy rights of people, but also that there are things too important to leave to trust.

Robin views privacy as a priceless possession that must be valued and protected, recognizing that personal information can be a weapon when it falls into the wrong hands and that once privacy is compromised, in today's world, it is often impossible to put it back together. Robin urges the reader to be skeptical when trading their prized personal information in exchange for convenience.

As the online and physical world becomes increasingly intertwined, Robin's multi-jurisdictional experience is particularly valuable. It is my hope that Robin's voice will help readers further understand the complexity and depth of this subject he cares so deeply about.

I wish my friend Robin all the very best.

Jacob Elberg Associate Professor Seton Hall University School of Law

Dedication:

To my Mom (Vinita Singh), Dad (Group Captain Madan G Singh),
&
Shree (Joginder S Dadyale), KY (Punita Dadyale)
&
Wify - Chill (Shilpa Uchil), Bani (Shanaya R Singh), and Rajvir R Singh.

GROUND ZERO

We live in a world where governments and organisations realise that data (i.e., information) is the key to remaining in power.

Here is one startling example of the power companies can wield based on the data they collect. A *New York Times* article explained how Target, a major US general merchandise store, could figure out whether a girl was pregnant even before she realised it. Target's baby registry promotion program tracked buying patterns, such as the type of lotion, fragrances, and medication a consumer would buy, and compare them with potential pregnancy symptoms to cross-sell their children's line of merchandise.

In another case, a man filed a lawsuit against a flower shop that exposed his purchase history (information!) to his wife, causing her to learn that he had purchased flowers for his girlfriend. This shows the significant impact of whether information falls into the wrong or right hands.

In the Target case, the information in question is not something likely to bother a general consumer. Still, the power of such information and the conclusions derived from it are things we all need to be circumspect about. Imagine the ways in which someone could be harmed if information about their personal life were revealed to bad actors in society. The same can be said of data in the hands of conglomerates and governments.

On the other hand, the incorrect flower bouquet transaction receipt case demonstrates that any person could end up on the path towards doomsday if private information is not managed correctly.

This book touches on various facets of information, privacy, data, security, and related legal issues. My goal is to encourage all of us to treat privacy issues with utmost importance. Information that even remotely concerns human life, irrespective of whether the person is rich or poor, is of paramount importance to companies and governments; all of us should consider the issue of data privacy with equal seriousness. We have been far too careless with our personal, emotional information, allowing entities such as Cambridge Analytica, Google, Facebook, and others to prey on the breadcrumbs of personal information that common people make available in their daily lives.

I was motivated to write this book by my travel and work experience across various jurisdictions and my experience in white-collar crime investigations, compliance, regulatory affairs, and ethics. I have seen information change the balance of power, sometimes in favour of the bad. The ways in which information, data, privacy, security, and law can be used are staggering and disturbing. On the one hand, I have seen information used to identify a pattern of facts and solve a crime; on the other hand, I have seen people use personal information to dominate their way to strong-arm the person to do their bidding by unfaithfully utilising their information and in some cases impacting people's lives. Having witnessed numerous issues surrounding privacy, data security, and cybercrime and frequently dealing with the human elements involved in these sensitive issues make my heart pound. I want to send everyone a simple message: Your privacy is your right, and you should safeguard it as carefully as you protect any of the other valuables in your life; thus *#MyPrivacy #MyRight*.

My desire to write this book is to make people aware of the importance of their data and various facts surrounding privacy, information, and data security. I have aimed the book at the general reader, taking you on a journey through what can go wrong if you do not safeguard your or your organisation's information and what you can do about the situation. I have seen excellent information technology (IT) people who might do their job superbly well but are careless with their own personal information. Whether you already know a lot about privacy issues or just want to understand the nuances surrounding the subject of privacy, data security, and law better, this book will empower you to be diligent and sceptical at the same time.

Two Laws to Be Familiar With

Governments around the world have sought to protect data privacy, although their efforts face opposition from companies that benefit financially from their ability to collect, analyse, and sell personal data. Two governmental actions stand out as the most wide-ranging measures and will be frequently cited in this book.

In this regard, the most comprehensive legislative effort is European Union's General Data Protection Regulation (GDPR), which took effect in 2018. GDPR exerts vast regulatory control over how businesses and government agencies handle consumers' personal information, and it gives individuals the ability to control how their personal data are collected, used, or processed.

The United States has no similar national framework regarding data privacy. The most significant US legislation in this realm has been the California Consumer Privacy Act (CCPA), which was passed in 2018 and took effect in 2020. Although passed by only one of the fifty US states, it has a wide-ranging impact since it affects all business entities in California. In November 2020, California voters further expanded data privacy protections by approving California Privacy Rights Act (CPRA) in a referendum. The passage of CPRA makes California's law comparable to GDPR. Because CPRA's approval occurred just before the publication of this manuscript, the text describes the provisions of the CCPA only.

To touch upon the upcoming legislation, such as the California Consumer Privacy Act (CCPA) of 2018, which was voted in on 3 November 2020 and approved to be signed as new legislation. The CPRA is expected to come into effect on 1 January 2023.

As an addendum to CCPA, CPRA seeks to tighten business regulations on using consumers' personal information while strengthening the data privacy rights of California residents. The act also establishes a new statewide enforcement agency in the form of CPPA (California Privacy Protection Agency). Additionally, CPPA will only strengthen the power residing in CCPA by ensuring the enhancements implanted in the new legislation - CPRA, such as more rights for the consumer and the alike. However, the basic would still reside within CCPA, and the spirit of the two legislations shall remain the same.

GDPR, CCPA, various US federal laws related to privacy, and provisions enacted in other countries are summarised in the Appendix.

The Organisation and Goals of This Book

I have two goals in this book: I want you to have the information you need to protect your own data privacy and that of the people you care about, and I want to motivate you to make this a high-priority issue in your personal behaviour, the opinions you express, and your public advocacy. Accordingly, you will find description information and passionate persuasion on these pages. Of course, you do not have to share my policy opinions to benefit from the factual information contained here, but I hope that you will be inspired to participate in some way in countering the threats to privacy that our technological age poses.

Chapter 1 provides a broad overview—and perhaps, for many readers, a rude awakening—concerning how current practices of data collection and use are endangering privacy. I follow that overview with a short chapter (2) in a more advocacy-oriented tone, warning that each of us (i.e., our personal data) is a product that companies want to exploit for profit.

Data-related threats include mostly legal behaviour by companies and illegal behaviour by hackers. Chapter 3 explains briefly why hackers want your data. In chapter 4, I return to my passionate style, pointing out the ways in which capitalism helps make protecting our privacy difficult.

Chapters 5 through 7 cover government regulation, data management complexities, and protecting privacy in the healthcare sector, respectively. I then turn to ethics-related issues in chapters 8 and 9.

Chapter 10 briefly considers how judges have viewed court cases related to data privacy; my primary purpose in this chapter is to clarify that we cannot rely on the courts to rescue us if we fail to protect ourselves.

Finally, chapter 11 provides a set of practical recommendations for individuals and businesses on how to safeguard privacy and protect data from misuse or unauthorised access.

As noted above, the Appendix presents more detailed information on existing data privacy laws in various countries.

I hope that you will find this book enlightening and that you will never again take your privacy or data security for granted. Thank you for being interested enough in the topic to pick up this book!

CHAPTER 1

HOW ARE EMERGING TECHNOLOGIES MAKING IT DIFFICULT TO MAINTAIN PRIVACY?

Is technology evolving faster than the privacy laws designed to protect personal data? Emerging technologies harness vast amounts of real-time data and communicate seamlessly through a complex network of connected technologies. Such data are valuable for research and commercial entities and offer improved knowledge, competitive advantage, and data-driven decision-making opportunities to businesses. However, they carry significant security and privacy risks for data subjects and the integrity of systems within organisations.

Enhanced connectivity of devices and mass data flows raises thorny questions concerning protecting individuals' right to privacy. Smart devices abound that record health patterns, lifestyles, and habits, while connected devices lead to an unprecedented data flow.

These data-heavy technologies present a host of unique privacy challenges. The digital boundaries of 'smart devices' are poorly defined, and communication between such devices is often automatically triggered. Additionally, from the manufacturers of intelligent device to application developers, various stakeholders carry out numerous activities within the life cycle of data processing. Intrusive practices are leading to the commercialisation of what was once considered insignificant or anonymised user data.

Lack of or poorly-defined user control is a considerable challenge across a wide range of technological developments. Obtaining specific and clear informed consent from end users for processing each type of data is far more complex than traditional consent mechanisms.

Many businesses, including IoT manufacturers who process personal data, remain under pressure to implement the new requirements in data privacy regulations. For instance, Articles 13 and 14 under GDPR place the burden on IoT manufacturers to give comprehensive information on processed personal data to end users. This obligation has resulted in significant administrative and workload challenges. Withal consent forms are also under review as businesses strive to provide complete, transparent, and clear information to enable users to declare consent.[1]

A. SMART WEARABLES

Smart wearables[2] offer innovative solutions in healthcare and well-being, along with the possibility of improved emergency

---

1   "IoT Update: The E-Privacy Regulation – Impact on the IoT Market," Liza Marie Herberger, 27 September 2018, https://www.natlawreview.com/article/iot-update-e-privacy-regulation-impact-iot-market.

2   "Reflection and Orientation Paper" by European Commission, Brussels,

management, safety at work, and medical monitoring. Smart electronic devices can collect, record, and monitor real-time biometric movement and location data and communicate the data wirelessly or through cellular communication.

Wearables are increasingly becoming an integral part of corporate wellness programs across the globe. According to a 2018 Gartner study,[3] for 2 million employees involved in physically-demanding or dangerous roles, such as firefighters or paramedics, wearing fitness and health tracking devices is a necessary condition of employment.[4] According to a study by Tractica, by the year 2020, with corporations focusing on employees' health and well-being as a means to higher productivity, reduced sick leave, and healthcare costs, 75 million wearables will be in use in workplaces.[5]

28 November 2016, https://ec.europa.eu/information_society/newsroom/image/document/2016-11/report_on_smart_wearables_information_and_stakeholders_day_14540.pdf *defines "smart wearables" as "As defined by European Commission in Smart wearables are body-borne computational and sensory devices which can sense the person who wears them and/or their environment. Wearables can communicate either directly through embedded wireless connectivity or through another device (e.g., a smartphone). The data collected by the wearable device about the user, or its environment is processed in a processing unit located locally or in an external server, and the results are ultimately provided to the wearer. Smart wearables may have control, communication, storage and actuation capabilities."*

3   "Gartner Predicts Our Digital Future," section "Gartner's Top 10 Predictions Herald What It Means to Be Human in a Digital World," Garner.co, 6 October 2015, https://www.gartner.com/smarterwithgartner/gartner-predicts-our-digital-future/.

4   "By 2018, Employees Will Be Required to Wear Wearables," *Mobility Management Solutions Review*, 8 October 2015, https://solutionsreview.com/mobile-device-management/by-2018-employees-will-be-required-to-wear-wearables/.

5   "More Than 75 Million Wearable Devices to Be Deployed in Enterprise and Industrial Environments by 2020, According to Tractica," businesswire.com, 8 April 2015, https://www.businesswire.com/news/home/20150408005309/en/More-than-75-Million-Wearable-Devices-to-be-Deployed-in-Enterprise-and-Industrial-Environments-by-2020-According-to-Tractica.

As with any other technology, smart wearables also raise concerns and questions concerning privacy, such as the following:

- *a.* What kinds of data are collected and shared?
- *b.* Who has access to the data?
- *c.* How securely are the data stored?
- *d.* To what extent are data controllers obliged to disclose their data access to the individuals involved or to people treating them, especially when adverse health conditions are involved?
- *e.* Can the data be used for secondary purposes?

I. How Safe Are Wearables?

The Centre for Digital Democracy, the leading non-profit consumer and privacy protection organisation in the United States, conducted a study along with the School of Communication at American University on smart wearables' privacy protection level. They found that US health privacy regulations do not provide a suitable level of protection. The study indicated that health wearable devices could result in a growing loss of Americans' most sensitive information.[6]

As one illustrative example of this problem, the Department of Defence issued an order requiring soldiers to stop using wearable devices in January 2018, following the discovery that the device revealed confidential locations through a fitness heat map. Military personnel deployed in "operational areas," including overseas US bases or war zones, have to leave their wearable trackers, which

---

[6] "How Data Breach Is Inevitable in Wearable Devices," Sam Draper, wearable-technologies.com, 9 August 2018, https://www.wearable-technologies.com/2018/10/how-data-breach-is-inevitable-in-wearable-devices/.

identify their location, at home pursuant to the order.[7] Eight
months after the discovery by a researcher, this order was issued
that the Strava fitness app had a heatmap feature that revealed
troop movement and location details in conflict zones in Syria
and other places. At the time of the discovery, *Wired UK*
reported that the tracker's application programming interface
(API) allowed de-anonymisation of data to reveal the user's
personal data, such as name, heart rate, and speed of travel.[8]
Strava's heat map showed 3 trillion or more GPS data points.
The map can be used by other fitness trackers, such as Fitbit, to
suggest running routes. However, military analysts noted that
the heat map was so detailed as to provide sensitive information
on military personnel and strategic locations.[9]

Even as smart wearables' popularity continues to grow, the
challenges in terms of data privacy and security are substantial.
Third parties can exploit poor data management and sell the
data to unscrupulous or malicious entities, which may grossly
misuse the information. Lack of adequate encryption in data
transfer processes makes wearables vulnerable to hackers.

7 "How Data Breach Is Inevitable in Wearable Devices," Sam Draper, wearable-technologies.com, 9 August 2018, https://www.wearable-technologies.com/2018/08/pentagon-tells-soldiers-to-leave-wearable-trackers-at-home-when-heading-to-warzones/.

8 "Fitness Tracking App Strava Gives Away Location of Secret US Army Bases," Alex Hern, *The Guardian*, 28 January 2018, https://www.theguardian.com/world/2018/jan/28/fitness-tracking-app-gives-away-location-of-secret-us-army-bases?awc=11152_1568006907_77e4bf372dcf5898f53eb2cd71d016a5&utm_source=afl&utm_medium=awin&utm_content=IDG+Communications%2C+Inc.

9 "Fitness Tracking App Strava Gives Away Location of Secret US Army Bases," Alex Hern, *The Guardian*, 28 January 2018, https://www.theguardian.com/world/2018/jan/28/fitness-tracking-app-gives-away-location-of-secret-us-army-bases?awc=11152_1568006907_77e4bf372dcf5898f53eb2cd71d016a5&utm_source=afl&utm_medium=awin&utm_content=IDG+Communications%2C+Inc.

Moreover, companies are ready to pay a fortune to have access to valuable personal information.

Additionally, the issue of continuity is a crucial concern. If you have chosen to share your personal data with a company compliant with privacy laws, no one can guarantee that the same company will be in existence a few years later. Bankruptcies, mergers, acquisitions, and companies' shutdowns raise more questions about what happens to anyone's personal data in these corporate rearrangements.

II. Deepfakes, Smart Speakers, and Privacy Challenges

The Centre for Data Ethics and Innovation (CDEI), a UK government advisory body composed of an independent team of experts, published a snapshot series on deepfakes and audiovisual disinformation. Deepfakes are audio and visual content manipulated through advanced software to modify the presentation of an object, person, or environment. Although the term is often used synonymously with face replacement technology, where a person's face is digitally swapped with another person's (commonly called face-swapping), deepfakes can also involve face re-enactment, face regeneration, and speech synthesis. The face re-enactment uses advanced software to manipulate a person's facial features.[10] Face regeneration produces entirely new face images that do not represent a real person, whereas speech synthesis creates a model of a person's voice. Think about that! The risks of deepfakes are twofold: First, the technology intrudes on individual rights because a person's likeness can be

---

10   "Deepfakes Deserve Policymakers' Attention, and Better Solutions," Joshua New, Centre for Data Innovation, 12 September 2019, https://www.datainnovation.org/2019/09/deepfakes-deserve-policymakers-attention-and-better-solutions/.

used for profit without their consent; second, the technology could become a powerful disinformation tool.

Such concepts are far-reaching, beyond imagination. Deepfakes are essentially corrupting the current worldwide records. When this has gone further into the future, this will need to be tackled through *evidence-triangulation[11] before being admissible in courts. However, these fakes will profoundly affect human behaviour and what they will do – for instance, recently, France trashed the AstraZeneca and now has a vaccination problem in its population as if they are refusing.[12]* Even when all the data (evidence) points to something else, the perception is causing a problem. This particular case is where the government caused the problem but could easily have come from somewhere else.

Similarly, sometime earlier, a video went viral, where during a political campaign, Biden fell asleep, and it was later identified to be manipulated.[13] When some of the people in the audience were confronted with the evidence, the troubling part is that they expressed doubt on the claim's validity and continued with the belief that could have happened. The impression is everything! Someone with advanced know-how was successful in achieving what they wanted.

Another technology of concern is *shallowfakes*. This term refers to visual or audio content edited with basic techniques

---

11   *International Encyclopaedia of Human Geography*, 2009, ScienceDirect, https://www.sciencedirect.com/topics/social-sciences/triangulation, defines triangulation as *"a technique to analyse results of the same study using different methods of data collection."*

12   "In Talking Down AstraZeneca's Success, The EU Has Sacrificed Lives for the Integrity of the European Project," Ross Clark, 19 February 2021, https://www.telegraph.co.uk/news/2021/02/19/talking-astrazenecas-success-eu-has-sacrificed-lives-integrity/.

13   "Fact Check: Video Showing Joe Biden Falling Asleep during Live Interview Is Manipulated," Reuters Staff, 1 September 2020, https://www.reuters.com/article/uk-factcheck-biden-asleep-altered-idUSKBN25S63S.

in which captions may be changed or the speed of footage slowed down to misrepresent people or events. A recent victim of a shallowfake was Nancy Pelosi, currently speaker of the US House. Footage of a panel event was slowed down to give the impression that she was inebriated and slurring her words when speaking.

In a similar shallowfake attack on Jim Acosta, a CNN reporter, footage from a presidential press conference was sped up to make him appear to have acted aggressively towards a White House staffer.

Across the world, legislators are mulling new laws to address such disinformation. Lawmakers in New York debated a bill to prohibit the use of digital replicas of individuals based on the principle that a living or deceased individual's persona is their private property.[14]

In 2018, US Senator Ben Sasse introduced the Malicious Deep Fake Prohibition Act, seeking to create deepfakes illegal if there is tortious conduct (intentional conduct causing harm). In June 2018, the Deepfakes Accountability Act was introduced and referred to the House Intelligence Committee; it proposed the inclusion of irremovable digital watermarks on deepfakes.[15]

Making deepfakes requires specialised skills, in addition to advanced professional software that is not yet widely available. However, the technology is on a path to becoming more sophisticated, presenting new challenges for data privacy regulators and controllers.

---

14   "Deepfakes Deserve Policymakers' Attention, and Better Solutions," Joshua New, Centre for Data Innovation, 12 September 2019, https://www.datainnovation.org/2019/09/deepfakes-deserve-policymakers-attention-and-better-solutions/.

15   "Deepfakes and Audio-visual Disinformation," White Paper produced Centre for Data Ethics and Innovation, September 2019, https://stip.oecd.org/stip/policy-initiatives/2019/data/policyInitiatives/26710.

Smart speakers similarly present exciting opportunities in terms of easy access to information and delivery of numerous services. These devices are increasingly prevalent in homes; a wake-up word such as "Hey, Google" prompts their response. The apparent flexibility and novelty of these devices add to their attraction. From playing favourite music to laughing on request, to telling jokes, the device has an almost human-like personality. Voice-enabled devices are fundamentally changing people's engagement with technology, but at the same time, this technology is unnerving to many.

With users increasingly relying on these devices in their daily routines, the constant monitoring of people's intimate environments seems intrusive. In one case, a resident of the US state of Oregon allegedly found that Echo smart speakers had recorded her private conversations with her husband and sent the recordings, without permission, to a random contact in the address book.

Voice assistants' audio snippet recordings from homes enable companies to obtain new types of data. Although such data are not currently used for advertising purposes, they can provide valuable insights into users' profiles that can impact other platforms' advertising. Data collected from online interactions, such as the content viewed, comments posted, or likes, have been a critical tool helping advertisers profile and target consumers. Online activities using voice assistants will add further to this complex advertising ecosystem. Smart speakers help marketers gather new insights about households, from their morning alarms to the music they stream.

Concerns have arisen about these devices' intrusive features and the volume of data captured. Questions also have been raised regarding their disruptive, long-term impact on information consumption, user profiling, and users' relationship with technology.

The snapshot series from the CDEI highlights these concerns regarding smart speakers:

a. Voice recordings are routinely processed by humans and machine learning models to improve services and drive further innovation. Devices at times detect the wake-up word wrongly and make intrusive recordings.

b. Voice assistants collect recordings, which create data troves used to profile customers in novel ways, including analyses of mental health status or sentiments. Although such applications may be beneficial, the use of voice data analysis to make inferences about individuals presents new data privacy challenges.

c. Smart speakers provide engaging ways to consume online material. These devices are rapidly becoming critical gateways to the online world. Data regulators need to consider the long-term impact of this emerging issue.

B. The Impact of the Internet of Things on Data Privacy

The Internet of Things (IoT) is set to interconnect billions or trillions of smart devices around us. With the capability to collect, process, store, and relay information about the physical environment and about themselves, IoT systems are poised to deliver a whole new way of doing everything, from simple everyday tasks to complicated healthcare services. In smart city services, building management systems, and public surveillance, IoT benefits are readily evident.

IoT devices not only monitor the user but also collect and communicate information about the user. IoT systems collect and relay personal information to connected devices where data are stored and processed. These devices can sense, gather, monitor, analyse, and distribute sensitive data on a massive scale. With more access points available, which means more points of a potential attack, IoT devices are highly vulnerable to security threats. Insufficient encryption or protection of IoT devices can lead to data breaches, with individuals' data being compromised or stolen.

The Internet of Things and artificial intelligence intersect seamlessly. While IoT connects machines and makes use of the data generated from devices, AI involves simulating intelligent behaviour in all kinds of devices. As IoT devices generate vast volumes of data, AI will become functionally necessary to handle and make sense of the immense amounts of data.[16]

RFID (radio frequency identification) technology is one evolutionary step in the IoT vision. Passive automatic identification is made possible by RFID at a nominal cost. Studies of the multiple privacy risks of RFID have revealed threats related to the automated tracking and identification of individuals through hidden tags, such as in clothes. The proposed countermeasures include tag encryption, reader authentication, blocking of tags, and randomising tag identifiers.

Wireless sensor network (WSN) technology is seen as the next evolutionary step. With augmented capabilities of sensing, communicating, and processing, the connected things become active. Sensor networks range from extensive industrial-scale monitoring to small-scale home devices.

Identification denotes the threat of associating a (persistent) identifier, such as a name and address or a pseudonym of any

---

16   "Internet of Things Remains Privacy Concern for Consumers," Stephen White, PrivSec Report, 14 May 2019, https://gdpr.report/news/2019/05/14/internet-of-things-remains-privacy-concern-for-consumers/.

kind, with an individual and data about that individual.[17] Thus, the threat lies in associating an identity with a specific privacy-violating context, enabling, and intensifying other risks, such as profiling and tracking individuals or combining different data sources for invasive purposes.

Identification is currently the most dominant threat to privacy in connected devices where vast volumes of data are concentrated centrally at a location out of control of the data subject. Surveillance camera technology, facial databases, and electronic identification camera images open enormous possibilities for identifying individuals.

Speech recognition is used widely in mobile applications where speech samples' databases are being built. The database could potentially also be used to identify individuals. With speech recognition becoming a dominant interaction mode through IoT systems and the growing use of cloud computing, protecting individual privacy is an immense challenge.

Users may have difficulty controlling their information because communication and data exchange between IoT devices can be triggered automatically and by default, without the individual being aware of it. Moreover, modern techniques related to data analysis and cross-matching may lend this data to secondary uses, whether or not they are related to the purpose assigned to the original processing.

As data exchange and communication between IoT devices are often triggered by default or automatically without the user being aware of what is happening, individuals have difficulty controlling how their personal information is collected, used, or distributed. Third parties may also request data collected by

---

17 "Privacy in the Internet of Things: Threats and Challenges," Jan Henrik Ziegeldorf, Oscar Garcia Morchon, and Klaus Wehrle, 10 June 2013, https://onlinelibrary.wiley.com/doi/full/10.1002/sec.795.

IoT devices for various commercial purposes. In the absence of informed consent or when data accuracy is questionable, such transfer to third parties is a serious threat to data privacy.

I. Low Levels of Trust in the IoT

Another incident highlighting the data privacy concerns raised by fitness devices is the My Fitness Pal (MyFitnessPal app) data breach that occurred in February 2018.[18]

This fitness app experienced a data breach that compromised the personal data of 150 million users. The compromised data included e-mail addresses, hashed[19] and salted[20] (or peppered[21]) passwords, and usernames.

---

18 "MyFitness Pal Breach Hits 150 Million: What to Do Now," Paul Wagenseil, *Toms Guide*, 29 March 2018, https://www.tomsguide.com/us/myfitness-pal-data-breach,news-26885.html.

19 According to theguardian.com, in an article by Samuel Gibbs, 15 December 2016, https://www.theguardian.com/technology/2016/dec/15/passwords-hacking-hashing-salting-sha-2#:~:text=When%20a%20password%20has%20been,key,%20using%20a%20set%20algorithm, *"When a password has been 'hashed' it means it has been turned into a scrambled representation of itself. A user's password is taken and—using a key known to the site—the hash value is derived from the combination of both the password and the key, using a set algorithm. To verify a user's password is correct it is hashed, and the value compared with that stored on record each time they login."*

20 According to theguardian.com, *"Salting is simply the addition of a unique, random string of characters known only to the site to each password before it is hashed, typically this 'salt' is placed in front of each password. The salt value needs to be stored by the site, which means sometimes sites use the same salt for every password. This makes it less effective than if individual salts are used. The use of unique salts means that common passwords shared by multiple users—such as '123456' or 'password'—are not immediately revealed when one such hashed password is identified, because despite the passwords being the same the salted and hashed values are not. Large salts also protect against certain methods of attack on hashes, including rainbow tables or logs of hashed passwords previously broken. Both hashing and salting can be repeated more than once to increase the difficulty in breaking the security."*

21 According to theguardian.com, in an article by Samuel Gibbs, 15 December

In the aftermath of this breach, an independent IT security research institute, AV-Test, evaluated fitness trackers. The agency found that of thirteen devices tested, nine trackers transmitted personal data from the smartphone; the rest did not.

The adoption of IoT is related strongly to trust amongst organisations and consumers. The 2017 Edelman Trust Barometer found that public trust in technological evolution was at a low level. A research study by ISACA, an organisation that focuses on IT governance, found that 39 per cent of consumers in Europe completely disagreed that IoT manufacturers provide sufficient information about personal data collected. In comparison, another 42 per cent somewhat disagreed.

A study conducted by Consumers International and the Internet Society found that consumers across the globe have reservations concerning the security of devices connected to the Internet of Things. Citizens from France, the United Kingdom, Australia, Japan, Canada, and the United States were polled regarding their views on security and trust in the IoT. Regarding the level of data that smart devices are collecting, 63 per cent of those surveyed in the study described it as creepy.[22]

2016, https://www.theguardian.com/technology/2016/dec/15/passwords-hacking-hashing-salting-sha-2#:~:text=When%20a%20password%20has%20been,key,%20using%20a%20set%20algorithm, *"Pepper is similar to a salt—a value added to the password before being hashed—but typically placed at the end of the password. There are broadly two versions of pepper. The first is simply a known secret value added to each password, which is only beneficial if it is not known by the attacker. The second is a value that is randomly generated but never stored. That means every time a user attempts to log into the site it has to try multiple combinations of the pepper and hashing algorithm to find the right pepper value and match the hash value."*

22 The Consumerinternational.org, https://www.consumersinternational.org/what-we-do/digital/internet-of-things/, defines the Internet of Things as *"Connections between devices and objects, 'the Internet of Things' (IoT), is rapidly expanding. Technology such as sensors are embedded in increasingly everyday things like cars, utility meters, white goods, wearable fitness trackers or home security systems. This makes objects capable of sensing and remotely communicating with*

Trust was also a concern, with more than half of the participants stating that they had no trust in their devices concerning privacy and responsible data processing. The study further found that 75 per cent[23] of those surveyed were significantly concerned about how the collected data were being used without their consent or awareness.

The study's findings reiterated the need for retailers, manufacturers, and data controllers to demonstrate their commitment to data privacy and IoT device security.

II. Questions IoT manufacturers Need to Ask

The legislation required that could force companies to adopt a labelling system that explains in a straightforward manner on how secure an IoT device is?

In my opinion, IoT gadgets need to have a unique default password, indicating how security updates are available, and provide contact details to consumers so that they can report cybersecurity problems to the concerned authorities.

In a survey conducted by ResearchGate.net, when asked who should take the lead in finding solutions to data security and IoT privacy problems amongst retailers, manufacturers, and regulators, 88 per cent believed it was the responsibility of data regulators to maintain the privacy standards. In comparison, 81 per cent of the respondents said manufacturers should take the lead in providing assurance.[24]

---

each other, with users or with a central system – for any purpose."

23   "Internet of Things Remains Privacy Concern for Consumers," Stephen White, PrivSec Report, 14 May 2019, https://gdpr.report/news/2019/05/14/internet-of-things-remains-privacy-concern-for-consumers/.

24   "Concerns over Privacy and Security Contribute to Consumer Distrust in Connected Devices" contacts: Allesandra deSantillana, and Suzi Price, Internet Society, 1 May 2019, https://www.internetsociety.org/news/press-releases/2019/concerns-over-privacy-and-security-contribute-to-consumer-

The ePrivacy Regulation, a complementary regulation to GDPR, has a broader scope and covers machine-to-machine communication or non-personal data communication between machines.

With growing concerns and unease surrounding connected devices, the following questions can help IoT device manufacturers review and strengthen data privacy and security:

a. What personal data does the IoT device collect on users?
b. Where are these data stored and sent?
c. How are such personal data used?
d. Is there any information that the IoT device is not authorised to collect?
e. Who else has access to the user's personal data?
f. How long are the IoT data stored?
g. Is there an expiration time for the data?
h. How secure are the users' data during storage or transfer?
i. How would consumers be notified in case of a data breach?

III. The Satellite and the New Challenges to Data Privacy

The United Nations Office for Outer Space Affairs (UNOOSA) maintains a register called the Index of Objects Launched into Outer Space. At the start of 2019, according to UNOOSA, 4,987 satellites were orbiting Earth.[25]

Satellite systems are critical to global communications, navigation, space science, technology development, earth observation, and earth science. Satellite technology has improved communication speed, optimised emergency responses, and

---

distrust-in-connected-devices/.
25 "How Many Satellites Orbiting the Earth in 2019?" Andy, Pixalytics.com, 19 January 2019, https://www.pixalytics.com/satellites-orbiting-earth-2019/.

enabled the highly-accurate determination of locations. Smart devices integrated with GPS satellite chips would allow people to know their exact location, guide travellers, and allow athletes and fitness enthusiasts to track their activities.

Although the benefits of such systems are apparent, unfettered access to data collected and transmitted by satellites leads to new ethical and legal concerns concerning data privacy.

Satellites pose diverse kinds of cybersecurity challenges. As satellite operations are based on technologies housed on earth, the entry points on earth offer enormous potential and multiple pathways for hacking by cybercriminals. The considerable number of entry points compounds the challenge of tracing and mitigating a cyberattack.

One critical weakness common to satellite systems relates to the long-range telemetry used for communicating with ground stations. The downlinks or uplinks are often transmitted through open network security protocols, which cybercriminals can easily access. IoT devices utilising satellite communications are additional points of entry for hackers.[26] Equally vulnerable are satellite ground stations, where interrupting the satellite signal help hackers gain access to downstream systems connected to the satellite. A hacker can trespass into the organisation's network through this channel, using the infiltrated ground station as the starting point.

Satellites can carry out continuous and advanced surveillance using thermal imaging, high-resolution imaging, and real-time video. Private satellites can create images at a resolution of 25 centimetres, enough to discern objects as small as a mailbox. Archived data sets that include private citizens'

---

26 "Cyber Concerns for the Satellite Sector," Francis Knott, Attila Security, 13 July 2020, https://www.attilasec.com/blog/satellite-cybersecurity.

data enable anyone with access to view past actions as far back as the operator has retained data.[27]

These data sets can be combined with data gathered from other surveillance technologies, such as street-level cameras, licence plate readers, and face or object recognition to arrive at a more accurate and detailed record of an individual's movements. In 2014, the US government lifted restrictions related to satellites' high-quality images, which could have profound privacy implications for individuals. Before lifting these restrictions, companies could not make use of sharp satellite images with a resolution of fewer than 50 centimetres. This meant that companies could not utilise images that would result in people being personally identifiable from services such as Google Earth.

GDPR has a direct impact on satellite telecommunications, direct-to-home (DTH), and geolocation services. In DTH, operators are obliged to inform subscribers or viewers about how their personal data are being collected, processed, and stored.[28]

However, GDPR does not apply to the European Global Navigation Satellite Systems Agency (GNSS) or the European Commission. These institutions are instead governed by Regulation (EC) 45/2001. GDPR or EU laws also do not apply to intergovernmental and international agencies such as the European Space Agency.

---

27 "Cyber Concerns for the Satellite Sector," Francis Knott, Attila Security, 13 July 2020, https://www.attilasec.com/blog/satellite-cybersecurity.

28 "GDPR Is Here, But What Does It Really Mean for Satellite?" Adrienne Harebottle, Via Satellite, 30 May 2018, https://www.satellitetoday.com/business/2018/05/30/gdpr-is-here-but-what-does-it-really-mean-for-satellite/.

C. Regulation of Privacy on Blockchain and Cryptocurrencies[29]

Blockchain is a distributed, secure ledger designed to maintain records of transactions without the need for intermediaries. Cryptocurrencies promise anonymous electronic transfers, unlike traditional modes of value exchange. From providing the infrastructure for cryptocurrency trading, blockchain has grown to become integral to many businesses. Blockchains hold vast amounts of data, including shipments, customer information, and value transactions. However, only authorised personnel from the company can use private blockchains, retail, or corporate blockchains to gather and store customers' personal data.

Under the sweeping provisions of GDPR, businesses must erase all the personal data of individuals who request such erasure. According to Bloomberg, companies that use blockchain with publicly-available data trails, including Ethereum and Bitcoin, completely erasing or purging such information may be impossible.[30] Some blockchains in their present form are deemed incompatible with GDPR's "right to be forgotten" (i.e., to have one's data removed), and distributed data make blockchains vulnerable to attacks from hackers, thereby potentially compromising vast amounts of personal data.

An essential transparency requirement under GDPR is set under Articles 13 and 14, granting individuals the right to

---

29 "Is Your Blockchain Business Doomed?" Olga Kharif, Bloomberg Businessweek, 22 March 2018, https://www.bloomberg.com/news/articles/2018-03-22/is-your-blockchain-business-doomed.

30 "Is Your Blockchain Business Doomed?" Olga Kharif, updated 22 March 2018, https://www.bloomberg.com/news/articles/2018-03-22/is-your-blockchain-business-doomed.

be informed about their personal data collection and use.[31] Individuals have a right to know not only about what data of theirs is processed but other elements too, such as but not limited to retention periods for their personal data, all who have access to their data, and to all whom it is shared.

The primary issue that comes to light brought about by blockchain is identifying the data controller and processor to a blockchain. We are aware that the key benefits some types of blockchain provide is that of decentralisation of transactions, but on the other hand, the concept of controller and processor is key to GDPR, which, in the case of blockchains, can lead to an undefined line of demarcation between the two concepts of GDPR.

If we dig deep into the concept of a private and public blockchain, one may argue that a private blockchain's demarcation could be identified since the chain is controlled and managed centrally, assuming the operator controls the blockchain. On the other hand, public blockchains usually lack centralisation with the number of parties involved and, thus, a more significant issue at hand.

The problem is twofold: One identifies the two concepts while it stems down to another issue, the issue relating to the consumer. If the line cannot be appropriately demarcated, then would the consumer reach out to exercise their right enshrined in the law?

An analysis carried out by Gartner indicated that by 2022, 75 per cent[32] of public blockchains would suffer *privacy*

---

31 "Individual Rights: Right to Be informed," Guide to the General Data Protection Regulation (GDPR) by Information Commissioner's Office, accessed 1 June 2020, https://ico.org.uk/for-organisations/guide-to-data-protection/guide-to-the-general-data-protection-regulation-gdpr/individual-rights/right-to-be-informed/.

32 "Gartner Predicts for the Future of Privacy 2019," Gloria Omale, Gartner,

poisoning. Once blockchain data are recorded, they cannot easily be modified or deleted. However, privacy laws grant individuals the right to be forgotten. This conflict will become a two-edged sword, raising the critical question of whether such systems will store, by design, personal data that can never be deleted or whether they could compromise the integrity of the chain. On the other hand, the Gartner study also suggests that the application of blockchain might change so as to become useful in cases of ground-up privacy, such that by 2023, over 25 per cent of GDPR-driven proof-of-consent implementations could involve blockchain technology, up from less than 2 per cent in 2018.[33]

D. What Happens with Artificial Intelligence?

AI and machine learning automate repetitive tasks by utilising massive volumes of data. The greater the amount of data consumption, the better the AI and machine learning algorithms recognise patterns in data sets. The very concept of AI is based on the use of redundant data to find regularities and structures, learn directly, and become able to predict what comes next.

The Council of Europe's statement on the protection of individuals about automatic processing of personal data[34]

---

14 January 2019, https://www.gartner.com/smarterwithgartner/gartner-predicts-2019-for-the-future-of-privacy/.

33 "Gartner Predicts for the Future of Privacy 2019," Gloria Omale, Gartner, 14 January 2019, https://www.gartner.com/smarterwithgartner/gartner-predicts-2019-for-the-future-of-privacy/.

34 "Report on Artificial Intelligence," Consultative Committee of the Convention for the Protection of Individuals with Regard to Automatic Processing of Personal Data, Council of Europe, 25 January 2019, https://rm.coe.int/artificial-intelligence-and-data-protection-challenges-and-possible-re/168091f8a6.

indicated that "personal data have increasingly become both the source and the target of AI applications." Furthermore, the adoption of a legal framework by the Council of Europe aims "to favour the development of technology grounded on these rights" and which is "not merely driven by market forces or high-tech companies." The convention mentions that protecting personal data under Article 8 should be an essential prerequisite when developing or adopting AI applications when used in decision-making processes.[35]

I. How Can AI Compromise Data Privacy?

AI is inherently capable of using copious amounts of data for analysis and can perform designated tasks without supervision. These are the very traits of AI that compromise data privacy in the following ways[36]:

a. **Data exploitation**: Many consumer products, ranging from computer applications to smart home appliances, have features that expose them to AI-based data exploitation. People are typically unaware of how much of their personal data these devices or applications generate or share.

b. **Tracking and identification**: AI is utilised to track, monitor, or identify individuals via multiple devices at work, at public locations, or at home. Even if personal data are part of an extensive data set and anonymised,

35 "New Guidelines on Artificial Intelligence and Data Protection," Council of Europe, 30 January 2019, https://www.coe.int/en/web/data-protection/-/new-guidelines-on-artificial-intelligence-and-personal-data-protection.

36 "Artificial Intelligence a Threat to Privacy," Tweak Team, Tweak Library, 4 April 2019, https://tweaklibrary.com/artificial-intelligence-a-threat-to-privacy/.

they can be de-anonymised by AI based on inferences and data gathered from other devices.

c. **Voice and facial recognition**: These methods can severely compromise anonymity in the online or public spheres.

d. **Prediction**: AI utilises machine learning algorithms to predict sensitive information. For instance, keyboard typing patterns are used to predict or infer an individual's emotional state, such as sadness, nervousness, or anxiety. Moreover, an individual's political views, overall health, or ethnic identity can be deduced from different metrics.

This technology has been growing at a rapid pace with speed bumps, but we all are tending to turn a blind eye to what we read in the news. In June 2019, Google confirmed that it took facial scans of people of colour, homeless people, and students in Atlanta, USA, to improve its face recognition program. People did not have a choice since their choice was coerced by Google, paying them $5 in the name of technological advancement in lieu of their personal identity – their facial scans.[37] Racial profiling has been at the forefront of many companies. It helps them segment, categorise, and offer products better, not realising that it does not depict equality and objectivity when offering such a service.

Things get glaringly annoying when similar systems are adopted by healthcare institutions, a place that inherently draws the trust from a common man by virtue of the business they are in – providing "healthcare." Well, if this would surprise you, there have been incidence surrounding the issue discussed herein. An algorithm was developed by UnitedHealth Group

---

37   "Google's 'Field Research' Offered People $5 to Scan Their Faces for the Pixel," Dieter Bohn, The Verge, 29 July 2019, https://www.theverge. com/2019/7/29/8934804/google-pixel-4-face-scanning-data-collection.

Inc., which was used by other hospitals. The algorithm ranked white patients with fewer chronic diseases and healthier vital signs the same as sicker patients of colour.[38] All algorithms and programs somewhere need some historical data and various parameters to analyse and provide results. Such an algorithm is filled with pitfalls, such as what if incorrect data was input by the registration desk or the historical data might not be adequate and the like. The algorithm used by UnitedHealth was no different: *Algorithm used past medical use and spending to predict patients' future healthcare costs, then used cost to rank their medical needs. But spending for black patients was less than that for similar white patients, giving healthier white patients an edge.* These were just not mere allegations, the study spokesperson validated "that the cost model within Impact Pro was highly predictive of cost, which is what it was designed to do."[39] Why would a healthcare provider of this magnitude not carry out appropriate testing?

Similarly, in another case, when the world was caught unaware during the Covid-19 pandemic initial wave, most healthcare institutions used a device called pulse oximeters, which measured blood oxygen level in a human body. Those who had blood oxygen levels below the expected threshold of 92–96 per cent of a healthy human being were admitted, while others were sent home to self-monitor. According to the researchers at the University of Michigan, which looked at nearly ten thousand patients through the USA, it was identified that

38 "New York Regulator Probes UnitedHealth Algorithm for Racial Bias," Melanie Evans and Anna Wilde Mathews, 26 October 2019, https://www.wsj.com/articles/new-york-regulator-probes-unitedhealth-algorithm-for-racial-bias-11572087601.

39 "New York Regulator Probes UnitedHealth Algorithm for Racial Bias," Melanie Evans and Anna Wilde Mathews, 26 October 2019, https://www.wsj.com/articles/new-york-regulator-probes-unitedhealth-algorithm-for-racial-bias-11572087601.

the device overestimated blood oxygen saturation levels more in patients of colour than in white patients.[40] This means that patients of colour would be in the range of normalcy and would have a less likely chance of being admitted. This also shows the lack of historical data on which the results are predicted. Possibly, this could have been based on two conditions:

  a. **Historical data.** Since patients of colour spend less on medical care, including lack of access and the inherent racial bias in treatment, which existed historically, thus, such patients had fewer previous expenses noted in the system.

  b. **System.** Most devices or systems are geared towards generating revenue. To accomplish that, the devices need to leverage historical data. If the inherent data is skewed in the first place or even to a small degree, it would impact future results.

In the case of pulse oximeters, there is an alternative school of thought too which believed that dark skin, being more pigmented, is harder to read for the device and, thus, the skewed-up results. However, if this was the case, why would the Food and Drug Administration (FDA) release a warning stating that "pulse oximeters have limitations and a risk of inaccuracy under certain circumstances that should be considered." This advice guided doctors to use pulse oximeter readings as an estimate.[41]

---

40 "How Medicine Discriminates against Non-White People and Women," *The Economist*, 10 April 2021, https://amp.economist.com/science-and-technology/2021/04/08/how-medicine-discriminates-against-non-white-people-and-women.

41 "How Medicine Discriminates against Non-White People and Women," *The Economist*, 10 April 2021, https://amp.economist.com/science-and-technology/2021/04/08/how-medicine-discriminates-against-non-white-people-and-women.

This would continue to happen until we as a society start to actually do something about it.

Additionally, one of the critical concerns with facial technology is that many government agencies are using such technology, and more often than not, a bystander gets hurt. Many of the US police force use such systems to identify bad actors in society. However, the system gives many false-positive results, resulting in incorrect arrests and, in many cases, incorrectly targeting people of colour.

The police, not surprisingly, have claimed otherwise, and as much as technology can be biased, it is not entirely worthless as depicted by the following information: In 2005, the police department of Memphis, Tennessee, made 1,200 arrests across the city under the operation Blue CRUSH (Criminal Reduction Utilizing Statistical History) and was hailed as a massive success. The succeeding police director quickly rolled out the scheme, and by 2011, crime across the city had fallen by 24 per cent.

The program was developed by criminologists and data scientists at the University of Memphis using IBM predictive analytics software.[42] The algorithms search for correlations in the data to identify crime-concentrated areas, much like Tom Cruise in the movie *Minority Report*. The problem of rules remains to be seen. If you tighten the limits on such a program, you are bound to miss out on many other crimes. On the other hand, permitting the program to operate freely might drag in many blameless people too. "Parole boards in more than half of all US states use predictions founded on data analysis as a factor in deciding whether to release somebody from prison or to keep him incarcerated."[43]

42 "How Algorithms Rule the World," Leo Hickman, *The Guardian*, 1 July 2013, https://www.theguardian.com/science/2013/jul/01/how-algorithms-rule-world-nsa.

43 "How Algorithms Rule the World," Leo Hickman, *The Guardian*, 1 July 2013,

This is just one realm of the usage of such technology. The creative industry has been using such technology to identify hit songs, melody, tempo, and the like across all the top hits. In my opinion, this all is taking too much away from the humans and placing it in the hands of the machine for the sake of profits.

The world around us uses AI in some form or the other such as predictive machine learning algorithms, automated approvals of bank transitions, robotics in medicine, and the like. We need to be more diligent as we continue to accept modern technology with a naive attitude in our lives.

II. AI and Data Privacy Acts

Data privacy protection laws are mainly concerned with the minimisation, protection, and deletion of data that contradicts the foundation on which AI and machine learning technologies are developed. As we are all aware that for AI to be effective, an AI system needs to access massive historical data for the purpose of learning and analysis to provide future predictive results.

Every year twenty-seven European Union countries, along with the United States and Canada, celebrate Data Privacy Day on 28 January. This is an ongoing effort to empower individuals, organisations, government officials, and consumers to protect data privacy, manage digital footprints, and make data protection a priority. The celebrations commemorate the first international treaty concerning data privacy protection signed in 1981.[44]

---

https://www.theguardian.com/science/2013/jul/01/how-algorithms-rule-world-nsa.

44 "Data Privacy Day," ITS Mississippi Department of Information Technology Services, 28 January 2020, https://www.its.ms.gov/Services/Pages/January-28th-is-National-Data-Privacy-Day.aspx.

Pursuant to the Convention for the Protection of Individuals, the Council of Europe, by a treaty entered into by the Council of Europe in 1981 to protect individuals' privacy rights, published "Guidelines on Artificial Intelligence and Data Protection" on 28 January 2019. The guidelines seek to assist AI developers, manufacturers, service providers, and policymakers in preserving individuals' right to data privacy.

The convention's committee emphasises the importance of personal data protection as a prerequisite for adopting or developing AI applications. The guidelines highlight the critical need for AI innovators to pay close attention to mitigating or avoiding the potential risks involved in processing personal data while enabling meaningful control over the data for data subjects.

In the United States, growing concerns about the lack of comprehensive Internet privacy regulations—particularly the use of AI to collect, use, or distribute consumer data—led to the introduction of a federal bill named the Future of Artificial Intelligence Act. The bill was introduced in 2017 in the Senate, but it did not make legislative progress.

E. NEW YORK'S LANDMARK CYBERSECURITY LAW

In July 2019, New York Governor Andrew Cuomo signed into law the SHIELD Act (Stop Hacks and Improve Electronic Data Security), which took effect on 22 March 2020. The state law requires companies to implement *reasonable safeguards* to protect personal data failings, lest they face legal consequences.[45]

The safeguards include the following:

---

45   "New York's SHIELD Act Heads to the Governor's Desk," W. Scott Kim and Alejandro H. Cruz, Data Security Law Blog, 9 July 2019, https://www.pbwt.com/data-security-law-blog/new-yorks-shield-act-heads-to-the-governors-desk/.

a. Ensuring that there is a designated employee/information security officer to oversee security programs
b. Establishing a cybersecurity program and having a written policy concerning cybersecurity
c. Training employees concerning the security program
d. Identifying foreseeable third-party risks
e. Monitoring and checking on the effectiveness of the data safeguards
f. Assessing risks within the network and software
g. Disposing of privileged information when it is no longer needed

Data covered under the SHIELD Act have been expanded to include biometric information, usernames with passwords, and credit card numbers. The extended definition of *private/ privileged information* incorporates two additional data identification provisions, one being the primary source of such privileged information, which is "any information concerning a natural person which, can be identified because of name, number, and/or personal trait or personal mark, or any other identifiers, can be used to identify such natural person," along with one of the following:

a. Social Security number
b. Driver's licence number
c. Account number
d. Debit or credit card number with or without code or password that would enable access to the account
e. Biometric information

Changes to prior law include enhanced civil penalties for breaches of notification obligation, application of the law to entities irrespective of their location, and expanded definitions of a data breach as well as of *privileged information.*

The law applies to New York State businesses and those who licence or own computerised data containing New York citizens' private information. Physical presence in New York State or doing business in New York is not a prerequisite for being covered under SHIELD. As long as people or entities maintain New York residents' private information, they are subject to SHIELD. Small businesses (defined as those with fewer than fifty employees and less than $3 million of yearly revenue) are required to implement a security program with their type of work, size, and types of data stored.

F. IoT and Data Privacy Breaches: Case Analyses

In 2018, a Portland couple reported that their Amazon Echo recorded their conversation and sent it to someone in the contact list without their consent. The incident made headlines as concerns over Alexa (Amazon's AI device) spying on personal conversations grew.[46]

A report titled "Clearly Opaque: Privacy Risks of the IoT" (2018) warns that the IoT could undermine personal privacy to an extent where advertisers could capture private thoughts and/ or conversations.

IoT-enabled devices are vulnerable to hacking, given the multitude of access points.

A case in point is an incident involving VTech Electronics, a manufacturer of electronic toys. The company reached a settlement reportedly worth $650,000 with the US Federal Trade Commission over a data breach in 2015 that exposed millions of children and

---

46 "5 Biggest IoT Security Failures of 2018," James Sanders, TechRepublic, 17 December 2018, https://www.techrepublic.com/article/5-biggest-iot-security-failures-of-2018/.

parents' personal information. The data breach resulted from IoT devices designed for children that included smartwatches, handhelds, and apps.[47] VTech collected information from the children without prior consent from parents, and the decryption keys of the data were readily available to hackers. VTech did not know about the data breach until a tech publisher reported on it online.

Another case in 2017 involved an Internet-connected fish tank that hackers used to gather data on patrons of a North American casino. According to a cybersecurity agency, Darktrace's report, hackers gained a foothold into the casino network through the fish tank's connected thermostat. Sensors on the fish tank were connected to a personal computer that controlled the tank's cleanliness, food, and temperature.[48]

Imagine the level of sophistication.

G. HOW CAN DATA BEHAVIOUR LEAD TO YOUR IDENTIFICATION?

Identifiability refers to the ability to distinguish one individual from other individuals using a set of identifiers. The individual's name, combined with another identifier, such as an address, is sufficient to identify the specific person.

Although a person's name is the conventional means of identification, by itself, it may not constitute personal data since many other people may have the same name. However, the name in combination with additional data, such as a

---

47   *"IoT Kids' Toys Privacy Breach Case Settles," George Khoury, Esq., Find Law, 10 January 2018,* https://blogs.findlaw.com/technologist/2018/01/iot-kids-toys-privacy-breach-case-settles.html.

48   *"How a Fish Tank Helped Hack a Casino," Alex Schiffer, Washington Post, 21 July 2017,* https://www.washingtonpost.com/news/innovations/wp/2017/07/21/how-a-fish-tank-helped-hack-a-casino/.

workplace, address, or telephone number can identify one specific individual.

An Internet user's online profile has several layers. *Online identifiers* is a term included explicitly in GDPR in its definition of personal data. These identifiers include information related to the device used by an individual, tools, applications, or protocols. Recital thirty gives a non-exhaustive list of online identifiers:

a. IP or Internet protocol addresses
b. Cookie identifiers
c. Radio frequency identification (RFID) tags
d. Advertising ID
e. Device fingerprints
f. MAC addresses
g. Pixel tags
h. Account handles

An individual leaves traces on the Internet when using any of these, and these data, in combination with unique identifiers and data received by servers, can be enough to create an individual profile while also identifying the individual.

The first layer is what you can control and relates to your inputs to social media or mobile applications. The data can include private messages, likes, profile information, public posts, search queries, surveys, and tests you took, photos you posted, events you attended, and websites visited.

Whereas the first layer deals with the conscious decisions you made, the second layer consists of behavioural observations. These are not particular actions but metadata[49] that provide a

---

49   The Electronic Frontier Foundation, at https://ssd.eff.org/en/module/why-metadata-matters, 3 December 2019, defines metadata as everything except the content of your communications. You can think of metadata as the

context for the actions taken. These observations can include your real-time location and an in-depth understanding of professional and personal relationships. Companies or entities track the time you spend offline or online, the content you click on, time spent reading it, keystroke patterns, shopping patterns, typing speed, and movements of fingers on a touch screen.

The third layer combines interpretations of the above two layers. The data gathered from the first two layers are analysed using algorithms and compared to obtain meaningful statistical correlations. The analyses infer conclusions concerning what we do and how we live.

I. Why Is Metadata Necessary to Understand?

We need to understand the difference between regular data and metadata. A call to your doctor about your diagnosis is data; information about the phone call, such as when it was made, to whom, or for how long, could be examples of metadata. The concept of metadata applies to just about everything. Digital content is organised through metadata. When metadata becomes personal, such as when they tell how a specific person uses a particular software program or how frequently the program is run, things get tricky. When you click a picture through your android or iOS devices, they all collect metadata about the photo, the time and date, how many clicks were made or settings used, how data were exchanged

---

digital equivalent of an envelope. Just as an envelope contains information about the sender, receiver, and destination of a message, so do metadata. Metadata means information about the digital communications you send and receive. Some examples of metadata include
Subject line of your e-mails
Length of your conversations
Time frame in which a conversation took place
Your location when communicating (as well as with whom)

amongst many systems with disparate operating platforms, and the like. Someone who does not know the actual content of your data may look at metadata to find vulnerabilities. For example, they may discover that you called a doctor (though they may not know the speciality), that you spoke to someone for thirty minutes every day, that you meet Jane/John Doe[50] at 3:00 p.m., and so on. Such information is enough to make you vulnerable even if they do not have the password to your vault.

We tend to care about our data but not about our metadata. As a result, we leave metadata as breadcrumbs when we use the software, devices, and other technology, without realising how these metadata can be reconstructed to learn things about us. When you buy a book from an online seller, the system shows other comparable items coupled with the book you are purchasing. In short, that system is tracking your activity, and it connects your actions based on its monitoring of visitors' behaviours to that site. As a result, the algorithm shows you additional, similar products to help you buy and produce an extra sale for the company.

When you use a search engine, metadata, combined with other factors, determines what is on the web page and how relevant it is for you. The system makes decisions based on your search choices and clicking behaviour, and it starts to offer preferences targeted at you specifically.

On the bright side, metadata can help replicate similar structures, extending your data's longevity and the devices storing them. The best example would be how Target, the megastore, used this information to its advantage. In *a New York Times* article, one Target employee gave a hypothetical

---

50 According to Wikipedia.org article "John Doe," 8 January 2014, https://en.wikipedia.org/wiki/John_Doe, "'John Doe' and 'Jane Doe' (for females) are multiple-use names that are used when the true name of a person is unknown or is being intentionally concealed."

example. Imagine a woman, age twenty-three, living in Atlanta. In March, she bought cocoa-butter lotion, a purse large enough to double as a diaper bag, zinc, magnesium supplements, and a bright blue rug. Based on these purchase decisions, there is an 87 per cent chance that she is pregnant and that her delivery date is sometime in late August. In fact, in a real case, a high-school girl's father gave a piece of his mind to the Target sales manager for sending coupons for maternity clothes and advertisements for cribs; he later learned from his daughter that she was due to deliver a baby that August.[51] So the actual data on which the algorithm made its decision was unknown. Still, some aspect of the data collected was just metadata, which is nothing but descriptive information that pinpoints certain concrete activities. This information, coupled with other parameters, helped Target develop an algorithm that delivered tangible results.

Metadata is such a powerful tool that, on its own, can give valuable information to people who own your metadata. In case of a phone call, the data of the actual conversation might or might not be essential, but the metadata—the cell towers you are connected to, with whom you spoke, what other devices are connected to your primary devices—are so rich with valuable information that are equal in weightage to the core information. The question we need to ask ourselves is, why metadata has gained so many advancements in technology? To me, the answer is simply because people do not care about metadata as the regular data, which opens an opportunity of the landscape for technology or tech enthusiastic companies to experiment and invest money in such technology since there is more financial

---

51 "How Companies Learn Your Secrets," Charles Duhigg, *New York Times Magazine*, 16 February 2012, https://www.nytimes.com/2012/02/19/magazine/shopping-habits.html?pagewanted=6&_r=1&hp.

benefit to be gained there than regular information. If you would look at most of the telecom providers, they are now reducing tariffs of calls, but the tariffs associated with Internet/data packages are increasing. This just supports my argument. The websites people serve, the type of preferences we use on our mobile devices, the apps we use, the VOIP calls being made, the online relationship that people have, such metadata holds tremendous potential for cross-sells of some products or another.

The power of metadata is far more durable than people generally realise, and one should watch closely for its influence since it is difficult to control the dissemination of metadata.

II. How Anonymous Are Your Data?

The amount of digital data produced across the world every day is close to 2.5 quintillion bytes. The new data add to the sea of information, including confidential information on individuals' habits, preferences, and health. Anonymisation of data is necessary for marketers and researchers so as to protect data privacy. Anonymised data are exempt from GDPR, CCPA, and other data privacy regulations.

Massive data repositories can reveal trends that help researchers and scientists gain insights into health or disease, demonstrate certain factors such as the impact of income inequality, teach AI systems to behave more like humans, and target advertising with more efficiency. The process of deidentification helps data brokers protect data when people unwittingly share their personal information. De-identification involves removing visible markers or identifiers such as Social Security numbers, names, and addresses, adding random *noise* data, or replacing specific details with more generic ones. For instance, "1 September 1997" could be replaced with "May–October 1997."

According to a new study, it is possible to reidentify an individual from a so-called anonymised data set even if the set is incomplete. Commonly-used techniques of anonymisation make it easy to link anonymous data to a specific individual. For instance, if a detective is looking for a male in Tampa, age thirty to thirty-five, with diabetes, it would not be possible to deduce the person's name. Nevertheless, if any other information such as birthdate, zip code, number of children, or employment details were known, it could be possible to identify the person.

A new study led by Yves-Alexandre de Montioye, an expert on computational privacy at Imperial College London, indicates that the risk is high. The researchers created a statistical model to discover the possibility that anonymous data could be linked to a person's true identity. They found that this was disturbingly easy even if one had only an incomplete data set.[52]

According to Montjoye, it is possible to reidentify an individual accurately 99.98 per cent of the time in the United States if one has fifteen pieces of data, including gender, age, or marital status. Fifteen demographic details may sound like a lot, but in 2017, anonymised data containing 248 attributes of 123 million households in America were published by a marketing analytics company.

In many instances, researchers have been able to identify individuals from public data sets. One of these relates to the reidentification of individuals from Netflix data sets by Arvind Narayanan. In a contest organised by Netflix to improve the movie recommendation engine, Narayanan's team reidentified individuals in the anonymous database. In another instance,

---

52 "Anonymous Data Won't Protect Your Identity," Sophie Bushwick, *Scientific American*, 23 July 2019, phttps://www.scientificamerican.com/article/anonymous-data-wont-protect-your-identity/.

researchers reidentified fifty individuals from DNA information in databases such as the one thousand Genomes Project.[53]

Montjoye suggests that one way to tackle the identification problem is to produce new anonymisation techniques while rigorously testing them to ensure individuals are not identified by third parties based on personal data sets.

---

53 "The Re-Identification of Anonymous People with Big Data," Dr Mark van Rijmenam, 10 February 2013, https://datafloq.com/read/re-identifying-anonymous-people-with-big-data/228.

CHAPTER 2

ARE YOU THE PRODUCT?

"THE PRYING EYES OF THE DIGITAL WORLD"

Most social media users are fearful of not getting likes on their picture, being accepted as a friend, or being tagged in others' photos, or not being commented on their social media post. Such user, without realisation, andin an effort to being more visible on the social media, are placing more of their personal information out there. For example, a better-clicked image uploaded on your social media from home, a catchy tagline posted from children's school building, or posting a private dinner celebration showing of their luxury with family and the like. If you reread my previous sentence, if you have left your geolocation switched on, a person seeing your post now knows where your home is, where your children study, or who your family members all are. Besides the location embedded in the image, the metadata of a picture also contains what kind of phone you have.

You might argue that this is all going into a black box supposed to treat information privately and people fairly. I certainly do not believe so. When someone writes a program, many predefined values are already baked into the code, ready to influence you. Again, look around, what does a pop-up on the latest Windows setup say? Cortana would say, "Go ahead, read the terms and accept the condition." If you do not, then no windows. Or look at the cookie pop-ups. They generally give you a choice to either read more or click okay. (Ahem!) When a choice box having options is default-selected on a particular option, these are choices already made for you. You might be able to tweak them but not block them. Thus, I believe all systems have a degree of biases of the programmer or prejudice of the company's objective for their balance sheet. The ethics are muddled in with the developers' expectations.

With time, the business models and revenue-generating mechanisms have changed, especially in the tech industry. Earlier business were developing software, such as Windows 95 or tally (accounting software), and selling those software. The job was defined, and the products have boundaries and limitations to be working as software. The industry did well by selling software, machines, and other business products. However, with time, all industries reach a saturation level, then what? Companies hunt for more enticing and intriguing products. In the current generation, it is the user data that is a hot commodity to be sold. Why? This product opens new possibilities for every business, no matter the industry or the product. The equation in my mind is simple: You were the adopter and buyer. Now the businesses and advertisers are the buyers. They are paying for services or products you use on social media or all over the Internet. How can software companies make these advertisers' money? The answer is complicatedly straightforward. By making you click the advertisement or product link upon something that interests you or something that draws your attention, they are able to generate revenue. Thus, most of these Internet-based solutions want you to continuously interact with their software by starting to play with your mind, physic, and alert the way you think. So how can they predict the appropriate advertisement? How do they know which brand were you looking out for or what product? It is through your engagement and clicks online. Your clicks on various websites and advertisements denote your behaviour, actions. The way your data is used and used for you as a carrot and everything online is so subtle that your mind and behaviour is not able to adapt and judge anything at that point in time, and somewhat subconsciously, you go with the flow.

Business are planning for the future without the consumer even realising it. Mobile industry has gone leaps and bounds ahead of time. Mobile phones have become an identity, not only because of the brand but also the data and reliance we are placing on them. They are already toying with the consumers. Look at the Samsung Galaxy, fold two (2) launched in September 2020. Fantastic piece of technology, but when you see the tech, you feel how refined it is from their gen one (1) product? There is no way they changed all that engineering so much, which took them years to develop the first time. My hunch is that they had this tech available with them. The Samsung Galaxy fold (generation 1) introduced the concept of the first folding mobile phone to humanity! Their phyolophy was to underplay the market and thought process of the consumers. YouTubers, in anticipation of technology, were estimating the cost of the device from \$2,300 to \$2,500. But they launched it for \$2,000 so that the consumers do not feel the pinch. They made the world settle in the thought of their first galaxy fold device and then releasing something they had the tech for such a price. Even though this device carries such a high price tag, its sale will go up.

Refer to any political campaign right from the time the political candidate wants you to perceive to the instance when or if a scandal breaks out. Everything is data-driven to influence the masses. It is estimated that fake news travels six times faster than the truth on Twitter, while truthful tweets take six times as long as fake ones to spread across Twitter.[54]

Three main forces shape how data affect people's lives, specifically their privacy: (1) laws and regulations; (2) business, society, and culture; and (3) technology.

KEY FORCES REQUIRED TO MAINTAIN PRIVACY

---

54   "Fake News Travels Six Times Faster Than the Truth on Twitter," Chris Stokel-Walker, 8 March 2018, https://www.newscientist.com/article/2163226-fake-news-travels-six-times-faster-than-the-truth-on-twitter/.

We do not live in a world of perfect privacy. Many people and organisations will have information about you—sometimes for good purposes, sometimes for evil ends. Data are continually being generated about you, and no one has complete control over how these data are used, except the person who possesses them. Yes, you do have a right to privacy, and many laws exist to protect it. But the right to privacy is not merely given to you on a silver platter. You must fight for it and earn it. Data are a major corporate asset. In many cases, data are of greater value than the technology that processes them. Google, Amazon, Facebook, Apple, all the technology giants, have gotten to where they are thanks to their ability to collect and manipulate data, including personal data on billions of individuals.

This exploding use of online services is opening a new black hole that we cannot avoid. Telemedicine, online shopping, online investigations, and many other activities are often without inadequate safeguards. Protecting people from being harmed by this proliferation of digital content will be challenging, but that does not mean it is impossible or that we should not try. We must realise that privacy is a fundamental right (the *what* and *why* of this book) and security (i.e., the technical aspects of data protection) is the *how*.

The more you take control of your privacy, the more you limit the power of those who wish to control your life. If a person knows everything about you, they can do a lot more to affect your life than if they do not know anything about you. Your reputation should be shaped by your own actions, not those of others.

We recently experienced a significant data fiasco involving a consulting firm, Cambridge Analytica. The personal information of more than 50 million Facebook users were harvested and offered to their clients. However, even after such events, most of us remain largely unaware of who knows who and who sees their data.

You should be in control of with whom you share your thoughts, ideas, and feelings. Protecting your privacy can give you a second chance in life should you happen to make a grave or stupid mistake. Without privacy, we all would be mere puppets in the hands of those who control our information, whether it be governments or private-sector tech giants. Without privacy, there is no free will.

Thus, we all need to be sensitive to privacy at an individual level if we wish to be protected from companies violating our privacy. Company employees can be instrumental in this regard since employees are the heart of any organisation. However, to use existing protections, you must be aware of them and how they can be applied. This book will guide you towards understanding the relevant laws so that you can exercise your rights and protect your privacy.

CHAPTER 3

WHAT DO HACKERS LOOK TO GAIN FROM AN INDIVIDUAL'S PERSONAL DATA AND INFORMATION?

Hackers search through data files to steal personal information, including name, address, credit card details, and phone number, along with other authentication credentials. The following are some of the typical gains hackers stand to achieve from stealing personal data:

Sale of personal information: Hackers obtain personal information and, typically, sell it in bulk. According to Quartz, an individual information package that includes birthdate, identification number, name, address, and possibly credit card details can fetch as much as $450, with the median price being more than $21.35.[55]

---

55 "The Many Motives of Hackers and How Much Your Data Is Worth to them," Navanwita Sachdev, The Sociable, 1 July 2019, https://sociable.co/web/the-many-motives-of-hackers-and-how-much-your-data-is-worth-to-them/.

According to a Google study, Symantec's "2019 Internet Security Threat Report" indicated that attacks on businesses had increased by 12 per cent in the previous two years, and the revenue from ransomware had reached $25 million in those two years.[56]

Social Security numbers can fetch $1 each, while each medical record generates revenue of $20–$50. Each credit card number brings between $2 and $5.

More lucrative information: Hackers will search for potentially lucrative accounts, such as military and government addresses and large corporations' e-mails and passwords. Hackers may either carry out the hack themselves or sell the credentials to the dark web for a higher price.[57] Stolen credit card information is typically sold in bundles of ten or a hundred. After buying physical items using the card, the hackers sell these through eBay or a dark website.

Blackmail and extortion: Following a data breach, two Canadian banks, the Bank of Montreal and Simplii Financial, were blackmailed by perpetrators who threatened to publicise data unless they were paid a million-dollar ransom.[58] In another case, hackers accessed the files of Radiohead, an English rock band, and threatened to make them public unless they were paid $150,000.

56 "Ransomware Has Made More Than $25 Million from Its Victims over 2 Years, Google Study Finds," Rob Price, Business Insider, 26 July 2017, https://www.businessinsider.com.au/ransomware-victims-25-million-ransomware-two-years-google-study-2017-7?r=UK&IR=T.

57 "Here's What Your Stolen Identity Goes for on the Internet's Black Market," Keith Collins, Quartz, 23 July 2015, https://qz.com/460482/heres-what-your-stolen-identity-goes-for-on-the-internets-black-market/.

58 "Two Major Canadian Banks Blackmailed after Alleged Data Breach," Jérôme Segura, Malwarebytes Labs, 29 May 2018, https://blog.malwarebytes.com/cybercrime/2018/05/two-major-canadian-banks-hacked-blackmailed/.

Information is loosely available to everyone. And if you are cheating on your wife, you must be incredibly careful about which flower service you use. Consider the case of *LeRoy Greer v 1-800-FLOWERS.*[59]

LeRoy buys flowers for a girlfriend. The wife finds out, calls 1-800-FLOWERS, and confirms the transaction. Files for divorce and gets it. After divorce, filed a lawsuit on 1-800-FLOWERS. The company says they need to sue us in New York. Leroy submits the case in Texas, and the judge dismisses the case.

LeRoy bought the flowers over the telephone. When his wife called to enquire about the flower shop, the vendor gave her details about the transaction. The injured party (the husband) claimed the disclosure to his wife violated his privacy, so he sued in Texas court. The court looked at the vendor's terms and conditions, posted on its website, and found that according to those terms, any dispute must be resolved in the courts of a different state, New York.

Now it is difficult to go to another state just to sue a flower shop. Thus, the vendor's publication of terms on the web was effective as a transaction. Furthermore, as a general rule, it is difficult for an insensitive party to win the case in the eyes of the jury.

In a similar case, covered by USAtoday.com, technology ruined another man's marriage. *The case was against Uber by a French businessperson for nearly $48 million,*[60] *claiming that a flaw in the ride-sharing company resulted in the marriage's dissolution. He claimed that the app's glitch caused it to continue to*

---

59 "Lawsuit of the Day: *Greer v. 1-800-Flowers,*" David Lat, Above the Law, 8 August 2007, https://abovethelaw.com/2007/08/lawsuit-of-the-day-greer-v-1-800-flowers/.

60 "A Man Sues Himself. A Docket of 25 of the Weirdest, Silliest and Frivolous Lawsuits," John Harrington and Hristina Byrnes, 3 February 2020, https://www.usatoday.com/story/money/2020/02/03/25-really-weird-lawsuits-you-wouldnt-believe-were-ever-filed/41083385/.

send notifications of his whereabouts to his wife's phone even after it was logged off because he used his wife's phone to book the ride in the first place.

Shaming and taunting: Sometimes hackers steal data to taunt or shame someone. In May 2019, the city of Baltimore experienced a ransomware attack in which the hacker tagged the mayor through tweets that released confidential information. In June, hacker Daniel Kelley said he was motivated by *revenge* for not being accepted into a college computer course when he carried out a hack worth £77 million ($99 million) on a mobile network.

Experimenting, bragging, and having fun are some other reasons for hacking. In the Equifax data breach of 2017, although hackers accessed sensitive information, they did not sell the information, possibly because they considered other purposes, including espionage.

One of the most significant data breaches ever recorded involved a Vietnamese national, Hieu Minh Ngo. He sold online the identities he stole from Court Ventures, a company owned by Experian, the credit reporting agency. Ngo was arrested in 2012 for accessing 200 million records, including Social Security numbers, from which he made $1.9 million in profits.[61]

In another case in 2016, Salah Sood of Baltimore was indicted for using the Social Security numbers and names of three elderly people at an assisted-living facility to obtain six credit cards. Sood made himself the authorised user of the elderly people's accounts and carried out purchases worth $75,000 using these accounts.[62]

61   "Vietnamese National Sentenced to 13 Years in Prison for Operating a Massive International Hacking and Identity Theft Scheme," Justice.gov, 14 July 2015, https://www.justice.gov/opa/pr/vietnamese-national-sentenced-13-years-prison-operating-massive-international-hacking-and.

62   "Assisted Living Facility Manager Indicted for Stealing Elderly Residents' Identities to Obtain Credit Cards" through US Department of Justice

He allegedly committed these crimes while managing Holland Manor Eldercare, where the elderly individuals lived. Sood could be looking at thirty years in prison and a $1 million fine for bank fraud.[63]

Can police ask you to unlock your phone? With the increasing use of encryption, law enforcement officials say compelling a person to cooperate in decryption, such as giving their fingerprints or face scans, can be a make-or-break for collecting key evidence. In one case of an alleged sexual assault, the police seized a piece of crucial evidence: the defendant's iPhone, which had a geolocation system that could place him at the crime scene. The prosecutor had to obtain an order from the magistrate to require that the phone be unlocked.

There are many different schools of thought on this issue. Some people believe that asking people to open their own mobile devices violates their rights not to engage in self-incrimination. In contrast, others believe it is a necessary evil to safeguard society. The courts have gone through a topsy-turvy journey on the question. A 2019 article in the *Washington Post*[64] argued that a fingerprint is not the same as a password. To ask someone for their password is to request that they disclose the "contents of their mind," whereas fingerprints are like a key that does not require people to divulge anything through a mental

(District of Maryland), 25 February 2016, https://www.justice.gov/usao-md/pr/assisted-living-facility-manager-indicted-stealing-elderly-residents-identities-obtain.

63 "Maryland Assisted Living Facility Manager Indicted For Stealing Elderly Residents' Identities" covered by Office of the Inspector General Social Security Administration, 25 February 2016, https://oig.ssa.gov/audits-and-investigations/investigations/feb25-md-id-theft.

64 "A Magistrate Said Police Could Force a Man to Unlock His Phone. Is That Legal?" Justin Jouvenal, *Washington Post*, 12 August 2019, https://www.washingtonpost.com/local/public-safety/a-magistrate-ruled-police-could-force-a-man-to-unlock-his-phone--is-that-legal/2019/08/10/7f78281e-b882-11e9-a091-6a96e67d9cce_story.html.

process. Nowadays, police have started seeking consent when they collect any digital evidence. Still, some people have fought back by claiming that collecting a device is not the same as reviewing the contents of the device.

To review a device, an investigator generally requires permission. In the United States, the Fifth Amendment to the Constitution gives all people the right to refuse to incriminate themselves. The same concept is encompassed in the European Convention of Human Rights (ECHR), in Article 6. The European Court of Human Rights (ECtHR) has affirmed that this concept is at the heart of fair procedure under Article 6. So one must be incredibly careful and attentive when dealing with authorities or investigators. Remember, it is #myprivacy #myright.

In another case, under US law, *where a wife passed away, leaving behind her husband and memories locked in the iCloud with its appropriate security, the judge ruled in favour of the husband's request for access to any photos behind the Apple ID, where Judge Rita Mella wrote, "Apple shall afford [Scandalios] the opportunity to reset the password to [Swezey's] Apple ID."*[65]

Surviving a ransomware attack: Criminals are becoming very sophisticated in their use of technology, and so are the mechanisms they have started using to encrypt a victim's data. Attackers start by observing their victim's behaviour. To be successful, an attacker needs to get into your head, and what better way to do it than by sending a message from a person who is close to you? While receiving your e-mail, if you receive an e-mail from a familiar name, you will invariably download an attachment without giving the e-mail a second thought, and

---

65   *"Apple Must Give Grieving Husband Access to Cloud-Stored Family Photos, Judge Rules," Andrew Keshner, 26 January 2019,* https://www.marketwatch. com/story/apple-must-give-grieving-husband-access-to-cloud-stored-family-photos-judge-rules-2019-01-25.

even before you realise it, kaboom! Your data are encrypted. This method can encrypt virtually any device, from a desktop to a server. The idea is to encrypt your data and ask you to pay for a decryption key.

According to survey data in Radware's 2018 "Executive Application and Network Security Report," for the first time in the survey's five-year history, a majority of executives (53%) reported paying the ransom to a hacker following a cyberattack. This comes as technology and privacy concerns present more significant challenges in improving overall security postures. Additionally, the respondents stated that their biggest concerns associated with cyberattacks were customer loss (~41%) and brand reputation loss (~34%).[66]

It is of paramount importance to do all you can to safeguard your privacy and data. So what should you do to protect yourself?

a. Back up your data: I would suggest not to pinpoint critical, essential, and other forms of data, but rather to back up everything. Cloud storage has gone down in cost year after year, and it is going to get cheaper.

b. Where to back up: I would suggest that you back up your data on the cloud as well as on a hard drive.

c. What to do when you receive a suspicious e-mail: Use a medium other than the one through which the suspicious attachment has arrived. I would suggest making a phone call. There is a possibility that the hackers might be tracking you through your device. If you try to use the same medium to enquire, the attacker is smart enough to respond with a convincing answer

---

66 "Radware Survey Finds Majority of Companies Paid a Hacker's Ransom over the Past Year," Rad Hardware, 12 June 2018, https://www.radware.com/newsevents/pressreleases/2018/majority-of-companies-paid.

since you are using a device that has been compromised in the first place.

d.   Should you pay? If you think that once you pay these hackers money or digital currency, they will give you the decryption key, then you are wrong. They never will, and the ransom for your data will always keep growing.

e.   What to do once your system is infected: Just restore everything to factory settings and restart your life with your backed-up data. If you do not have a backup, start from scratch. If you pay, they will never go away, and if you back up your data later, they might encrypt your data again and even encrypt other devices. Sometimes, in life, taking one step back is the only way to take two steps forward.

f.   Know the law: This does not mean you need to be a lawyer. Read blog articles, such as www.whitecollar. org, whitecollarinvestigator.com, and the like, to stay abreast of what is happening in your state or country. Then if tomorrow you were to be trapped in a breach, you would not have been sitting idle.

CHAPTER 4

DOUBTING CAPITALISM?

This chapter is dear to my heart, as it reveals the depth of privacy concerns plaguing societies across the globe. Here, I present the human, technology, and legal system's emotional side and what privacy means to other determined advocates and me for privacy protections. I use somewhat less formal language to let my emotions come through. If you do not share some of my policy views, I will ask for your forgiveness in advance. You do not have to agree with this chapter to benefit from the information I have provided throughout the book.

We live in a world dominated by capitalism, and in such a world, privacy can never be 100 per cent guaranteed unless you disconnect yourself from the world or are a Secret Service agent.

If you have any doubts, take a look at your smartphone, a mobile device used to carry out so many activities and other elements associated with our lives, such as personal diaries, passwords, private pictures, and the like; on the other hand, it is used to store information such as day-to-day tasks, social media interaction, social contacts, health information, and much more.

This powerful pocket tool can easily be used as a surveillance mechanism. Under Covid-19, many governments have opted to use such devices to carry out contact tracing. If you are diagnosed with the virus, the government can easily track where you have been and with whom you had contact, basically tracking your interaction, networking, and social presence. But this procedure poses enormous security and privacy risks, albeit with good intent. Any activity you carry out, from a basic request for an Uber or Lyft ride to placing an online order for something delivered to your doorstep, enables others to track your location with pinpoint precision. The question we must ask ourselves is what all your personal data, in the hands of people who are financially motivated, can do to you and your life. This chapter explains the various elements of behavioural tracking and how it is being used to sway the decisions of a typical person.

A. THE SNOWDEN EFFECT

Edward Snowden is viewed as a knight and a protagonist for an individual's privacy. He took on one of the strongest governments of the United States for the people to be aware of what is at stake and how the government was exploiting their own personal data without any due process. The effect was he is currently living his life in exile. The ripple effect created is too huge to be ignored.

So will tomorrow be any different? I start with this question because this is the idea that underpins the concept of capitalism. Capitalism has done well over a few hundred years, in selected countries, such as the West or developed nations, where this economic system has provided wages, jobs, and the like. Most economists would argue that it strengthens economies, though it by itself does not eliminate poverty. Another idea underpinning capitalism is the freedom to choose from a plethora of products because of the availability of alternatives. Through the resulting growth in markets and competition, capitalism incentivises innovation as a way to make money.

Capitalism, generally, is a good thing and a barometer of growth for a country. But in today's world, capitalism incentivises large companies to take advantage of their ability to obtain personal information. That is, the money drives new investment with dubious innovation, which leads to a lack of alternatives, in the true sense of freedom, to choose amongst multiple options. And because of the lack of choices, the end user has no choice but to opt for the single option represented in many ways to entice the customer. For me, the process implies nothing but this: no choice, no freedom. Isn't this the case with all the privacy policies that force the users to click "I agree" when you open websites or any software? Though the privacy policy is right in front of us, we cannot reject it because the consequence would be the unavailability of a service or upgrade, rendering our device or software inoperable. So you have a choice but actually no choice in the practical sense.

I suspect that the great majority of people think that corporations collect only information that people have provided to them directly. But such information has limited gain. Google knows where you are virtually every second of your life through Google Maps and various Google devices as many of the related apps require location accuracy. Similarly, Facebook knows your likes, dislikes, types of friends, and so on. The companies or tech giants are incentivising you so that they can get not only your personal information but behavioural information too. Once your behaviour is known, they virtually control your future actions. But most users of social media apps and other technologies do not worry about keeping such information private because they do not understand the related privacy concerns. People cannot fully assess the impact of their information being disclosed to such companies.

As a general process, everyone believes the technology to be neutral and objective. We all believe what we want to believe, or we believe what we are told to believe, as most humans are not qualified to look beyond that black box, such as computers or mobile devices or other advanced devices. It is time that we question each and every element of the black box and build on our understanding of the impact it might carry on our personal lives.

Edward Snowden (the former US National Security Agency employee who exposed that agency's intrusive data collection practices) has started a wave to show the world that your data are essential. Many others have followed in his footsteps, creating a "Snowden effect" by fighting for people's right to privacy. So why should the billions of users of such devices not take their own actions and information that they give out seriously? We must tackle technology as a child, recognising that just as a father and mother are responsible for creating life, humans have developed technology and not the other way around.

One must deal with technology in the same way that a father deals with his son or daughter. When a parent wants to get a message through to a child, the parent must convey the message in a language that the child would understand, but to do so, you need to understand the child's thought process that instigated his or her action in the first place. Technology is no different, but to understand its effects, one must go beyond the black box and understand it in detail to tackle the situation.

Let us drill down into this scenario in more detail. If the child is not bound by any learnings, they would virtually do what they want to do. The same applies to technology. Various fields, such as science and medicine, which have impacted society in myriad, have gotten through different hopes and channels and regulatory compliance. One wonders why there are no regulatory constraints in the field of technology. When a modern technology is introduced as the impact of the data, metadata will create on a common man. Without appropriate rules, the potential is limitless, and coupled with the concept of capitalism, where the only driving force is money, it does not leave any choice for the society to exercise their freedom of choice.

My objective here is to show that we must all be sceptical, though not paranoid, in our outlook when dealing with technology relating to privacy matters, especially when it comes to data. Scepticism is an art when using technology. Ways of exercising scepticism range from thinking twice before giving your information to sometimes saying no to a service because they ask for too much intrusion into your privacy.

If you still believe that your indirect information cannot create or force you to buy anything, let me take you through some concepts that can show you the light at the end of the tunnel.

I. Advanced Psychological Theories Used to Manipulate Human Behaviour

This short section explains the importance of your behavioural data. Information on our behaviour is derived from what you like, dislike, subscribe to, the ads you click on, and so on. Obviously, there is an algorithm running in the background, but in simple words, what you do in the online world is tracked and is used to derive your behaviour. Studies have shown that the data we disclose without giving any consent can do wonders for large corporations, even to the extent of predicting your mood. That is because your attitude is affected by your recent activities, such as which book you are reading, where you bought from, which TV series you are watching, how you have spent your day by clicks, where you have gone, what orders you have placed, what household items you bought, and so on. If this is not scary enough, consider the case cited earlier, reported by the *New York Times*, where Target figured out a way to find if a girl was pregnant even before she began to realise it herself. Target's baby registry promotion program was tracking buying to such an extent that they knew that pregnant women buy unscented lotion, calcium, magnesium, and the like.

This web of dilemmas keeps on growing and entangling people, where systems can now predict the gender of the unborn child on the colour of the rug purchased by the pregnant lady, amongst other factors. Now, when you play a behavioural game on Facebook, such as "What do you think?" or "What animal are you?" or anything that asks you to give your birthday and other personal information, think twice.

On an organisational level, companies are using chatbot services, where there is no requirement for a physical representative; artificial intelligence analyses previous queries and answers the customers who ask product-related questions. This overall mechanism may be described as surveillance capitalism. Though such activities may be perceived by many people as a process or outcome of a mere machine learning algorithm, people forget that for any machine learning algorithm to be successful, it requires a plethora of data. To further attain the best results, one must gain more insight into an individual's personal data. A simple application as chatbot requires your name, e-mail, and optional mobile number. The moment it gets these parameters, it starts referencing to your previous request made with the mentioned parameters to yield results favourable to your request. That is fine, but what happens to this data or the metadata surrounding all these machine learning algorithms or the cookies you accept while using such services? Such data and similar data are stored for future reference, and many users do not even care.

Microsoft had launched an artificial intelligence chatbot named TAY (Thinking About You) in March 2016. Within sixteen hours of its launch, it was shut down because the chatbot started posting provocative and insulting tweets through its Twitter account. The chatbot learned from the politically-incorrect phrases that were posted on Twitter. As a result, the chatbot started posting racist and sexually-charged messages in response to other Twitter users.[67] Roman Yampolskiy,[68] an artificial intelligence researcher, mentioned that TAY's reaction was understandable because it was programmed to impersonate the deliberate and offensive behaviour of other Twitter users, which indicated that the chatbot wasn't given an understanding of what is considered inappropriate behaviour and, thus, to omit the same.[69]

People do not care because they do not have the foresight of what could potentially go wrong, and no one wants to let go of their convenience factor. There is no doubt that when you try using a browser like Google Chrome, which stores your data and with their robust algorithms, they can yield a perfect result favourable to your request, while on the other side, if you use a DuckDuckGo browser, which blocks all tracking request (the

---

67 "Microsoft Is Deleting Its AI Chatbot's Incredibly Racist Tweets," Rob Price from Business Insider, 24 March 2016, https://web.archive.org/web/20190130071430/https://www.businessinsider.com/microsoft-deletes-racist-genocidal-tweets-from-ai-chatbot-tay-2016-3.

68 "Roman Yampolskiy," Wikipedia.org, last edited on 2 October 2020, https://en.wikipedia.org/wiki/Roman_Yampolskiy.

69 "Tay (bot)," Wikipedia.org, last edited 7 April 2021, https://en.wikipedia.org/wiki/Tay_(bot).

majority of them, at least), the search result that you might get is scattered. You have to leave your convenience and take the pains of looking for the correct search results, ultimately losing your convenience, however, safeguarding privacy to a great extent.

Let us look at one of the most famous games of all time, Pokémon Go. It was not developed by just any gaming company but initially by Google, which brought the game forward under the shadow of its Niantic lab—a fact that was not widely known. The game was much bigger than the screen on which people played it. It was an augmented reality game that could emulate people or children visiting places and, thus, increase patronage at a coffee shop or mall. And people were travelling in groups wherever the game directed them to go, which was basically where investors or businesses wanted them to go. The whole idea was to silently influence people's habits of shopping and the like. If people became aware of what was going on, users would become opposed to it and discover the threats involved in subliminal advertisements.[70]

Subliminal advertisements hit people's subconscious in such a subtle manner, considering your actions, which users of technology might find not worth paying attention to. As an example, Benson & Hedges[71] produced a subliminal advertisement in which a man was holding a woman wearing a backless one-piece dress. This advertisement was released in the early 2000s. The ad displayed excitement, but on an unconscious level, it stimulated anxiety for physical intimacy. The advertisement did not leave much to the imagination

70 "How Companies Learn Your Secrets," Charles Duhigg, 16 February 2012, https://www.nytimes.com/2012/02/19/magazine/shopping-habits.html?pagewanted=6&_r=1&hp.

71 "6 Examples of Subliminal Advertising, from Spooky to NSFW," Dan Shewan, Word Stream, 24 October 2017, https://www.wordstream.com/blog/ws/2017/10/24/subliminal-advertising.

once you noticed it. This is because this type of anxiety is associated with maladaptive behaviours like smoking, drinking, and overeating. And they wanted you to smoke more of their products. Their sales actually went up.

Similarly, Marlboro's marketing team produced a visual message to convey the Marlboro brand using the company logo. Marlboro developed a logo in a barcode-style design and placed it on the Formula 1 car representing Ferrari. The logo was clearly visible at high speeds, creating the same subconscious impact as in the Benson & Hedges ad. This subliminal visual messaging drives people subconsciously to buy or get attracted to a brand, much as Professor X from movie *"The X-men"* could control people's minds and actions.

Another famous psychological theory of relevance is B. F. Skinner's theory of behaviour modification, which emphasised the use of positive reinforcement to encourage the desired behaviour, much in the same way as many parents treat their children. Positive reinforcement starts off with baits, like the ones used by fishermen while fishing. Technology developers use this theory to their advantage, producing enticing content when the user aimlessly swipes down from the top of the screen to refresh the notification or the page. When you get some content you like as a response, such as a gadget to be bought, a post with your named tag, or some likes or someone forwarding your picture, you are subconsciously guided to look at those actions, and this reinforcement keeps you hooked on the mobile device. Some of the notable examples could be photos refresh of people in your network, clickbait, headlines pop-up on a stock you are invested in, and the like.

Today's social media employs the same positive reinforcement technique. They have taken the theory of positive reinforcement to the next level. For instance, when someone likes or forwards your picture, you would subconsciously be forced to look at those actions. Once you are on that app, you would subsequently start scrolling, clicking on others' feeds and then some advertisements, and so on and on, helping tech giants make money by clicking those posts or those advertisements. The tech companies' advanced algorithms are designed to simulate this behaviour repeated over and over. Food apps have used a similar positive reinforcement technique. Swiping to refresh on apps such as Zomato or Uber Eats uses your historical data to present pictures of yummy-looking food items. You will click on and be enticed to buy because such advertisements are selected for you based on what they have learned from your past behaviour. Our online behaviour has been manipulated to the extent where the choice for the user has been made even before you click "accept."

And now, with the pandemic, we are more engrossed in our electronic devices than ever before. We are giving out unwanted data that helps the technology companies analyse you, dissecting your behaviour and your thought process. Most people out there think, "So what?" as if this all does not matter to them. Well, an impact on behaviour comes at a price that could be too high to pay for some families. It can even cause deaths. Yes, information has been utilised to track teenage girls' posts on social media, leading to sad consequences for the girls, some of whom have committed suicide.

Even when companies are required by law to give their users choices, they do it in a manner such that the user still does not have any option. As an example, take the privacy policy. You will invariably find a statement relating to the collection of data for quality and improvement purposes. But how many people read it? Companies would often be sending data to multiple companies, and those companies, in turn, send the data to other such companies, and if you do not consent to it, then your devices will not get updated or might even start having glitches. I believe users of technology are held at gunpoint or, in effect, forced to accept the privacy policy. Can you imagine Google cars moving around collecting road data and other information we still do not care about? So much information is being collected; some for focused research, while other data are preserved for future experiments. And since this is all metadata, the data which users do not care much about, corporations feel if others are not going to own it, why should they own it?

With mobile devices as the people's next best friend, we have opened a gateway to unimaginable amounts of data that are difficult to keep control of. Companies are vested in ramping up technology for mobile devices and coming out with lucrative offers for users. Over time international calling has become cheap or even free with some providers. However, the price of data packages has steadily ramped up because that's how companies can obtain your behavioural information and sell it to prospective customers, who can further sell their goods— you. Reliance Communication in India tried to do a similar thing, took the first bite at the apple, so to speak. They gave out mobile phones for free and charged only for the package. However, because of poor execution, they failed. But Google, with Android, will not fail. Phones are getting cheaper, and the race towards surveillance between giant companies from countries such as China and the United States is increasing. And we are handing over our data on a silver platter, and then we ask ourselves why we are getting this advertisement. It is easy for the tech giants now to replicate search results which you asked your mobile phone assistant ("Hello, Google" or "Hey, Siri") to carry out on your laptop while visiting various sites on the Internet after a few days.

Let us not forget the case of Chris Wiley, who followed in the steps of Edward Snowden. He was the whistle-blower against Cambridge Analytica. One of the things he mentioned that they could identify as a company was people and their emotions, fears, or paranoia. With those as targets, they used intelligence to manipulate what to do with their prospective customers, right from whom they should meet to what they should do next and (as we have seen) whom to vote for as well. Similarly, as many have claimed, the fake Facebook voting groups created incorrect perceptions. This has shifted the focus from commercial outcomes to political outcomes to destabilising economies by creating mass chaos.

As we can see now, governments across the globe are gaining a keen interest in such surveillance. It is about which country can use these tools to their advantage to cast semi-accurate news that can create disruption and sway emotions. The key to solving the problem is knowing the truth, but the fact seems to be long lost amongst the information produced by online media.

B. BIG BROTHER IS WATCHING

All our actions are being monitored: which picture have you clicked, when you clicked it, what did you see before that, how long did you see it for. Check it for yourself: On Facebook, when you see a video online, it stops after a few seconds, then you click on it, go to the main view, and you see the whole video. It gives whatever stimulates you, what you like, when you are depressed, when you are lonely, what advertisement will go with that video, all customised to your thought process. Let me depict a practical scenario showing how multiple apps across the mobile device can be utilised to sway your behaviour.

Imagine you are seeing an ex-boyfriend or ex-girlfriend's picture over the phone or laptop on a social media app. The algorithm knows what type of picture you are looking at because the other person does not tag you anymore; your face scan does not seem to fit with the new person who features in pictures with your ex-partner. The following action your mobile phone records are the food you ordered through the food app, such as chocolate ice cream, which points to the fact that you are sad and depressed. This would lead the system to reflect the advertisements of relationship experts or antidepressant or dating websites being displayed to the user. Those would be the best sale for them now. This is one such scenario out of millions, and the algorithms are working on them as we speak or as I am authoring this book. This is how much our lives are connected, and we still do not care about the data.

A 2018 case against the UK government focused on the surveillance and collection of information by the Government Communication Headquarters (GCHQ), Britain's signal-intelligence agency. The European court ruling sided with the plaintiff as the government action violated Article 8 of the European Convention of Human Rights (ECHR) and Article 10 on the right to freedom of expression. This was the first mass surveillance case decided against the UK government after the Edward Snowden revelation.

To reiterate some facts, I believe Edward Snowden was a revelation in breaking the chain of causation and monopoly regarding surveillance carried out by the American and British governments. However, the residual effect caused many governments to be taken aback by his action and its impact. Now courts are stepping in, as we saw with the aforementioned case, where they are trying to limit the powers of government on surveillance.

Masses have a short memory, and they will forget all these whistle-blowers, and the monopoly of power would corrupt the minds of people. The surveillance might begin again, especially if there is another attack on their soil by a terrorist. As depicted in Edward Sowden's interview with Joe Rogan, available on YouTube, situations such as these, unfortunately, give the administrations a free pass as happened after 11 September 2001.[72]

With the street surveillance cameras powered by AI that tracks you physically, scans you, matches your face ID to available databases, such as citizenship records, police records, and the like, control is placed in the hands of a few people. The rich would become more affluent, and the politically more potent would become even more influential. If a few people were to have the information about the masses—what they do, how they behave, eat, react, play, and buy—then such people can orchestrate their biddings to do anything to satisfy their financial motivations. The world needs to know, understand, and learn. The impact and the wave created by Edward Snowden are too significant to be ignored.

C. CAN WE BE SPIED UPON?

This question is on everyone's mind, but no one has a concrete answer. The answer lies in whether you are a person of interest to the government. I would define a person of interest as a person whom the government thinks might have been involved in affairs, work, or tasks against the interest of the state or country. The key phrase here is "acts against the state or country," but authorities might now have concrete evidence

---

72 "Summary: Big Brother Watch and Others v. the United Kingdom," Chinmayi Sharma, Law Fare, 12 October 2018, https://www.lawfareblog.com/summary-big-brother-watch-and-others-v-united-kingdom.

to hold the subject person responsible for that act. Legitimately, everyone would understand that. The problem is when this definition expands to everyone without any concrete evidence or substantiation of when the people are being tracked, and this is where it starts to take the form of invasion of privacy. In the government's argument, the terrorist and illegal activities have increased so much that they have no clue what can come up next, and thus, they would need to put everyone under their radar, which is where I believe things start to go wrong for everyone.

In the United States, a news report covered by *The Guardian* mentioned that the National Security Agency (NSA) uses a program called PRISM to tap into user data of Apple, Google, and others.[73] The news agency claimed that it "verified the authenticity of the document, a 41-slide PowerPoint presentation—classified as top secret with no distribution to foreign allies—which was apparently used to train intelligence operatives on the capabilities of the program. The document claims collection directly from the servers of major US service providers." However, when *The Guardian* approached the intelligence agency personnel for comments, they obviously denied such claims. This is just the tip of the iceberg, as the article indicated, "The program facilitates extensive, in-depth surveillance on live communications and stored information. The law allows for the targeting of any customers of participating firms outside the US or those Americans whose communications

---

73   "NSA Prism Program Taps in to User Data of Apple, Google and others," Glenn Greenwald and Ewen MacAskill, *The Guardian*, 7 June 2013, https://www.theguardian.com/world/2013/jun/06/us-tech-giants-nsa-data#:~:text=7%20years%20old-,NSA%20Prism%20program%20taps%20in%20to,of%20Apple%2C%20Google%20and%20others&text=The%20National%20Security%20Agency%20has,document%20obtained%20by%20the%20Guardian.

include people outside the US. It also opens the possibility of communications made entirely within the US being collected without warrants." The article mentions that the tech giants are claimed to be part of the information-sharing program since its introduction in 2007.

I am sure everyone would have gotten goosebumps when seeing the movie *Snowden*, released in 2016. Even though the movie was a dramatised version of the true story, it depicted how agencies use a program called XKeyscore, which runs like a search engine to detect and analyse voluminous data on people's communications through mobile phones and their online information. Then on the other hand, the movie shows a paranoia effect of Snowden, where he covers the door with pillows to create dampness to reduce radio frequencies that could hear him speak with reporters, or when he covers his webcam as there are programs, such as QUANTUM, that can access webcams remotely.[74] All this seems so personally impactful.

If you are vigilant and smart enough, you can identify any indications of external usage or spying. Everything requires technology, from your day-to-day usage to hacking to spying. Everyone must play on the same platform. And your platform—Google, iOS, or Blackberry—has limited resources, so you will need to keep an eye out if you notice any changes in your data usage or consumption; everything requires data to be transmitted, so be watchful. See what you give consent to, such as cookies (covered in a different chapter of this book). As an individual who values his privacy, I strongly recommend being

---

74 "New Film Tells the Story of Edward Snowden; Here Are the Surveillance Programs He Helped Expose," Jenna McLaughlin and Talya Cooper, The Intercept, 16 September 2016, https://theintercept.com/2016/09/16/new-film-tells-the-story-of-edward-snowden-here-are-the-surveillance-programs-he-helped-expose/.

vigilant about your metadata (covered in the previous chapter). This is the only element of your information that is not direct and is not readily encrypted, like your standard regular data in a database. Be watchful if your mobile or laptop device camera (the light on your webcam) is turning on or off; always cover it with a sticker, use it when needed only. Otherwise, keep it protected. Well, there have been reports that special government agencies can turn your webcam on without triggering the webcam light. The FBI has been able to use spyware technology for years and put it in place in terrorism cases or the most serious crime investigations; Marcus Thomas, former assistant director of the FBI's Operational Technology Division in Quantico, told this to the *Washington Post*.[75] Keep an eye out on your car's GPS: Has it been reset, showing you unusual pathways or routes? Always question why. Be observant: Do you see the same people around you in your neighbourhood whom you never saw living in or around you? The average person might not notice, but such people are trained long and strong and are great with social skills and easy to blend into your surroundings.[76] Don't ignore it if you hear funny noises, such as popping, clicking, and the like on your phone or unusual disturbance or keywords you used to pop up as a search result.[77] It is claimed that officials have devices such as a Stingray, a device that acts as a fake cell

---

75 FBI's Search for "Mo," Suspect in Bomb Threats, Highlights Use of Malware for Surveillance," Craig Timberg and Ellen Nakashima, *Washington Post*, 6 December 2013, https://www.washingtonpost.com/business/technology/2013/12/06/352ba174-5397-11e3-9e2c-e1d01116fd98_story.html.

76 "FBI Surveillance Team Reveals Tricks of the Trade," Dina Temple-Raston, NPR, 5 July 2008, https://www.npr.org/templates/story/story.php?storyId=92207687.

77 "Listen Up: 17 Signs That You Are Being Wiretapped" covered by Toolbox. com, 23 July 2012, https://www.toolbox.com/collaboration/telephony/blogs/listen-up-17-signs-that-you-are-being-wiretapped-072312/.

tower.[78] Be wary of the unusual behaviour of your smart TVs. In 2012, it was identified that Samsung TVs' vulnerabilities could open the door for hackers to access files on connected USBs and gain control of the TV itself.[79] A simple word that can be mistaken by your phone as "Okay, Google" or "Hey, Siri" can gain access to what you say. Your Google account includes a complete list of requests (no matter how embarrassing) you have made and archives them in your phone's history.[80]

Do not be careless about your wearables and health devices; they can be as susceptible as other devices discussed above. The US Food and Drug Administration came out with a statement that cardiac devices, including pacemakers and defibrillators, could be hacked by a third party.[81] Do not be over-reliant on baby monitors, as they can be risky too; make sure you change the password regularly. A security company, Sophos, released a video[82] showing how one could guess a CCTV password in less than a minute, not only sending the video stream to their own computer but also giving them to camera points.[83] If you

78   "Cellphone Data Spying: It's Not Just the NSA," John Kelly, *USA Today*, 8 December 2013, https://www.usatoday.com/story/news/nation/2013/12/08/cellphone-data-spying-nsa-police/3902809/.

79   "8 Things in Your Home That Could Actually Be Spying on You," Marissa Laiberte, *Reader's Digest*, Business Insider, 19 March 2018, https://www.businessinsider.com/8-things-in-your-home-that-could-actually-be-spying-on-you-2018-3.

80   "8 Things in Your Home That Could Actually Be Spying on You," Marissa Laiberte, *Reader's Digest*, Business Insider, 19 March 2018, https://www.businessinsider.com/8-things-in-your-home-that-could-actually-be-spying-on-you-2018-3.

81   "8 Things in Your Home That Could Actually Be Spying on You," Marissa Laiberte, *Reader's Digest*, Business Insider, 19 March 2018, https://www.businessinsider.com/8-things-in-your-home-that-could-actually-be-spying-on-you-2018-3.

82   "8 Things in Your Home That Could Actually Be Spying on You," Marissa Laiberte, *Reader's Digest*, Business Insider, 19 March 2018, https://www.youtube.com/watch?time_continue=1&v=rZoslioj1zg.

83   "8 Things in Your Home That Could Actually Be Spying on You," Marissa Laiberte, *Reader's Digest*, Business Insider, 19 March 2018, https://www.businessinsider.com/8-things-in-your-home-that-could-actually-be-spying-on-you-2018-3.

are surrounded by the Internet of Things (IoT), that could be a human landmine for you and your family. A small thing such as a thermostat, refrigerator, coffee machine, and the alike, working on IoTs, can also be easily hacked.[84]

Again, your privacy is your right, and you need to find ways to protect it. If you let it loose, you would be a slave to an unknown master who would guide you and your family's actions for the rest of your life on planet Earth.

D. Cross-Border Data Transfer

Now let us move back and see where a common person fits into the big picture. With the continued growth, globalisation, and movement of goods across jurisdictions, data flows across continents. On the one hand, this creates and increases the value of data. Moreover, data sitting alone in a single server are by themselves of no importance. As more business continues with the model of business-to-business (B2B) or business-to-consumer (B2C), more companies rely on the Internet to move their data. For them to improve efficiency, innovative technologies have come into play, such as cloud computing, big data, and the IoT. The problem is that such business and interactions generate even more data; thus, governments have started to step in to manage this problem, which some people have begun calling a hindrance. The effect is that governments have begun to put in requirements for localisation and underlining regulations, making it difficult for companies to transfer data while protecting privacy. Thus, companies and organisations argue that only a specific type of data should be excluded from movement across the border.

---

84   "8 Things in Your Home That Could Actually Be Spying on You," Marissa Laiberte, *Reader's Digest*, Business Insider, 19 March 2018, https://www.businessinsider. com/8-things-in-your-home-that-could-actually-be-spying-on-you-2018-3.

In contrast, a different kind of data should be allowed. I thought that if we all could learn to scrub and de-identify the data, and only such data could be traded, then such a thing would support privacy and make the organisation straightforward to deal with. Companies and organisations will always argue that they need complete data to assist or support their customers' requirements. This, to me, sounds like companies jumping up and down to say, "Give us rights to do what we feel like." But common people and even managements of companies forget that it might be okay to do so with the selected data, but the same rules might not apply to other data sets, such as medical records. Medical records are confidential and need to be encrypted when transferred from one jurisdiction to another. Unlike different data sets, such data should be bound by a legitimate purpose as to why such a request was made in the first place. This is just the beginning, and we will be caught up in more dilemmas as time goes on. The line between right and wrong is getting blurred with the amount of data being generated and used.

It is better to be sceptical of posting your data on the Internet because once our digital identity is available on the Internet, no matter how hard you try, you can never scrub it off the Internet thoroughly.

E. So What Does It Boil Down To?

All countries need laws to protect their sovereignty. The harsh reality is that laws developed to protect countries from acts that might constitute terrorism might have unforeseen consequences against the bystander.

One must consider why laws such as the Patriot Act in the United States or POTA (Prevention of Terrorism Act) in India came into existence. These came into existence because of some sort of terrorist activity carried out on their home soil, such as 9/11 in the United States or the terrorist bombing in Mumbai, India.

The spirit of such laws was to protect countries from acts of terror or similar situations from reoccurring. However, with the lapse of time, such laws have grown in their magnitude of coverage, making the lines between citizens' civil liberties and acts that may be antisocial or against the country blurred.

Article 22 of the US Patriot Act gives the agencies a blank check to oversee each and every individual's activity. In India, POTA itself provides police and various agencies with many teeth to bite with.

The laws themselves are not responsible for the overreaching invasion of privacy measures, but it is the technology. Technology, from being a blessing in disguise, has moved to be a necessary evil. The technology supporting the execution of laws is like a megalodon eating away any type of data that comes their way, irrespective of who it is coming from or whether it is needed.

The effect of this is that any and all data have become essential for patterns to be created, relationships to be deciphered, interpreting activities to be carried out. Eventually, a court will ask agencies and lawmakers, if all data are important, then what or which types of data are not consequential? If such a thought process brewed amongst the legal society, it would give temporary relief to the masses. I say temporary because the legal structure of common law or civil law will not allow for changes to make a permanent impact. Yes, the court decisions are binding, but then a few tweaks in the law and a selected section with a new name would be enough ammunition for the army of lawyers serving the government to prove that the new law is different and, thus, dodge the preceding case law, and then it is business as usual.

The actual effect of such a law would only see the light of day if the spirit of the law changes, which requires the "tone at the top" thought process to change. The actual difference in culture and tone at the top would help change the spirit of such laws and make a better impact while caring for people's civil liberties.

I remember a web page that was very famously a part of President Obama's campaigns, which was developed to promote the masses' civil liberties and the importance of protecting whistle-blowers. However, this never happened in Edward Snowden's case.

In general, we are at an interesting crossroads when we speak of laws under discussion, especially regarding people's rights and protection for whistle-blowers against what is at stake for the country. The law needs to establish a legal test that would consider motive when an act of leaking a confidential/ classified document takes place. Definitely, some people reveal confidential or classified documents for publicity and money. Still, others, such as Edward Snowden and Julian Paul Assange, are, in my view, driven to commit such an act for the greater good or the betterment of the public interest.

However, the current legal regime is more focused on the act than the outcome. Thus, I believe we might be embarking on an era that would see a change in applying such laws.

CHAPTER 5

WHAT ARE GOVERNMENTS DOING TO REGULATE CYBERSPACE?

From election interference to NotPetya ransomware, from healthcare data hackers to digital financial fraud, cyber insecurity has pushed governments worldwide towards a cohesive and authoritarian approach to cyberspace.

Cyberspace regulation comprises regulations that aim to safeguard information technology and information in the systems from cyberattacks and unauthorised access. Various governments have collaborated in many attempts to strengthen cybersecurity. US provisions on cybersecurity include the Health Insurance Portability and Accountability Act (HIPAA), Homeland Security Act of 2002, Gramm-Leach-Bliley Act of 1999, and Cybersecurity National Security Action Plan (CNAP) of 2016, amongst others. In 2018, the Cybersecurity and Infrastructure Security Agency Act was signed into law, aiming to strengthen the United States' defences against digital threats.

The European Union and the United States reaffirmed their commitment to secure and stable cyberspace in May 2019 at the sixth US-EU Cyber Dialogue held in Washington. The European Union and the United States are looking to develop a new UN Group of Governmental Experts (GGE), pursuant to a US-drafted resolution on Advancing Responsible State Behaviour in the Context of International Security. They have both pledged to engage constructively in increasing the international community's awareness of, adherence to, and implementing the GGE's recommendations. Additionally, both have called for substantial progress in the development and implementation of cyber confidence-building measures (CBMs) to reduce misperceptions and the risk of escalation stemming from the use of information and communications technologies.[85]

Current debates over cybersecurity also raise the challenge of framing security policies while differentiating from concerns over cyber-surveillance and invasion of privacy. To create a balanced action plan to tackle cybersecurity threats, it is essential to ensure human rights are at the core of policies. The US government's Foreign Intelligence Surveillance Act (FISA) and the Data Retention and Investigatory Powers Act of 2014 in the United Kingdom regulate the surveillance of private citizens' Internet records, personal data, and website browsing activities.

---

85 "Joint Elements Statement on the Sixth EU-US Cyber Dialogue" covered by Xavier CIFRE QUATRESOL, European Union External Actions, 21 June 2019, https://eeas.europa.eu/headquarters/headquarters-homepage/64495/joint-elements-statement-sixth-eu-us-cyber-dialogue_en.

A. Smart Cities and Privacy Challenges

Today

Tomorrow: Smartness of technology without appropriate comprehension

The director of privacy at a smart neighbourhood project based in Toronto, Ann Cavoukian,[86] resigned after learning that not all the data collected from the neighbourhood's residents would be de-identified. Dubbing the project "smart city of surveillance," she highlighted the transparency and privacy concerns for such smart cities.

Today's smart cities have a plethora of networks and connected technologies capable of generating real-time and actionable data on their citizens. These smart cities routinely collect data on a host of parameters, including noise, traffic, air quality, temperature, and emergencies, amongst others, using low-power sensors, mobile devices, web-based applications, and wireless networks. Much of the information collected deal with the citizens' and visiting tourists' daily activities.

Sensors in smart cities are used to detect transportation congestion and bottlenecks in traffic. Connected cameras enforce traffic and watch for speed infractions; in doing so, they also gather real-time information. Self-driving cars, lighting, energy monitoring, fire detection, wastewater monitoring, bridge inspection systems, and waste management are just a few of the other benefits of smart sensors.

Surveillance cameras that ensure security, drones for law enforcement, body cameras worn by safety officers to capture footage of their interactions with others, and wearables that enable communication within the city are some of the more intrusive uses of the Internet of Things in smart cities.

---

86 "Google's Smart City of Surveillance Faces New Resistance in Toronto," Ava Kofman, Monitor (Policy Alternatives), January/February 2019, https://www.policyalternatives.ca/sites/default/files/uploads/publications/ National%20Office/2019/01/CCPA%20Monitor%20Jan%20Feb%20 2019%20WEB%5B1%5D.pdf.

This can be a double-edged sword. This can give insight into police conduct and misconduct, especially when a government official can turn off the recording devices. Think about that!

A prominent case that comes to my mind is the shooting of Jean Charles de Menezes. It was claimed that the person under discussion was killed by officers of the London Metropolitan Police Service at Stockwell Station on the London Underground after he was wrongly deemed to be one of the fugitives involved in the previous day's failed bombing attempts. The surprising fact was during the judicial enquiry. Evidence surfaced seemed to suggest a technical problem with the CCTV equipment on the same platform where the shooting took place simultaneously, and thus, no footage was available. However, it was later confirmed that the videotapes had been changed by a station supervisor in three video recorders monitoring the station CCTV.[87]

Such advancement does open society to a different type of intrusive behaviour.

According to the International Data Corporation (IDC), in 2009, the volume of digital information generated in a year, also called the digital universe, increased by 62 per cent, and in 2010, it reached more than 1.2 million. The IDC estimates that by 2020, the digital universe will grow to forty-four times than what it was in 2010. An estimate by Business Insider indicates that there were nearly 2 billion connected devices in 2013. According to Statista figures, the global spending on smart cities is an astounding $34.35 billion for that year, and the number of installed, connected devices was around 463.5 million between 2015 and 2018.[88]

---

87 *"Shooting of Jean Charles de Menezes," Wikipedia.org, last edited on 24 February 2021,* https://en.wikipedia.org/wiki/Shooting_of_Jean_Charles_de_Menezes#Missing_CCTV_footage.

88 "Installed Base of Connected Things within the Utilities Sector of Smart Cities from 2015 to 2018," Statista, December 2015, https://www.statista.com/

Chicago has adopted smart city principles, intending to be the "most data-driven" city in the world. At the core of any smart city is the Array of Things (AoT) project, composed of a network of sensors (or nodes) mounted on traffic signal poles. The nodes will measure barometric pressure, temperature, vibration, light, carbon monoxide, sulfur dioxide, ozone, nitrogen dioxide, ambient sound intensity, and vehicular and pedestrian traffic.

The project's stated goal is to "measure the city in sufficient detail to provide data to help engineers, scientists, policymakers, and residents work together to make Chicago healthier, more livable and more efficient."[89]

Policy groundwork is also taking place to support Chicago's smart city development. The mayor issued an executive order in 2012 concerning an open data policy to provide residents with all the information needed to participate in governance, promote social progress, and collectively solve problems. The executive order also required the creation of an online data portal to share public data.

The key commitments of the project were open government and transparency. The AoT project also established data privacy policies of its own. The privacy policy includes details on what steps will be taken to secure and manage personally identifiable information (PII), which would also be placed in a secure facility with restricted access. The images collected by sensors would be converted to numerical data before their deletion from the nodes.

---

statistics/423063/smart-cities-connected-things-installed-base-utilities-sector/.

89   "The City of Chicago and Its Array of Things Project," Yezi Peng, Harvard Business School, Digital Innovation and Transformation, 4 April 2017, https://digital.hbs.edu/platform-digit/submission/the-city-of-chicago-and-its-array-of-things-project/.

The architecture of data collection in smart cities spans several layers.[90] The first is the perception layer, where RFID tags, smartphones, or sensors perceive the environment and generate data in response. Second, the integration layer is composed of communication protocols into which the data generated are fed from the perception layer. A diverse array of communication protocols is employed by devices based on their capabilities; these protocols include Bluetooth, RFID, Wi-Fi, Zigbee, and others. This layer integrates the data received with the cloud layer, the primary layer of the system, which has multiple components concerning analytics, storage, and computation. Data fed to this layer from the integration layer are further processed for smart city applications.

The application layer relates to the operations of different smart city applications, including analytics performed on collected data. Finally, the business layer creates different business models based on the smart city system's services. The processed data are used to develop various value-added services for smart city users.[91]

Connected devices in smart cities, though beneficial in many ways, raise concerns about privacy, freedom of choice, and autonomy. The risk is real and intelligent cities could lead to a situation in which everyone is watched continuously. Governments face the challenge of navigating complex vendor

---

90   "Security and Privacy in Smart Cities: Issues and Current Solutions," Talal Ashraf Butt and Muhammad Afzaa, ResearchGate, January 2019, https://www.researchgate.net/profile/Talal_Butt/publication/325452315_Security_and_Privacy_in_Smart_Cities_Issues_and_Current_Solutions/links/5b0ed7b64585157f87245ffa/Security-and-Privacy-in-Smart-Cities-Issues-and-Current-Solutions.pdf?origin=publication_detail.

91   "Smart Cities: Privacy, Transparency, and Community," Kelsey Finch and Omer Tene, SSRN, 3 April 2018, https://papers.ssrn.com/sol3/papers.cfm?abstract_id=3156014.

relationships, variable regulatory regimes, and dynamic community norms and viewpoints around surveillance, openness, public safety, and privacy.

The overarching debate relates to how communities can leverage the apparent benefits of data while mitigating threats to civil liberties and individual privacy. Smart cities can succeed only when they can offer the required level of security. Privacy and security requirements include integrity, availability, data privacy, confidentiality, control, and access.

Sensors gather data from physical spaces in smart cities that contain granular details on inhabitants. The data's journey begins at the sensor node and concludes at the user application. With multiple nodes and entry points, any device with software has a risk of exposure to vulnerabilities. These risks increase many-fold in a network, as the possibilities of remote hacking increase as well. With millions of connected devices in smart cities, a single compromised device could leave the entire system vulnerable to cyberattacks and other intrusions on privacy.

There are three categories of cyberattacks. Availability attacks take the system down entirely or deny certain services. Confidentiality attacks refer to unauthorised information access and monitoring. Integrity attacks break into the system to modify or alter information or configurations by infecting them with viruses or stopping critical services.

Weak encryption and the security vulnerabilities of various communication technologies used by IoT devices further raise the risk of cyberattacks. Whether the communication protocol is an NFC,[92] RFID,[93] Wi-Fi,[94] Bluetooth,[95] or low-power wide area network, all of them are exposed to security vulnerabilities.

---

92   As defined by Android Authority in an article by Robert Triggs, 30 June 2019, What is NFC and how does it work? Here's everything you need to know (androidauthority.com), *"NFC stands for Near Field Communication and, as the name implies, it enables short-range communication between compatible devices. This requires at least one transmitting device, and another to receive the signal. A range of devices can use the NFC standard and will be considered either passive or active. Passive NFC devices include tags, and other small transmitters, which can send information to other NFC devices without the need for a power source of their own. However, they do not process any information sent from other sources, and can't connect to other passive components. These often take the form of interactive signs on walls or advertisements. Active devices are able to both send and receive data, and can communicate with each other as well as with passive devices. Smartphones are by far the most generic form of active NFC device. Public transport card readers and touch payment terminals are also good examples of the technology."*

93   As defined by Abr.com in an article by unknown author, https://www.abr.com/what-is-rfid-how-does-rfid-work/, *"RFID is an acronym for radio-frequency identification and refers to a technology whereby digital data encoded in RFID tags or smart labels (defined below) are captured by a reader via radio waves. RFID is similar to barcoding in that data from a tag or label are captured by a device that stores the data in a database. RFID, however, has several advantages over systems that use barcode asset tracking software. The most notable is that RFID tag data can be read outside the line-of-sight, whereas barcodes must be aligned with an optical scanner."*

94   Cisco.com (https://bit.ly/33M9szh) defines Wi-Fi as *"a wireless networking technology that allows devices such as computers (laptops and desktops), mobile devices (smart phones and wearables), and other equipment (printers and video cameras) to interface with the Internet. It allows these devices—and many more—to exchange information with one another, creating a network. Internet connectivity occurs through a wireless router. When you access Wi-Fi, you are connecting to a wireless router that allows your Wi-Fi-compatible devices to interface with the Internet."*

95   As described by Lifewire.com in an article by Malanie Uy, 2 February 2020, https://www.lifewire.com/what-is-bluetooth-2377412, *"Bluetooth is a short-range wireless communication technology that allows devices such as mobile phones, computers, and peripherals to transmit data or voice wirelessly over a short distance. The purpose of Bluetooth is to replace the cables that normally connect devices, while still keeping the communications between them secure. The 'Bluetooth' name is taken from a 10th-century Danish king named Harald Bluetooth, who was said to unite disparate, warring regional factions. Like its namesake, Bluetooth technology brings together a broad range of devices across many different industries through a unifying communication standard."*

B. Vulnerabilities of a Complex System

Smart cities rely on a complex, large-scale system composed of heterogeneous devices and multiple networks, where each layer of the city's architecture has a plethora of devices. The interdependencies between various networks and devices pose colossal security and privacy challenges to stakeholders. The multiple links expose such systems to security risks, even if each device in the network is independently secure. And with human beings still in the loop of all decision-making, alongside automated technologies, errors, whether unwittingly committed or deliberate, can also sabotage data privacy in the system.

Threatcare (a Texas-based data breach solutions company) and IBM X-Force Red discovered in 2018 that smart city sensors across the world had seventeen zero-day vulnerabilities or software flaws unknown to those responsible for fixing such flaws.[96] According to the researchers, these vulnerabilities, if unpatched, could let hackers obtain access to the system and manipulate data.

IBM's team of researchers explored the vulnerabilities of smart cities for a report titled "The Dangers of Smart City Hacking."[97] Some of the critical vulnerabilities in smart cities include

    a. Creating traffic gridlocks: Hackers can create simultaneous traffic gridlocks by accessing the traffic control infrastructure in smart cities to delay law enforcement from reaching the scene of a crime.

---

96 "IBM & Threatcare Discover 17 Zero-day Vulnerabilities in Smart Cities," Memoori, 16 August 2018, https://memoori.com/ibm-threatcare-discover-17-zero-day-vulnerabilities-smart-cities/.

97 "The Dangers of Smart City Hacking," IBM (IBM X-force Red) https://www.ibm.com/downloads/cas/B1JZXRZG.

b. Simulating disasters or creating real ones: Attackers can access disaster detection sensors or alarm systems, such as wind speed sensors, radiation detectors, or water level gauges, to report incorrect data and cause an evacuation. Delayed response to actual disasters as a result of inaccurate data is the other real danger.

c. Manipulation of agriculture: In smart farming, sensors are used by farmers to measure rainfall, temperature, and humidity to enhance the efficiency of irrigation and optimise harvest times. Hackers can manipulate these data, causing irreversible crop damage in a specific area or globally.[98]

C. What Are an Individual's Rights Concerning Data?

I. Rights under the European Union's General Data Protection Regulation

Under the GDPR, individuals are guaranteed the following rights:

a. The right to information about data collection, disclosure, and storage

b. The right to rectify incorrect data;

c. The right to access one's own data

d. The right to the deletion of data

e. The right to restrict data processing

f. The right to portability of data

g. The right to be forgotten

---

98 "The Security Challenge for Smart Cities: How Sensors and Control Devices Can Be exploited," Andrew Ross, Information Age, 9 August 2018, https://www.information-age.com/the-security-challenge-smart-cities-123474071/.

h. The right to object to processing or withdraw consent

i. Rights concerning automated decision-making.

II. Rights of Consumers under the California Consumer Privacy Act

Under the CCPA, consumers have the right to request the details of the specific pieces and categories of personal information a business collects about them. Companies are obligated to notify consumers about the kind of data they collect. Consumers have a right to request such information, and on receiving the request, organisations must provide details as to how data is processed. Consumers have the right to know sources of specific categories of information collected, the particular purposes for selling or collecting personal information, and with whom the data is shared.

Consumer rights under the CCPA fall into these categories:

a. Right to notice
b. Right to access
c. Right to opt in and opt out
d. Right to request the erasure
e. Right to equal prices and services
f. Right to portability

The Breach Notification Statute Revision was introduced in February 2019 and passed to become a part of the CCPA, expanding the scope of *personal information* in the CCPA's breach notification section. Per this bill, breach notification obligations are not limited to personal identifiers but also include "other government-issued identification numbers" and "unique biometric data generated from measurements or technical analysis of human body characteristics, such as a fingerprint, retina, or iris image, or other unique physical representation or digital representation of biometric data."[99]

Data breach notification under the CCPA should include the following:

a. A description of the data breach
b. The nature of information compromised in the breach
c. Steps being taken by the entity to resolve the problem
d. What steps victims can take to protect themselves
e. Where victims can find more information related to the data breach

Additionally, the CCPA provides residents with the right to file suit in case of data breaches where their non-encrypted personal data has been compromised as a result of inadequate security procedures. Victims of a data breach can claim from $100 to $750 per breach incident.

Similarly, under GDPR, there is detailed guidance on notifying a data breach to individuals without undue delay if the breach is likely to impact an individual's freedoms and rights. A personal data breach is defined as one that affects sensitive data, financial data, or any information that can lead to exclusion, identity theft, or stigmatisation. The notification must be comprehensive and precise so that individuals are clear about what it says and how they can mitigate the consequences.

California SB 1386, which took effect in 2003, requires any agency or individual who owns, licences, or stores residents' personal data in unencrypted form to disclose a breach of security. Entities that do not comply with notification obligations for a security breach can face private lawsuits for damages. The bill

99 "Under California's New Privacy Law, HIPAA Is Not a Fail-Safe for Compliance," Louise Rains Gomez - Thomas Hiney, 10 March 2020, https://www.lawtechnologytoday.org/2020/03/hipaa-is-not-a-fail-safe-for-compliance/.

mandates that in the event of a security breach, residents must be notified in "the most expedient time possible and without unreasonable delay."

III. Exclusions under the CCPA

The CCPA does not restrict a business's ability to collect or sell a consumer's personal information if every aspect of that commercial conduct takes place entirely outside California. That implies that the information can be harvested while the person is outside California, as the CCPA is focused on California rather than on the whole United States.

Also, the CCPA does not apply to information that is subject to other federal regulations; such as the Health Insurance Portability and Accountability Act (HIPAA), the Fair Credit Reporting Act (FCRA), the Gramm-Leach Bliley Act (GLBA), or the Drivers' Privacy Protection Act (DPPA), all of which are federal statutes. The CCPA, however, will apply to entities covered by these laws to the extent they collect and process data from consumers.[100]

D. DIGITAL SIGNATURE AND IDENTIFICATION AND HOW THEY HELP IN E-COMMERCE BUT ALSO RAISE CONCERNS

Digital signatures are *electronic seals* used by contracting parties to authenticate a user's identity or the origin of a document or other electronic data. As digital signatures are vulnerable to forgery, much like written signatures, the PKI

---

100 "United States: California's Data Privacy Law: What It Is and How to Comply (A Step-by-Step Guide)," Sara H Jodka, Mondaq, 17 July 2018, https://www.mondaq.com/unitedstates/data-protection/720066/california39s-data-privacy-law-what-it-is-and-how-to-comply-a-step-by-step-guide.

system (public-key infrastructure) is used to encrypt the message. Digital signatures are one of the critical technologies in use today to secure e-commerce transactions.

E-commerce involves a frequent exchange of documents containing sensitive information, such as financial transactions, details related to technological innovations, or legal contracts. E-commerce is as vulnerable as other electronic data exchange platforms to hacking.

In one such case, an individual associated with the Registration Authority in India was accused of misusing a company secretary's digital signature to sign MCA (Ministry of Corporate Affairs) certificates. In another instance, a company's directors allegedly used the deceased director's digital name to transfer ownership.

E. EU-US "Safe Harbour"

The Safe Harbour agreement was developed as a middle ground between the European Union and the United States to ensure adequate privacy protections when EU citizens' data are transferred beyond the European Union's jurisdiction. This allowed companies, such as Facebook and Google, to self-certify and move data beyond the European Union's borders to a data centre based on US soil.

Patrick van Eecke, co-head of the global privacy practice DLA Piper, said, "The advantage of safe harbour was that it functioned as a kind of 'one-stop shop' allowing for the export of personal data to the U.S., whoever in Europe it came from, without the need to ask for consent, or to enter into bilateral agreements, over and over again."[101]

---

101 "What Is 'Ssafe Harbour' and Why Did the EUCJ Just Declare It Invalid?" Samuel Gibbs, *The Guardian*, 6 October 2015, https://www.theguardian.com/ technology/2015/oct/06/safe-harbour-european-court-declare-

In July 2020, the Court of Justice of the European Union invalidated the Commission Implementing Decision (EU) 2016/1250, which had initially indicated that the EU-US Privacy Shield Framework (the official name of the Safe Harbour agreement) was adequate to enable transfers of personal data from the European Union to the United States.[102] This decision will have a massive impact on US business, and companies, such as the tech giants, will now have to abide by the high standards set by the GDPR.

The core principles of privacy protection remain the same[103]:

a. The data subject should give explicit consent to such transfer.

b. The data transfer must be necessary for the performance of a contract.

c. The person must have the ability to opt -out

d. There must be encryption measures and a privacy-focused system in place.

e. Circulate a message about the privacy practices incorporated in a corporation to your counterparts, involved in the contract with you, so the data subject knows the practices and can approach the corporation with questions.

f. The data transfer is needed for important reasons of public interest, such as protecting public health.

g. It must safeguard or defend against a legal claim.

invalid-data-protection.

102 "EU Court Strikes Down EU-US 'Privacy Shield,'", Matthew Sweet, RichMay Law, 17 July 2020, https://www.richmaylaw.com/eu-court-strikes-down-eu-u-s-privacy-shield/.

103 "EU Court Strikes Down EU-US 'Privacy Shield,'" Matthew Sweet, RichMay Law, 17 July 2020, https://www.richmaylaw.com/eu-court-strikes-down-eu-u-s-privacy-shield/.

h. The transfer of data is necessary to protect the vital interests of the data subject, such as in a hospital transfer or if the person is in a vegetative state or unconscious of rendering consent.

F. Comparing GDPR and the CCPA[104]

GDPR and CCPA are designed to guarantee reliable protection of individuals' personal data. Both laws apply to entities that collect, share, or process consumer data online or offline.[105]

There are also some critical differences between GDPR and CCPA, particularly related to scope, nature, collection limitations, and accountability. Whereas GDPR mandates appointing data protection officers, maintaining a record of data processing activities, and carrying out impact assessments concerning accountability obligations, there is no specific focus on these issues in CCPA. However, it does specify the need to train employees who handle consumer data.

Another noteworthy difference concerns the core legal framework of these two privacy laws. Under GDPR, a "legal basis" is required to process any type of personal data, but CCPA does not mention any legal basis. At the same time, GDPR applies to any business irrespective of its size, turnover

---

104 "Comparing Privacy Laws: GDPR v. CCPA," DataGuidance: Alice Marini, Alexis Kateifides, Joel Bates
   Future of Privacy Forum: Gabriela Zanfir-Fortuna, Michelle Bae, Stacey Gray, Gargi Sen, Fpf.org, 1 July 2020, https://fpf.org/wp-content/uploads/2018/11/GDPR_CCPA_Comparison-Guide.pdf.
105 "Comparing Privacy Laws: GDPR v. CCPA," DataGuidance: Alice Marini, Alexis Kateifides, Joel Bates
   Future of Privacy Forum: Gabriela Zanfir-Fortuna, Michelle Bae, Stacey Gray, Gargi Sen, Fpf.org, 1 July 2020, https://fpf.org/wp-content/uploads/2018/11/GDPR_CCPA_Comparison-Guide.pdf.

or volume of personal data handled, and whether it is for-profit or not; CCPA applies only to for-profit entities with revenue above $25 million and processes personal data of more than fifty thousand consumers.

Additionally, CCPA excludes specific categories of data covered in other sector-specific laws, such as medical data covered under HIPAA and credit-related information processed by reporting agencies.

A notable difference between the two privacy laws also relates to CCPA's requirement that a "Do Not Sell My Personal Information" link must be displayed on the home page of a website. GDPR does not mandate the inclusion of such a link. Also, CCPA has specific provisions related to data transfer as a result of mergers and acquisitions, ensuring that consumers have the right to opt out if there are any deviations in how the third party shares personal information as compared to what was promised at the time of data collection.

Whereas GDPR applies to any entity within or outside the European Union that handles the personal data of EU citizens, CCPA provisions concerning territorial scope are unclear. GDPR and CCPA do not apply to the national security and law enforcement sectors, although they do cover service providers for national security or law enforcement agencies. GDPR is also not applicable in a household or purely-personal activity; CCPA exempts non-commercial activities. The difference between these two approaches lies in the fact that the exemption of "purely-personal activities" applies only to individuals under GDPR and businesses in California.

Another essential difference between the two data privacy laws relates to penalties. GDPR mandates penalties that can be as much as 4 per cent of a business's annual global turnover or €20 million, whichever is greater. The fines under CCPA apply per violation, with a maximum penalty per violation of $7,500. Consumers can also sue the entity for a breach that compromises their personal data under CCPA. Whereas CCPA considers a violation to have occurred only at the time of an actual breach, under GDPR, a company can be sanctioned if a risk of a breach or irresponsible behaviour is determined.

G. How Would California Privacy Protection Act (CPPA) Change the Landscape?

Californians voted on 3 November 2020, to approve the ballot measure to create CPRA or California Privacy Rights Act. CPRA that comes into effect on 1 January 2023, expands and amends CCPA (California Consumer Privacy Act of 2018).

As an addendum to CCPA, CPRA seeks to tighten business regulations on using consumers' personal information while strengthening the data privacy rights of California residents. The act also establishes a new statewide enforcement agency in the form of CPPA (California Privacy Protection Agency).

I. Will CCPA Remain or Be Abolished?

CPRA is intended to augment and strengthen CCPA and will not replace or repeal the latter. CCPA also does not add a new private right of action for unauthorised use of PI.[106]

II. How Does CPRA differ from CCPA?

CPRA redefines covered businesses as those that process PI of equal to or more than one hundred thousand consumers

---

106 "The CCPA Wheels Keep Turning: The Addition of CPRA," Sheppard Mullin Richter & Hampton LLP, 6 November 2020, https://www.jdsupra.com/legalnews/the-ccpa-wheels-keep-turning-the-75222/.

per year. The act also introduces SPI, or sensitive personal information, that includes geolocation data, login information, genetic data, contents of the text, e-mail, and mail messages, health, sexual orientation, and biometric data.

Additionally, four new data privacy rights have been added to the act:

> *a.* California's residents can request correction of any personal information that is inaccurate.
> *b.* California's residents can opt out of automated technology used for consumer "profiling" that guides decisions related to health, location, work performance, personal preferences, economic situation, and interests.
> *c.* Consumers also have a right under CPRA to request access to the automated decision-making processes and their likely outcomes.
> *d.* Consumers can restrict the use of their sensitive PI that includes the prohibition of its disclosure to third parties.

III. Modified and Expanded Rights under CPRA

The scope of several rights has been expanded or modified under CPRA.

Right to Know - Under CCPA, if a California resident requests a business to disclose the exact personal information collected about them, the disclosure was limited to twelve months prior to receiving the request. This time frame has been expanded under CPRA, where businesses must disclose upon request what PI they collected beyond the period of twelve months.

Opt Out - While CCPA provides opting-out rights to consumers, CPRA expands it to cover the sharing of personal information relating to "cross-context behavioural advertising," a new term defined by CPRA as any advertising that uses the personal information of a consumer to target them based on their activities across businesses, applications, websites, and services.

IV. What Does CPRA Mean for Businesses?

CPRA impacts employers and businesses in many ways[107]:

a. **Applicability** - The act applies to large businesses that generate a majority of revenue from not just selling PI but also sharing, releasing, renting, disseminating, transferring, making available, or communicating in written, oral, or electronic means.

b. **Increased security measures** - The act makes it easier for California residents to file against businesses for data breaches or for accessing SPI without authorisation, including login information, account name, and passwords, as well as security questions.

- This means that businesses need to strengthen security protections to avoid new penalties that CPRA has created.

c. **Discrimination** - CPRA strengthens privacy protections for California consumers while extending privacy protection for independent contractors, job applicants, and employees. Apart from updating or creating new processes to exercise their rights, businesses also have to

---

107 "California Approves Even Tougher Privacy Laws," Taylor C. Day, Gregory T. Parks, and W. Reece Hirsch, 10 November 2020, https://www.lexology.com/library/detail.aspx?g=549144f3-7eaa-4dae-aa38-63a1c7ba887b#:~:text=The%20CPRA%20refines%20and%20expands,sale%20of%20their%20personal%20information.

build processes to allow consumers to correct inaccurate data.[108]

d. **Process for disposal or deletion** - There are limits on how long a business can hold PI under the new act. While informing consumers about how long they intend to retain each PI category, companies will have to create mechanisms for destroying or deleting the information after a designated period.

e. **Privacy policy and website updates** - Covered entities will have to update privacy policies and websites to comply with the new regulations under CPRA. Additionally, a method or website functionality has to be implemented that allows consumers to opt out of selling or sharing PI.

f. **Enhanced penalties** - While each CPRA violation imposes a fine of $2,500, each intentional violation of PI of those below the age of sixteen will incur a $7,500 penalty. CPRA has also eliminated the thirty days for "curing the breach" provided under CCPA, which considerably raises businesses' compliance risk.

g. **Audit requirements** - Businesses need to carry out independent cybersecurity audits and privacy impact assessments concerning high-risk activities and send them to CPPA. If the agency decides that the risks outweigh the benefits of information collection, businesses will have to stop processing PI.

---

108 "CPRA Series: Extension of CCPA's Anti-Discrimination/Retaliation Provision to Employees, Applicants, and Independent Contractors," Jerel Pacis Agatep, 13 November 2020, https://www.workplaceprivacyreport. com/2020/11/articles/california-consumer-privacy-act/prop-24-california-privacy-rights-act-extends-ccpas-anti-discrimination-retaliation-provision-to-employees-applicants-and-independent-contractors/.

V. What Does the Difference between the Two Means for People's Privacy?

CPRA expands the protection significantly with new data privacy rights and modification and strengthening of existing regulations. Individuals in California have more control than ever on their PI, including new categories of sensitive personal information, data deletion, right to opt out, correcting inaccurate information, and requesting information collected beyond twelve months.

With new regulations on cross-context behaviour advertising, consumers can gain control over targeted advertising and opt out of such behavioural advertising. Another critical protection consumers have received under CPRA is abolishing "dark patterns," which are manipulative interface designs, such as navigation of multiple screens or multiple clicks for opting-out buttons. Internet users in California can no longer be tricked into giving consent to which they do not intend.

H. How Can Companies Balance between Collecting Individual Data and Meeting Regulatory Obligations?

Businesses collect vast volumes of consumers' personal data to achieve various marketing objectives, such as personalising messages, improving consumer's experience on their website, or making relevant product suggestions. In the past decade, businesses have exploited innovative marketing technologies to collect data that helps them target consumers effectively. The promise of increased revenue or loyalty drove enterprises to obtain a vast array of personal data without the consumer's consent or knowledge. Furthermore, many businesses bought data from third-party brokers without the consent or knowledge of the individuals concerned. With the advent of stringent data privacy laws, such as GDPR and CCPA, businesses must rethink how to balance collecting necessary individual data with regulatory compliance.

I.   Legal Bases for Data Collection

The all-important question for businesses that collect personal data is, "What data are the most valuable of all?" Apart from e-mail address and name, the other valuable information businesses need depends on what products or services they sell. For a retailer or e-commerce entity, the most valuable personal information to collect is the transaction history, which can be used to upsell or cross-sell.

According to GDPR, there are six legal bases for collecting and processing data in Europe:

a. Individual's vital interest;
b. Public interest;
c. Legal obligations;
d. Contractual necessity;
e. Unambiguous consent by the data subject; and
f. Data controller's legitimate interest

The above six bases have equal value and are independent of one another. For businesses that collect personal data and for the digital marketing industry, the most important legal bases are unambiguous consent by the consumer and the data controller's legitimate interest.

The data controller's interest can be deemed a legitimate justification only when the purpose behind collecting and processing data is reasonably expected by data subjects. Personal data processing for direct marketing may qualify as a legitimate interest. However, it cannot override data subjects' privacy rights, and businesses must implement appropriate security measures to mitigate potential data privacy risks to users. The basic standards companies must meet before they claim legitimate interest are discussed below.

First, companies must explain what type of data are collected and a specific purpose for the collection. The statement should also include details on how the data collection affects the user's online experience. For example, "We use cookies for the purpose of advertising. This enables us to display relevant advertisements that are based on your browsing behaviour. To opt out of these services or to know more, please read our privacy policy."

The choice to opt out must be easy to access and use, and it must be easy to understand how this choice affects a user's ad experience. Also, consumers must have easy access to the website's privacy policy and information on the privacy standards the business has adopted.

Every business can ask the following questions to establish their legitimate interest in collecting what it considers necessary personal data:

a. What is the purpose of data collection?
b. Are the data needed to fulfil specific organisational objectives?
c. Does the GDPR or other legislation identify the processing activity as legitimate?
d. Can the corporate goal be achieved in any other way?
e. Does the individual expect data processing activity to occur?

f. What kinds of data are processed, and do such data have special protections and provisions under GDPR or other data privacy laws?

g. Does data processing undermine or limit the rights of individuals?

II. Minimising Data

Data minimisation is an essential principle in GDPR, which states that businesses should obtain only the data required to achieve the stated objective of collecting and processing the data. GDPR also mandates that data collected for a specific purpose cannot be used for another purpose without consent.

Data minimisation,[109] under GDPR, is referenced under five sections. Businesses must implement these rules of data minimisation at every step of the data life cycle. In other words, companies or marketers must limit the collection, storage, and usage of data to what is adequate, relevant, and necessary for the stated purpose of data collection.

Understanding the context of data is the first step towards achieving data minimisation. Typically, there are three environments where a company's data exists: development and testing, production, and data storage and analytics.

In the first environment, development and testing, it is necessary to suppress any personal data, which creates a dilemma as to what data to use and to what extent. Although leaving sensitive data out of the testing environment can be an easy solution, it does not support realistic scenarios. On the other hand, using fictitious data sets enables testing scenarios, but these data sets do not accurately mirror production data.

---

109 "Data Minimization in the GDPR: A Primer," J T Sison, Data Guise, 15 February 2017, https://www.dataguise.com/gdpr-compliance-data-minimization-use-purpose/.

A balance can be found by obscuring sensitive data to comply with GDPR requirements while at the same time effectively simulating a real data set.

Data minimisation in production environments entails limiting the amount of data collected rather than obscuring it. Traditionally, the tendency has been to collect every single piece of data available, but the amount of personal data required for business purposes is relatively concise. Asking whether a particular data point is needed represents the first step towards minimising data in production environments.

It is again important to ask if the retained data are still needed at the data storage and analytics stage. Only accurate and timely data can provide meaningful insights. Data collected years ago soon becomes unnecessary or irrelevant to current purposes. Wherever possible, businesses can minimise exposure of personal data in storage and analytics environments by employing anonymisation, encryption, and monitoring. For instance, credit card numbers are generally not required to analyse purchase trends. If they are needed, obscuring the data can ensure compliance with GDPR.

To achieve the right balance between what is collected and what is necessary, organisations can eliminate third-party data collection. By using only the personal information they collect directly with explicit customer consent, businesses can also build trust. Consumers must be made fully aware of how their data are being used. A study shows that using personal information without consumers' knowledge would cause 79 per cent to stop patronising the brand.

III. Best Practices in Data Collection

A *Harvard Business Review* article suggests the following best practices regarding collecting valuable data from consumers:

a. **Explain how customers will benefit by giving their consent for the collection of personal data.** These incentives can be in the form of exclusive rewards, personalised offers, or recommendation engines. For instance, Netflix provides an incentive in the form of a more robust recommendation engine in return for access to user data. The engine is an excellent way for users to discover content that is relevant and personalised.

b. **Give customers complete control over what kinds of data they choose to share.** For instance, an individual may be comfortable sharing their name and date of birth but not a phone number or address. Offering flexibility in what data the customer can choose to share will help build trust and obtain "necessary" personal information.

c. **Make it easy for customers to control their data choices by providing a digital privacy centre.** Customers need to be able to configure who controls their personal data in the organisation. Additionally, a "download my data" option can be provided. This option allows customers to know quickly what types of personal information a company has collected.

Maintaining consistency in data privacy policies is an essential ultimate step. Although incentivising can be one way to get consumers to agree initially to data sharing, it can be challenging to persuade them to continue to share their data.

Marketers need to keep the relationship healthy and build trust by strictly adhering to data privacy policies and maintaining consistent communication.

As a first step, companies should assess their digital assets or a digital footprint, including cookies, forms, analytics, domains, and IP addresses. Second, list the type of personal data that the business collects. Third, assess the purpose of collecting personal data. Instead of the traditional approach to gathering as much information as possible, marketers must shift their thinking towards "Is this information needed, and if so, why?"

Under GDPR, companies need to take the following steps in defining the need for collecting or processing data:

a. Be clear concerning data collection or processing purposes from the start.
b. Record these purposes and specify them in the business website's privacy information.
c. If you collect personal data for a different purpose that is in line with your original intention, obtain consent and ensure that it has a legal basis.
d. Conduct audits of data collected to evaluate how each data set is currently being used and which ones are needed.
e. Be transparent with data subjects regarding the use of data.
f. Ensure that the data collected translates to a more favourable, personalised experience for users.

I. What Are Cookies, and Why Are Websites Looking to Get Consent?

Cookies are small files that live on the computer and are created when you enter a website.

They consist of messages passed on to the browser by the web servers when a user visits any Internet site. The web browser stores these messages in a small file known as cookie.txt. The browser sends back the cookie to the web server when the user revisits the website.[110] Cookie files contain information on an individual's visits to web pages, along with any personal information, such as name or address, volunteered by the user. When the data are sent back on the user's return visits to the site, the web server gathers information on the user's web activity, such as which page was visited the most and which websites get the most repeat hits.

The term "cookie" is based on "Fortune Cookie," a Unix program that produces a different message each time it runs.

Businesses use cookies to store information about users' interactions with their websites. Various websites use them to facilitate online shopping, recording the personal data entered by the shopper, along with the items in the shopping cart. In this way, users do not have to enter this information every time they visit the website. Servers use cookies as well to offer personalised web pages. When the user selects preferences on a website that offers such options, the server stores this information in a cookie. When the user returns to the website, the server then draws on that information to provide a customised page.

The cookie can be read by only the website that created it, so other servers will not have access to the information. Moreover, web servers can use only the information the user provides when visiting the website, which is then stored in these cookies.

In some instances, cookies do not come from the visited website but rather from advertising companies that manage banner advertisements for a group of websites. These companies can build detailed profiles of individuals who select ads on their clients' sites.

Accepting a cookie alone does not provide access to a user's computer or any personal information other than voluntarily

---

110 "What Are Cookies?" Knowledge base, 18 January 2018, https://kb.iu.edu/d/agwm.

disclosed, such as in online shopping. Moreover, cookies cannot be used to infect the computer with a virus or to execute code.

Two diverse types of cookies are covered under the European Union's ePrivacy Directive, namely session and persistent cookies. Session cookies are strictly necessary for website functionality, and once the user closes the browser window, the cookie cannot track user activity. Examples include user authentication cookies, shopping cart functionality cookies, and cookies required for playback of multimedia.

Persistent cookies track user activity after the browser window is closed or after the user has moved on from the website. Examples include advertising tracking cookies and the cookies that analytics programs use.

GDPR and the ePrivacy Directive mandate the use of cookie consent banners on websites. In other words, website owners may only use cookies necessary for website operation and must request and obtain consent from website visitors for any other cookies. Website owners should also remove cookies that track data that could identify a person and update their cookie policy.

GDPR mentions cookies only once, although the repercussions of the regulation are significant for websites that use cookies to track users' browsing activity. GDPR's Recital 30 states,

> Natural persons may be associated with online identifiers . . . such as internet protocol addresses, cookie identifiers, or other identifiers . . . This may leave traces which, in particular when combined with unique identifiers and other information received by the servers, may be

used to create profiles of the natural persons
and identify them.[111]

In other words, since cookies can collect and share personal
data, websites need to have a cookie policy.

The ePrivacy Directive, also known as the Cookie Law,
was designed to ensure citizens' digital data privacy within the
European Union. It was passed in 2002 and amended in 2009.
The law applies to any organisation physically located within
the European Union with a website or any other international
website targeting consumers in the European Union.

The Cookie Law also requires websites to let users know
whether cookies are being used, explain what kind of data is
gathered through cookies, and indicate how the website owner
uses the data.

The user consent per GDPR and ePrivacy Directive must
have these characteristics:

a.   Transparent: Based on specific and clear information on
     the purpose and types of data collected.
b.   Prior: Must be obtained before processing, except what
     is strictly necessary for website functionality.
c.   Unambiguous: Consent is given with affirmative and
     decisive action; implied consent is not sufficient.
d.   Documented: Consent must be recorded and stored
     securely as evidence.
e.   Reversible: Users can withdraw consent at any time.
f.   Renewed: According to the ePrivacy Directive, the
     consent must be renewed once a year.

---

111 "How the GDPR Affects Cookie Policies," Luke Irwin, 12 May 2020, https://
     www.itgovernance.eu/blog/en/how-the-gdpr-affects-cookie-policies.

Website owners' compliance with the Cookie Law in GDPR entails the following:

a. Revealing to the user all the operating trackers and cookies on the website in plain language enables the user to make informed choices about giving or revoking consent.

b. Withholding trackers and cookies on the website apart from those strictly necessary for the website's functioning until the user's explicit and unequivocal consent is obtained for each type of tracker and cookie.

c. Consent must be freely given and cannot be a prerequisite for services offered.

d. Website owners are responsible for the information contained in cookies and must protect the same from unauthorised third-party harvesting.

J. The Importance of Having Terms and Conditions on the Website

Although terms and conditions are not a legal requirement, there are many reasons why legal experts encourage companies to have a set of comprehensive terms and conditions. The agreement on terms and conditions typically includes details on the following items:

a. Rights and responsibilities of the user
b. Expected or intended use of the website
c. Potential misuse
d. Accountability for online behaviour, actions, and conduct
e. Privacy policy that includes how personal data is collected and used

f. Payment details

g. Opt-out policy and account termination

h. Disclaimers

i. Limitation of liability

Having comprehensive terms and conditions agreement can help companies achieve the following goals:

a. Preventing abuse or misuses, such as spamming, posting of defamatory content, or theft of content

b. Terminating a user's account in case of misuse or abuse

c. Identifying the governing law and jurisdiction

d. Making disclosures concerning intellectual property

e. Limiting a business's liability

f. Ensuring that privacy policies and consent are explained clearly

I. Do Laws Allow You to Attack the Hacker?[112]

Can a victim of the hacking resort to retaliation? This topic has garnered significant attention in recent times.

In the United States, the Computer Fraud and Abuse Act of 1986, the Wiretap Act of 1988, and the 2015 Cybersecurity Information Sharing Act authorise companies to employ countermeasures against malicious malware on their networks but criminalise counterattacks on others.

The International Court of Justice, on the other hand, supports countering cyberattacks, provided that four elements of a legal countermeasure are followed. These elements are that the counterattack is directed at the entity responsible for the

---

112 "A Question about 'Hacking Back' — Is it Legal?" Brad Puckett, Global Knowledge, 9 April 2019, https://www.globalknowledge.com/us-en/resources/resource-library/articles/is-hacking-back-legal/.

initial attack, asking the attacker to discontinue the attack, ensuring that the counterattack is in proportion to the original act and that the counterattack is reversible.

Although "hacking back" has the sole objective of identifying the attacker and recovering stolen data, it must be done in an environment of legal protection. The Active Cyber Defence Certainty Act (ACDCA) was introduced in 2017 and again in 2019 in the US House of Representatives. The bill seeks to confer upon individuals or businesses the right to retaliate when they experience a data theft or breach. The bill was introduced in the wake of the WannaCry ransomware attack, which infected more than four hundred thousand systems across a hundred and fifty countries before it was killed. But (unfortunately, in my opinion), such a bill never passed, which could have assisted in fundamental safeguards. I understand politics well enough to recognise that if it did not get any traction in Congress, probably someone's political gain was at stake.

A cyberattack victim would be allowed, under this bill, to access information on the attacker's computer for attribution, retrieval, or destruction of stolen data, to monitor the attacker's behaviour, and to use beaconing technology.[113] In the event that

---

113 Wordstream.com, in an article by a guest author, 24 June 2020, https://www.wordstream.com/blog/ws/2018/10/04/beacon-technology#:~:text=Beacons%20are%20small,%20wireless%20transmitters,to%20other%20smart%20devices%20nearby.&text=Put%20simply,%20they%20connect%20and,interaction%20easier%20and%20more%20accurate, defines beacon technology as follows: "Beacons are small, wireless transmitters that use low-energy Bluetooth technology to send signals to other smart devices nearby. They are one of the latest developments in location technology and proximity marketing. Put simply, they connect and transmit information to smart devices making location-based searching and interaction easier and more accurate." Furthermore, in an article by Rightpoint.com, 16 November 2018, https://www.rightpoint.com/thought/articles/2018/11/16/beacon-technology, it explains, "Each beacon has a Unique ID made of numbers and letters and that identifying information

ACDCA passes, it could be possible for private companies to participate in a pilot program for two years, in which they would work in close coordination with the FBI. This would empower businesses to employ active cyber defence techniques without criminal repercussions. However, to count as active defence, the cyber defence measure would have to disrupt an ongoing attack, establish a cause of the attack, or monitor the attacker's behaviour to help develop more effective defensive methods. Active defence does not include causing a threat to public safety or health, causing financial harm or physical injury, accessing a computer deliberately, or destroying information stored on the attacker's computer that does not pertain to the victim. The new bill also specifies that revenge cannot be a lawful motive for hacking back.

Since the bill has not passed, there is currently no legal right for a US company to "hack back" in response to a cyberattack. In any case, if we decide that we must go to the dark side to protect ourselves—as sympathetic as I am creating safeguards, as I have noted above—it could become hard to distinguish our actions from those of the hackers.

---

is broadcasted by Bluetooth several times each second. If you have never seen a beacon before, they are quite simple devices and only consist of three parts: batteries, a central processing unit (CPU), and the radio. All beacons are BLE which stands for Bluetooth low energy (you may have also seen it called 'BTLE'). This is especially important because the use of less energy means the ability for the beacons to be actively used for longer periods of time, often years without changing the battery. If you hear BLE with regards to Bluetooth beacons, know that all Bluetooth related beacons are technically considered low energy beacons . . . There are many different types of Bluetooth beacons out there, but the most popular configurations are either iBeacons or Eddystone beacons. iBeacon was created by Apple and Eddystone by Google."

CHAPTER 6

DIFFICULTIES IN MANAGING DATA

We have seen the risks that emerging technologies pose to individuals. But on the other end of the exchange, those who process personal or digital data are also caught in a problematic situation regarding how to make sense of the data collected. It is exceedingly difficult to manage vast amounts of data for many reasons:

a. **Low quality of data:** Perhaps the data are not adequate, or information collected through metadata and other forms are incomplete.

b. **Growing volumes of data:** Since data may be personal, generated, or company-owned, the data are spread across disparate sources in a way that is difficult to comprehend. That is why big tech giants come into play, such as Google, Apple, Microsoft, and the like, because they can summarise and make meaning of your data and then use their advanced knowledge to generate revenue.

c. **Bias:** People processing data may be subject to discrimination because of their background or the type of company where they work, their values, and ideologies. These factors can dilute the true essence of the data collected. Incorrect tagging of someone's profiles can lead to a perception of someone in the online world that is not aligned with reality.

d. **Managing data stored in the soft-copy form:** Cloud storage is the preferred means of computer data storage. In cloud storage, digital data are maintained in logical pools across multiple servers managed by the hosting company. Making the data accessible and available and protecting the physical environment become the responsibilities of the cloud storage providers. Organisations or people lease or buy storage capacity from these providers to store and manage data.

An international bank with customers in Germany and Switzerland had to meet two stringent laws regarding data privacy and residency when implementing software-as-a-service (SaaS) applications. Concerning German customers, the Federal Data Protection Act had to be followed; meanwhile, it was also mandatory to adhere to the Swiss Federal Act on Data Protection when dealing with Swiss customers.

The duty of confidentiality in the common law legal systems is owed to service users is satisfied by protecting their privacy. The service provider platform should ensure that only de-identified data is available for research and service evaluation purposes. *R (Source Informatics) v Department of Health [2001] QB 42* clarifies to the courts that this can be done. Additionally, service users should be informed about the use of their data, so they reasonably expect their information to be used in such a way, the service provider's platform allows for an easy opt-out for anyone who wishes for their data not to be processed for this purpose. The common law legal systems categorise the duty of confidentiality is separate and is in addition to data protection legislation (DPA, UK GDPR). It requires that information given in confidence must not be shared with a third party without the individuals' valid consent or some other legal basis, such as overriding public interest, statutory basis, or court order.[114]

In Microsoft v United States,[115] *an appeals court blocked a law enforcement agency from obtaining user data outside US jurisdiction with the use of a search warrant, which requires only a demonstration of probable cause. In this case, the government argued that this restriction would hamper their investigations since criminals keep their information in cloud storage on servers beyond the physical US border. Microsoft contends that the government has no jurisdiction over servers physically located in other sovereign nations, even if the data relate solely to American users.*

Many countries or government entities mandate that personal data should not be disclosed abroad. This is a challenge as far as cloud storage is concerned as it cannot be guaranteed that private data will always remain within a region or country. Although SaaS providers have built data centres in some countries in Europe, including Switzerland, to provide within-region or within-country location data storage, this fails to address the backup data centre's location in case of an outage. Besides, the providers may have employees from other regions who need access to the stored data for operational reasons, but

---

114 "Data Protection Impact Assessment (DPIA)" published in https://www.nhsdatasharing.info/, https://www.nhsdatasharing.info/DPIA/OCS_DPIA_DC.pdf.

115 "The Year Ahead in Cybersecurity Law," Tara Swaminatha, CSO Online, 9 January 2018, https://www.csoonline.com/article/3245743/the-year-ahead-in-cybersecurity-law.html.

this would violate data privacy. There is no reason this access would be required unless the company that owns the data in the first place would request some assistance.

SaaS has gained much momentum because of its portability. However, security remains the number-one concern for buyers. Additionally, SaaS providers rarely accept full accountability in their service-level agreements (SLAs) to protect their customers' data, leaving the customers with the entire liability exposure in the event of a breach. SaaS has become a multibillion-dollar industry, and to accommodate their customers, SaaS providers have met on the common ground of a security concept called encryption and tokenisation. However, encryption is one of two mechanisms to make information inaccessible. It uses algorithms to transform data into a non-readable form called the ciphertext. A company entering into an SLA can offer confidentiality, which is a measured concept, at least contractually, but not "integrity," which is an intangible concept, as no one would know what a person on the job might/would/could do deliberately or otherwise.

KNOW YOUR BASICS: CIPHER TEXT

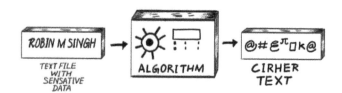

Moreover, a similar process governs the decrypting of the data. Algorithms are developed based on robust mathematical research to make it exceedingly difficult, though not impossible, to decipher and decrypt data. Generally, an algorithm uses a key, a virtual equivalent of a house key used to open a lock, to encrypt and a different key to decrypt; this is known as multi-key encryption and is generally more reliable than single-key encryption and decryption.

KNOW YOUR BASICS: LOCK KEY AND UNLOCK KEY

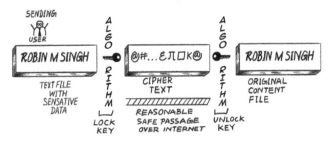

On the other hand, tokenisation is the process of randomly generating a substitute value or token used in place of actual data, where the token[116] is not computationally derived in any way. The most common form of tokenisation uses a highly-secure lookup table, called a vault, to track the relationships between actual data and substitute token values. In an entity that is well established, the client is expected to provide an additional server to keep the sensitive data for tokenisation.

---

116 As defined by techterm.com, 9 April 2009, https://techterms.com/definition/token, and in the context of networking terminology, a token is a series of bits that circulate on a token-ring network. When one of the systems on the network has the "token," it can send information to the other computers. Since there is only one token for each token-ring network, only one computer can send data at a time. In the case of security systems, a "hard token" is a small card that displays an identification code used to log into a network. When the card user enters the correct password, the card displays the current ID number needed to log into the network. This adds an extra level of protection to the network because the IDs change every few minutes. Security tokens also come in software versions called soft tokens.

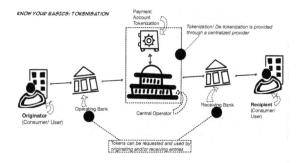

When using these security tools, you would need to identify which level you wish to encrypt: the database level, where the data are stored; field-specific level, individual values; or multiple levels.[117] You would then need to define what type of encryption you would select. Options would include FIPS 140-2, the US federal government encryption standard; FIPS 197, an algorithmic option that addresses the advanced encryption standard (AES); and many others available for personal or organisational use as a Google search will demonstrate.

An important concept to keep in mind is "who holds the key." One can develop a company policy to rotate the keys amongst selected members, just as two people may hold a secret launch code, one fixed and the other on a rotation basis. This always needs to be supported by a proper risk assessment to identify if a separation of duties would add remediation to the situation.

　　a.　**Data storage in the hard-copy form:** Hard copies offer many advantages over soft copies for data preservation. Document storage services in a specified location provide access only to individuals with official clearance,

---

117 "Data Privacy and Compliance in the Cloud," Symantec Corporation, Broadcom, 23 January 2020, https://docs.broadcom.com/doc/data-privacy-and-compliance-in-the-cloud-en.

unlike digital copies that can be hacked from anywhere. Some big-time businesses do still make hard copies of critical documents simply because paper documents or hard copies can also be destroyed entirely by shredding, thereby meeting data privacy regulations. However, hard copies have their own set of challenges.

Lost records can impact businesses in a big way. Although hard copies may be needed for legal matters, such as a lawsuit, the absence of appropriate documents may mean the dissolution of the business or additional cost. Keeping track of inventory on a daily basis can be a challenge for small companies, and depending on how long the data must be stored, companies may run out of storage space or filing cabinets. Moreover, the haphazard storage of hard-copy records with personal information increases the risk of a data breach.

A. What Are the Key Regulations That Govern Document Compliance with Privacy?

GDPR lists six principles concerning data processing. Data must be

a. Processed transparently, lawfully, and fairly;
b. Collected for legitimate purposes only;
c. Adequate and limited to only what is necessary;
d. Accurate and up to date;
e. Stored only for the required duration; and
f. Protected with appropriate security.

Documenting policies and activities: GDPR and CCPA mandate businesses or entities should:

a. maintain a detailed record or data inventory of data processing activities and

b. document data protection procedures and policies.

Post-mortem documentation: GDPR requires businesses that have experienced a data breach to document the breach details and the remedial action they have taken to prevent a recurrence.

Data encryption: In the case of electronic or cloud storage of personal data, encryption has been mentioned as one possible measure to protect data under Art. 32(1) of GDPR.[118]

B. An Example of a Company Spanning Multiple Jurisdictions

The case of Arthur Andersen LLP v United States *is an example of conflicting jurisdictions and their legal consequences in a case involving data protection and document retention policies.*[119]

Arthur Andersen was the Chicago-based accounting firm for the Enron energy company. Before Enron went bankrupt in 2001, its fraudulent accounting activity came to light.[120] *When Arthur Andersen learned of the US Securities and Exchange Commission's*

---

118 "GDPR Encryption," published at Gdpr-info.eu, https://gdpr-info.eu/issues/encryption/.

119 "United States: The Supreme Court's Decision in Arthur Andersen LLP v. United States: An Important Development Regarding the Legal Consequences of Document Retention Policies," Gregory Castanias, R Cook, Louis Fisher, and David Horan, Mondaq, 14 June 2005, https://www.mondaq.com/unitedstates/white-collar-crime-anti-corruption-fraud/33117/the-supreme-courts-decision-in-arthur-andersen-llp-v-united-states-an-important-development-regarding-the-legal-consequences-of-document-retention-policies.

120 "Arthur Andersen LLP v. United States, 544 U.S. 696 (2005)," covered by Justia (US Supreme Court), 7 January 2005, https://supreme.justia.com/cases/federal/us/544/696/.

impending investigation, the firm ordered its employees to destroy all records about Enron.

A charge of wilful obstruction of the investigation was filed against the accounting firm in 2002 in a Texas district court. After the firm was found guilty by the jury, it surrendered its licence and went out of business. Arthur Andersen petitioned the Supreme Court, stating that the instructions provided to the jury were inappropriate as they were told they could convict the defendant even if the defendant sincerely and honestly believed that its conduct was lawful. Arthur Andersen argued that although it had instructed its employees to destroy Enron's records, this was done per its document-retention policy, which was designed to keep its clients' information private.

The Supreme Court held that the firm's instructions to shred documents did not amount to being "knowingly corrupt." The court held that the firm was not guilty, as it was not conscious of any wrongdoing and merely impeding the proceedings by destroying documents was innocent conduct.

This decision does not clarify when a firm's document-shredding activity is indeed "dishonest" or "subverts the integrity of" as opposed to only "impeding" a legal proceeding. Regardless of this unresolved issue, the decision clarifies that developing and adhering to a clear set of document retention policies is of critical importance.

CHAPTER 7

WHY PRIVACY IN THE HEALTHCARE SECTOR IS SO IMPORTANT

Healthcare is an extraordinarily complex industry, as multiple service lines or stakeholders are involved in delivering one outcome for a single sick patient. When a patient visits a healthcare facility, the physician is not the only person responding. The patient may see only the physician who provides direct service. However, the visit also requires an independent entity that facilitates the scheduling of the visit, an electronic medical record (EMR) vendor that provides software and storage to save patient medical records (including their history, diagnosis, and doctor's notes), and then an interaction with a health information exchange (HIE) entity as well, which shares the data with other physicians if a second opinion is needed or the patient is transferred to a hospital, and then requires one more party that handles billing. This complex process is further intertwined with the insurance company that pays the bills and, occasionally, a collection agency for a patient who defaults or does not pay on time. As the complexity of medical services increases, the number of entities involved in providing them also increases.

Thus, it is essential to have a comprehensive understanding of the system and the interconnected relationships amongst its parts when addressing any breaches.

A. The Importance of Managing Patient Data[121]

Protected health information (PHI) is a valuable commodity in the underworld market or the dark web for hackers. PHI can be stolen from various places or held hostage via ransomware to obtain the desired payoff. In the United States, the HITECH Act requires business associates to comply with the HIPAA security rule regarding ePHI and report PHI breaches. Business associates must also comply with HIPAA privacy rule requirements that apply to covered entities when the associated act on behalf of those entities.[122] In addition to personal healthcare data, medical devices, which are increasingly becoming more and more digitally connected, are highly vulnerable to hackers because the healthcare systems are still learning to dance to the tune of technology.

In the financial world, stolen identity can be an inconvenience that can cost a considerable amount of money. However, in healthcare, the potential damage from a compromised medical device is exponentially higher. For instance, malicious hacking

---

121 "The Importance of Healthcare Data Security," Cprime | Archer, https://archer-soft.com/en/blog/importance-healthcare-data-security.

122 "HITECH (Health Information Technology for Economic and Clinical Health) Act of 2009," Scot Petersen and Tayla Holman, January 2018, https://searchhealthit.techtarget.com/definition/HITECH-Act.

of a heart rate monitor, which carries numerous data, could compromise a patient's well-being.[123]

Apart from these considerations, healthcare data breaches also have high financial costs. According to an IBM study, healthcare organisations incur the highest costs relating to data breaches in 2018 for the eighth consecutive year, to the tune of $408 per stolen record.[124] Stolen medical records are precious in the dark web marketplace as they can be leveraged to commit insurance fraud. Worse still, the records can be altered while in possession of an identity thief, compromising healthcare delivery in emergencies or affecting a person's eligibility for insurance.

Here is what the pattern looks like for breaches that have been identified. This summary does not contain any information on violations that were identified but not reported.[125] But the trends are headed in only one direction—upward.

THE TREND – SEE FOR YOURSELF

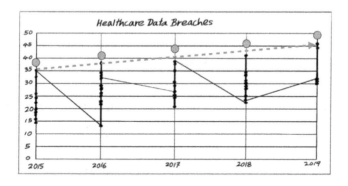

123 "Data Privacy & Security in Healthcare," Ian Terry, 23 October 2018, https://hackernoon.com/data-privacy-security-in-healthcare-8bb15e203e56.

124 "Healthcare Data Breach Costs Remain Highest Among Industries," Fred Donovan, Health Security, 12 July 2018, https://healthitsecurity.com/news/healthcare-data-breach-costs-remain-highest-among-industries.

125 "June 2019 Healthcare Data Breach Report," *HIPAA Journal*, June 2019, https://www.hipaajournal.com/june-2019-healthcare-data-breach-report/.

From 2015 to 2016, there was an increase of 21 per cent in healthcare breach cases, followed by an 8 per cent increase in 2017 and then roughly a levelling off in 2018. The chart shows data for only the first six months of 2019, and it reflected that more than 9 million Americans' records were compromised in some form or another, which was double the impact sustained in 2017.

The highest recorded number of breach incidents from 2014 to 2018 was forty-one cases in April 2018, but April and June 2019 had forty-six and forty-four breaches, respectively.[126]

There are numerous reasons why these breaches are occurring. One breach suffered by ZOLL Services, which notified 277,319 patients that their personal and medical data had been compromised, was caused by a server-migration error.[127] Some other prominent reasons were improper disposal, loss, theft, inappropriate disclosure, and hacking.

Privacy of patient data/records is at par, if not more, to those data of the very, very important (VVIP) personnel (governor, attorney general, cabinet ministers, prime minister/president, and the like officials). We physically place higher emphasis and safeguards on protecting access to such data by ensuring that a third party has biometric logging in process or facial recognition when accessing people's credentials. Patient records gain a higher level of confidentiality in a healthcare system than anything else.

---

126 "June 2019 Healthcare Data Breach Report," *HIPAA Journal*, June 2019, https://www.hipaajournal.com/june-2019-healthcare-data-breach-report/.

127 "The 10 Biggest Healthcare Data Breaches of 2019, So Far," Jessica Davis, Health Security, 23 July 2019, https://healthitsecurity.com/news/the-10-biggest-healthcare-data-breaches-of-2019-so-far.

B. WHAT DO HACKERS GET FROM PATIENT DATA?

In 2017, the healthcare industry experienced 750 cyber
incidents, of which 536 involved data breaches. Miscellaneous
errors, privilege misuse, and crimeware accounted for 63 per
cent of healthcare-sector cyber incidents. Just as in the financial
industry, data related to healthcare fetch immense value in the
dark web marketplace.

*In February 2016, hackers disrupted the IT systems at Hollywood
Presbyterian Medical Centre in California and demanded a
ransom. According to initial reports, hackers demanded nine
thousand in Bitcoin payment, equal to $3.6 million. The hospital
paid $17,000 to the hackers to end the electronic shutdown.*[128]

*In the same year, Marin Medical Practices (MMP) was hit
by ransomware affecting the healthcare data of 2,934 patients at
Marin Healthcare of Prima Medical Group physicians. Although
the exact amount was not disclosed, MMP ended up paying a
ransom to get the data back from the hackers.*[129]

These two healthcare providers were lucky to pay a ransom,
apparently satisfied the hackers. But in general, I would maintain
that paying a ransom is rarely, if ever, the right solution because
hackers often just come back again looking for more. Kansas
Heart Hospital paid an unknown "small amount" of money
to hackers; however, instead of restoring full access to the files,
the hackers demanded another ransom, according to a report.
Kansas Heart Hospital said it would not pay again. One of the
hospital representatives made the following statement: "Kansas

---

128 "Hollywood Hospital Pays $17,000 in Bitcoin to Hackers; FBI Investigating,"
Richard Winton, *Los Angeles Times*, 18 February 2016, https://www.latimes.
com/business/technology/la-me-ln-hollywood-hospital-bitcoin-20160217-
story.html.

129 "Marin Patients' Medical Data Lost after Cyber-Attack," Richard Halstead,
Marin Independent Journal, 29 September 2016, https://www.marinij.
com/2016/09/29/marin-patients-medical-data-lost-after-cyber-attack/.

Heart Hospital, in conjunction with our consultants, felt this was no longer a wise manoeuvre or strategy," which sums up the whole event.[130]

Healthcare data contain valuable information, such as Social Security numbers, passport or country identification card details, insurance details, and home addresses; thus, they are worth more to hackers than other types of data. Hackers make money by selling these data for a premium price on the dark web; they have a strong economic incentive to focus on the healthcare sector's hacking attacks. Additionally, being one of the oldest professions in history, the healthcare professions are not as tech-savvy as many other sectors.

The healthcare industry continues to be plagued by data and privacy breaches involving sensitive patient information. Protenus, Inc., in collaboration with DataBreaches.net, reported[131] that the impact of patient records being stolen is also increasing, with 15 million patient records breached in 2018.

As shown by a Technology Innovation at Brookings study,[132] not only have hacking incidents been increasing at a crazy pace, but also the loss ratio is even higher because a single hacking attack can seize millions of records at once.

The relationship between the type of incidents or breaches and the total number of individuals affected is correlated. Hacking requires to be sophisticated and technologically-advanced

---

130 "Kansas Heart Hospital Pays Ransom, Then Hackers Came Back for More," Becker's Health IT, 23 May 2016, https://www.beckershospitalreview.com/healthcare-information-technology/kansas-heart-hospital-pays-ransom-then-hackers-came-back-for-more.html.

131 "Protenus 2019 Breach Barometer," Protenus, 2019, https://www.protenus.com/resources/protenus-2019-breach-barometer/.

132 "Hackers, Phishers, and Disappearing Thumb Drives: Lessons Learned from Major Health Care Data Breaches," Niam Yaraghi, Bookings, May 2016, https://www.brookings.edu/wp-content/uploads/2016/07/Patient-Privacy504v3.pdf.

thinking, but a small number of hacking incidents can involve a sizeable number of individuals. In contrast, a mechanism such as theft might require multiple attempts to gain access to an individual's files.[133]

C. IMPORTANCE OF RIGHT RESTRICTIONS ON PATIENT DATA

In the healthcare industry, where the focus is on saving lives, securing access to sensitive private data, such as medical records, is the top priority.

Although extensive digitisation in the healthcare sector has enhanced its efficiency, it has also raised the information security risk. In 2016, data breaches in the industry impacted at least 27 million US patients.[134]

Given healthcare data's sensitive nature, healthcare providers must adopt a robust data security service. The strategies chosen should protect healthcare data from any attacks by hackers. If the government were to ease regulations on patient data, one could only imagine the magnitude of resulting risks to PHI.

The years 2015 and 2016 were significant years for data breaches in healthcare. According to a Ponemon Institute study, 90 per cent of organisations in healthcare suffered data breaches in these years, and 45 per cent experienced five or more data breaches. Estimates put the cost of such healthcare data breaches

---

133 "Hackers, Phishers, and Disappearing Thumb Drives: Lessons Learned from Major Health Care Data Breaches," Niam Yaraghi, Bookings, May 2016, https://www.brookings.edu/wp-content/uploads/2016/07/Patient-Privacy504v3.pdf.

134 "Report: Healthcare Data Breaches Hit All-Time High in 2016," Pajiv Leventhal, Healthcare Innovation, 4 May 2017, https://www.hcinnovationgroup.com/cybersecurity/news/13028482/report-healthcare-data-breaches-hit-alltime-high-in-2016.

at close to $6.2 billion.[135] The primary concerns for healthcare organisations, according to a survey, were careless employees, cyberattackers, insecure mobile devices, malicious insiders, and data theft.

I. Why Is HIPAA Important?

In the United States, secure storage of healthcare data has gained traction for organisations since the passage of acts like HIPAA (Health Insurance Portability and Accountability Act) and HITECH (Health Information Technology for Economic and Clinical Health). In healthcare, sensitive data include protected health information (PHI), such as medical histories, demographic data, mental health conditions, laboratory results, payment records, insurance data, and medical devices' data.

Enacted in 1996, HIPAA was designed to ensure sensitive patient data security and prevent healthcare fraud. The HITECH Act emphasises the adoption of Electronic Health Records (EHRs) to promote safety, efficiency, and quality of healthcare apart from improving healthcare data privacy and security.

HIPAA provides essential benefits to the healthcare industry while helping agencies transition to electronic health records from paper records. HIPAA streamlines administrative functions in healthcare and improves efficiency while ensuring that PHI is collected, shared, and stored safely and securely.

The act established rules that make it mandatory for healthcare agencies to control access to health data while restricting who views and shares sensitive information. HIPAA

---

135 "Sixth Annual Benchmark Study on Privacy & Security of Healthcare Data," Ponemon Institute, Ponemon, May 2016, https://www.ponemon.org/local/upload/file/Sixth%20Annual%20Patient%20Privacy%20%26%20Data%20Security%20Report%20FINAL%206.pdf.

aims to protect information created, stored, or transmitted by health plans and care providers. Patients retain control over their personal data and decide with whom they share their personal data.

II. How Does HITECH Benefit Society?

The HITECH or Health Information Technology for Economic and Clinical Health Act was signed into law by President Obama on 17 February 2009. The HITECH Act aims to promote and expand technology adoption in healthcare, particularly the adoption of electronic health records (EHRs). Before the HITECH Act, only 10 per cent of US hospitals had adopted EHRs. HITECH sought to provide incentives to adopt EHRs to improve efficiency and patient care coordination and facilitate seamless sharing of health information between different covered entities.

The HITECH Act helped ensure the implementation of safeguards to keep sensitive patient health information confidential and private and restrict disclosures and uses of health information while also ensuring that healthcare agencies were honouring the obligation to give medical record copies to patients on request.

D. HEALTHCARE EXCHANGES AND PRIVACY CONCERNS SURROUNDING THEM

The need for interoperability has fuelled the growth of healthcare data sharing. Exchanging patient information helps healthcare providers avoid duplicate testing, reduces readmissions, and helps prevent medication errors. Data sharing also offers many other benefits, including large-scale analytics, disease tracking, population health management, genetic studies, and chronic disease registries, to name a few. Data exchange enables healthcare organisations to share and adopt best practices.

Covered entities are exploring how health information exchange (HIE) can help enhance patient care. At the same time, there are concerns as to the security of exchanged healthcare data. In 2018, 15 million patient health records were compromised in 503 breaches; in 2019, close to 25 million records were breached. In June 2019, because of a system hack, medical information, Social Security numbers, and personal data of 12 million patients of the blood-testing company Quest Diagnostics were compromised.[136] Unauthorised access and disclosure, vulnerable IT systems, phishing attacks, and third-party vendors were behind many such security incidents, which raise concerns about unwanted consequences of data sharing.

E. DATA PRIVACY OBLIGATIONS IN CLINICAL RESEARCH

GDPR has many implications for clinical trials by research organisations as well as for sponsors. A sponsor is a person legally obliged by the Clinical Trials Regulation (CTR)[137] to carry out a range of activities (e.g., reporting trial results, performing safety reporting, and archiving the trial master file or TMF for

---

136 "11.9M Quest Diagnostics Patients Impacted by AMCA Data Breach," Jessica Davis, Health IT Security, 3 June 2019, https://healthitsecurity.com/news/11.9m-quest-diagnostics-patients-impacted-by-amca-data-breach.

137 Pursuant to the European Commission directorate-general for health and food safety, https://ec.europa.eu/health/sites/health/files/files/documents/qa_clinicaltrials_gdpr_en.pdf, the Clinical Trials Regulation defines by law certain processing activities that are necessary for the performance of a task carried out in the public interest for purposes outlined in the approved clinical trial protocol, in this case to pursue the general public interest of the Union in safeguarding public health.

twenty-five years). Subjects should be adequately informed with regard to the processing of their data.

In January 2019, the European Data Protection Board released an opinion concerning the intersection between the CTR and GDPR. The board highlighted the fact that "consent" to participate in clinical research is different from consenting to data processing under GDPR. For researchers and sponsors, obtaining consent for data processing is one way to ensure that personal data processing is lawful under GDPR. Significantly, anonymised data do not come under the lens of GDPR. Suppose the sponsor intends to use personal data for secondary uses (outside the protocol of the clinical trial) under GDPR. In that case, it is necessary to obtain specific consent from the trial participants for this activity.

The sponsor is also obliged to inform trial participants as to the processing of personal data. The data controller (investigator or sponsor) must implement the relevant organisational and technical measures to demonstrate and ensure that personal data from subjects are processed per GDPR mandates.

Researchers must also ensure that proper safeguards (technical and organisational) are in place when processing patient data, including pseudonymisation that ensures confidentiality with key-coding of data. Anonymising of data is also encouraged where possible to ensure that the patient is not identifiable from the data sets at all.

Although GDPR does not explicitly address what happens to data in case of a particular drug or treatment failure in a clinical trial, Article 17 upholds the data subjects' "right to be forgotten" or data erasure. Participants have the right to be forgotten if "there is no longer a purpose for processing [the data], following the principle of limited storage and data minimization."

Furthermore, the sponsor may seek subjects' consent for secondary use at the beginning of a clinical trial, as covered by Article 28(2) of the CTR. However, the sponsor of the research must separately request consent for data processing within a secondary use. Nevertheless, there are sometimes emergencies in a clinical trial, and this possibility is covered in one of the conditions of Article 35. However, the choice is up to the human subject. If a human subject or his legal representative does not consent to the terms and conditions, the participation by the human subject cannot be continued. If a data subject dies before the consent could be confirmed or refused, GDPR no longer covers the processing of the data.[138]

F. Revisiting the IoT from the Perspective of the Ownership of Healthcare Data

I. The Human Body as a Source of Data

Our bodies are the source of big data, which is being collected by all the apps and wearables we use. However, if the device malfunctions or data are compromised because of network issues or the like, the person harmed would have the right to file a civil lawsuit.

All the data collected could reduce lead times and identify root causes, thus allowing healthcare providers to react quickly to a medical condition. For the caregivers, this data would be a boon in disguise because a healthcare provider would analyse health information for a larger population and react accordingly. Possibly, once all this becomes a commodity, it will reduce the cost of care as well and boost positive outcomes. In

---

138 "How Does the GDPR Impact Clinical Trials?" ECA Academy, 15 May 2019 https://www.gmp-compliance.org/gmp-news/how-does-the-gdpr-impact-clinical-trials.

fact, industries with access to these shared data sources consider them part of their primary data streams, and they are leveraging the data towards developing new business models.

Figure I Emergency medical treatment scenario

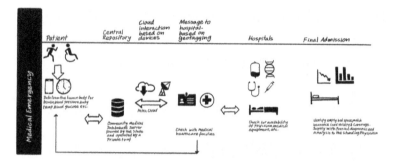

As noted earlier, Protenus, Inc., in collaboration with DataBreaches.net, reported[139] a total of 503 healthcare data breaches in 2019, up from 477 in 2017, in the United States alone, affecting more than 15 million patients. Insiders, in some form, caused about 28 per cent of these breaches; about 44 per cent were brought about by hacking, and 27 per cent of these were caused by ransomware attacks. Again, this is just the beginning. It is estimated that 20–30 billion devices in the healthcare Internet of Things (IoT) or the Internet of Medical Things (IoMT) will be part of this growing ecosystem. What that means is that hackers will have untold billions of data points to exploit. In short, hackers are likely to have a field day.

Closed-circuit TVs (CCTVs) have reaped an environment of caution with the use of IoT devices. In a car, a simple accelerometer and a gyroscope are capable of analysing people's driving habits. Imagine what happens when the data available

---

139 "Protenus 2019 Breach Barometer," Protenus, 2019, https://www.protenus.com/resources/protenus-2019-breach-barometer/.

extend to sleep patterns, smoking levels, physical activity, movement, or location.

Data previously considered non-identifiable can become identifiable with the use of IoT devices; for example, patterns as simple as voice data and habits can be used to identify individuals.

II. Why IoT Privacy Breaches Occur

The main reasons why IoT security breaches occur are as follows:

Sparse classification of data. It is easy to create data packets to extract customer information without having a valid user in the current state of health data management. This information might fall under secondary information, i.e., information not relating to direct diagnosis and, thus, a lack of security could result.

Lack of foresight. Providers may have never thought, a few years ago, that they would soon be in a situation where the intermingling of health with technology would be so great and where privacy, which should be at the heart of healthcare, would be so vulnerable. But of course, this is true in all fields. Just a couple of decades ago, nobody anticipated highway tollgates that would scan RFID tags for toll fees—and store vehicle information, driver information, driving patterns, and the like. As in the movie *The Net*, starring Sandra Bullock, when you cross an electronic tagging/RFID machine, the chips inside your credit cards or other electronic items can be used as a messaging system to track your location.

Not easy to upgrade. IoT devices, such as CCTVs, are not upgraded and are patched primarily in healthcare institutions to monitor patients or expansive healthcare devices. That is why ransomware attacks hold up many hospitals from their routine operations. A healthcare device, such as a blood glucose meter, is expected to help guide patients with managing their diabetes, not divulge the blood group, any prevalent diseases, family history, and the like.

Not much processing power. IoT devices do not possess much processing power to manage data and run security portals. Moreover, cost factors always serve as a hindrance to security features, which leaves this market vulnerable. Example A: The refrigerator keeps track of the remaining number of eggs, milk, and the like. Who would have thought that anyone would want to put a thunderbolt port into it to connect it to various providers and encrypt the information being sent for security purposes?

The diversified interest of healthcare institutions. In the machine-to-machine (M2M) model, where one company sends the encrypted data while the other company that receives the information decrypts the data to fulfil their obligation. For instance, if Fitbit, a smart wearable manufacturer, handles one aspect of storing your health data, such as (but not limited to) vital, blood oxygen levels, and the like, while Google Cloud stores the information (hopefully in an encrypted format) and your Internet provider ensures that it can move from one place to another, then it would be challenging to get all the data decrypted and under one roof. Considering the above refrigerator example, if prominent companies, such as Samsung and Whirlpool, started to encrypt their information, would the local grocery store that delivers the groceries need to invest in a system to decrypt the same? So an imbalance of technology is created: Either you can go along with the modern technology and choose a high-end grocer or stay with your local grocer and not use all the features of the latest technology.

Poor culture towards data subject rights. If the culture is set in stone to protect the privacy rights of individuals, patients, or customers, or about the privacy practice itself, there will be fewer questions or complaints, and this will create a strong level of consumer trust towards a manufacturer's brand.

The US Federal Trade Commission disciplined a company called TRENDnet[140] that marketed its Internet camera for various security purposes, even baby monitoring, while also claiming that their cameras were secure. In reality, they were sending unencrypted data and failing to fulfil consumers' privacy settings. Thus, hackers were able to get live video feeds from these cameras and upload them for online viewing.

The US Food and Drug Administration (FDA) issued guidelines to define when a technological item constitutes a medical device and when it does not. This is a complicated issue because the software that analyses multiple physiological signals to monitor whether a person has a heart attack should be treated differently from one checking if a person has a narcoleptic episode. Furthermore, that is where the playing field opens up for the hacker. Managing all the data is an arduous task; Fitbit, the smart wearable manufacturer, markets a device called the Health Solution that investigates sleep disorders, diabetes, cardiovascular health, and mental health, and this device has been profitable because of the intensive details that the medical device on your wrist can capture; their latest advancement, a medical device to detect a type of heart arrhythmia by screening for sleep apnea (a severe sleep disorder) through a blood oxygen sensor. Therefore, such devices need to be regulated by the FDA to ensure a higher standard of privacy and security. There is no

---

140 "FTC Approves Final Order Settling Charges Against TRENDnet, Inc.," Federal Trade Commission, 7 February 2014, https://www.ftc.gov/news-events/press-releases/2014/02/ftc-approves-final-order-settling-charges-against-trendnet-inc.

exact way to determine who owns the data in this scenario. It is a far more complex issue than initially imagined. The rule of thumb suggests that the person with the title to the device (or the original purchaser who registers their device) or the machine owns the data. Until it can be objectively determined who owns the data, there will be a strong need for vendors, developers, and lawmakers to focus on establishing effective data exchange regulations.

Contracts must be drafted to protect the consumer and the ever-expanding sphere of data generation and exchange. Read all your contracts associated with mobile devices; do not just click "I Agree" blindly.

CHAPTER 8

THE GRAY AREA BETWEEN ETHICS AND PRIVACY?

Data privacy relates to the collection of, use of, and access to data and the legal rights of the person whom the data concern. Those rights include

  a. power to prevent unauthorised access to personal data;
  b. right to prevent inappropriate use of private data;
  c. completeness and accuracy of data collection;
  d. right to update, inspect, or modify data; and
  e. right of ownership of and access to personal data.

Privacy, security, ethics, and law are interlinked. In many ways, the effective implementation of provisions concerning data security and confidentiality relies on trust. For instance, an individual may allow trusted entities or individuals to access data that are not accessible to anyone. Similarly, confidence in the security provider contributes to a feeling of security.

In contrast, violation of privacy is a threat to security. Although ethics provides a context for the framing of laws, the law provides a formal resolution that ethics cannot offer by itself. For instance, ethics tells us that stealing is wrong, but the law includes punishment. Similarly, the law permits specific actions; ethics motivates us to ensure that those actions are legitimate. Privacy breaches are not only illegal but also violate ethical principles.

Although there is some variation in attitudes towards privacy across cultures, there is a broad consensus on the intrinsic, social, and core value of privacy. It is, therefore, possible to formulate a privacy principle that is in accord with generally accepted standards of ethics, the framework of law, and societal concerns.

A. Data Brokers: Revere or Relieve?

Data brokers are the companies or intermediaries that collect and sell consumers' personal information. They are significant contributors to the Big Data economy, but consumers are not aware of their existence or the practices brokers adopt.

Not only is the broker industry complex, made up of multiple layers of brokers sharing data, but an FTC study also found that in most cases, brokers collect data from consumers without their knowledge. Although some data brokers' products are beneficial to consumers in preventing fraud, improving product offerings, and offering personalised advertisements, there are potential risks from the surreptitious collection and use of personal data.

The FTC recommends a series of best practices for data brokers, including these three:

a. implementing privacy by design, which requires brokers to focus on privacy issues at all stages of product development;
b. implementing measures to avoid collecting personal data of children and teens; and
c. taking reasonable precautions to make sure the data they sell downstream are not used for unlawful purposes.

Although there are a growing number of rules and regulations concerning data privacy, ethical considerations and consumer participation are equally essential to ensure that data brokers play a healthy, non-intrusive role in the Big Data economy.

B. What Are the Ethical Obligations Related to Tracking Technologies, iPhone Face Recognition, and Android Biometrics?

In 2015, social media giant Facebook faced a lawsuit under the Biometric Information Privacy Act in Illinois for using a facial-recognition feature without users' consent.[141] Under this law, companies must have a public policy on collecting, storing, and using biometric data, including face recognition scans. With this technology, Facebook can suggest tags in photos. In August 2019, a three-member appeals court rendered a unanimous decision, stating, "We conclude that the development of a face template using facial-recognition technology without consent (as alleged here)

---

141 "Facebook to Pay $550 Million to Settle Facial Recognition Suit," Natasha Singer and Mike Isaac, *New York Times*, 29 January 2020, https://www.nytimes.com/2020/01/29/technology/facebook-privacy-lawsuit-earnings.html.

*invades an individual's private affairs and concrete interests."[142]
The appeals court stated that the company's use of the feature
without consent invaded an individual's privacy. The penalties per
violation range between $1,000 and $5,000 under Illinois law.*

This case highlights the privacy concerns around facial-
recognition features that collect and use vast amounts of sensitive
personal information. Although Apple assured buyers and
privacy experts that facial data would be stored securely within
the phone, this assurance does not extend to app developers who
can access the data to build entertainment features. App makers
can capture a user's face and fifty different facial expressions,
which can be stored on the developer's servers, and then use
data to monitor the frequency of the user's blink, smile, or other
expressions.[143]

For all intended purposes, irrespective of blatant personal
information, this is a personal profile, which is unique, and
should come under the same protection.

Biometric authentication involves using a measurable
biological characteristic, such as a fingerprint, to unlock a phone,
to authorise payment, and to verify identity in other processes
that previously required a password. Android manufacturers are
committed to providing fingerprint sensors in-screen.[144]

---

142 "Facebook Could Pay Billions after Losing Facial Recognition Privacy Appeal,"
     Colin Lecher, The Verge, 8 August 2019, https://www.theverge.com/2019/8/8/
     20792326/facebook-facial-recognition-appeals-decision-damages-payment-
     court.
143 "Why Some Privacy Experts Are Spooked by iPhone X's Facial Recognition
     Feature," Reuters, *New York Post*, 2 November 2017, https://nypost.
     com/2017/11/02/why-some-privacy-experts-are-spooked-by-iphone-xs-
     facial-recognition-feature/.
144 "Council Post: iOS Vs. Android: Biometric Authentication As…," Justin Wetherill,
     Forbes, 1 November 2018, https://www.forbes.com/sites/forbestechcouncil/
     2018/11/01/ios-vs-android-biometric-authentication-as-a-strategic-
     differentiator/.

Although not many other privacy laws cover facial-recognition or biometrics, GDPR lists ethical and legal obligations while considering biometric data as personal data that enables identifying an individual. This particular category of personal data can be processed once the following steps have been concluded[145]:

a. Explicit consent from the data subject has been obtained
b. Processing helps protect the data subject's vital interests
c. Processing helps establish and defend legal claims
d. Public interest reasons
e. Lawful ground for biometric data processing

In all these "violations," I very rarely see restitution to the individual in any sense.

Fines go to the government, and in many ways, development is rarely stopped or reversed. Another recent scenario that comes to my mind is Google grabbing all the books out of copyright from around the world, which commenced in 2002. It led to an epic legal battle between Google and the authors and the publishers for copyright violations.[146] In 2013, Google came out victorious; a decision allowed Google to continue scanning the books. What benefits do individuals gain in terms of proceeds/profits earned is yet to be seen.

As opposed to America versus other countries' companies, American companies and their treatment are blatantly apparent.

---

145 "GDPR: Things to Consider When Processing Biometric Data," Luke Irwin, IT Governance European Blog, 15 September 2017, https://www.itgovernance.eu/blog/en/gdpr-things-to-consider-when-processing-biometric-data.

146 "What Happened to Google's Effort to Scan Millions of University Library Books?" Jennifer Howard, 10 August 2017, https://www.edsurge.com/news/2017-08-10-what-happened-to-google-s-effort-to-scan-millions-of-university-library-books.

C. CHILDREN'S PRIVACY ON THE INTERNET

In August 2019, the Federal Trade Commission imposed a fine of up to $200 million on Google for its subsidiary YouTube's violations of children's privacy. A coalition of twenty consumer advocacy groups had filed a complaint, stating that YouTube had collected and used children's personal information, which was a violation of online privacy law. This fine far exceeds the approximately $6 million that the FTC levied against the owners of TikTok in 2020 for violations of children's privacy.[147]

Lawmakers have recognised the need for children to receive special treatment concerning their data privacy on the Internet. The Children's Online Privacy Protection Act (COPPA) of 1998 was designed to protect the confidentiality of personal data collected online on children below the age of thirteen. The principal objective of this US law is to require parental consent for collecting, using, disclosing, sharing, or tracking the private information of minors as defined under COPPA.

Violation of COPPA carries a penalty of $40,000 per violation. This means that if a company's app or website violates COPPA by collecting just ten children's personal information, it faces fines of up to $400,000.[148]

COPPA's primary purpose is to protect children from such threats as paedophiles, porn purveyors, trauma, and the like. Just as children often hide behind a parent when a stranger enters, the law tries to create similar protection.

---

147 "YouTube Said to Be Fined Up to $200 Million for Children's Privacy Violations," Natasha Singer, Jack Nicas, and Kate Conger, *New York Times*, 30 August 2019, https://www.nytimes.com/2019/08/30/technology/youtube-childrens-privacy-fine.html.

148 "Costs of Non-Compliance with Privacy Laws," Elizabeth, Privacy policies, 18 February 2020, https://www.privacypolicies.com/blog/costs-non-compliance-privacy-laws/.

GDPR includes essential provisions related to the data privacy of children. Unlike COPPA, GDPR does not set an applicable age for data consent but leaves it to the discretion of member states. In most EU countries, data consent must be obtained for children below age thirteen; the age limit is fourteen in Spain and sixteen in the Netherlands. Under GDPR, data subjects (children) must be given clear, straightforward, easily-understandable information about the planned use of their data.

D. Concerns Regarding Data Collected Beyond an Individual's Understanding

Article 4(11) of GDPR defines consent for data processing as "any freely given, specific, informed and unambiguous indication of his or her wishes by which the data subject, either by a statement or by clear affirmative action, signifies agreement to personal data relating to them being processed."[149] GDPR further states that "consent should not be regarded as freely given if the data subject has no genuine or free choice or is unable to refuse or withdraw consent without detriment."[150]

To comply with these provisions, all people involved in data collection and processing should follow the following principles when obtaining consent:

---

149 "GDPR Consent Examples and Innovative Methods to Opt-In," Tim Watson, ZettaSphere, April 2018, https://www.zettasphere.com/gdpr-consent-opt-in-examples/.

150 "[GDPR III] Obtaining Informed Consent – FormAssembly," FormAssembly, https://www.formassembly.com/blog/gdpr-obtaining-informed-consent/.

YOUR RIGHT – KNOW AND UNDERSTAND YOUR 'INFORMED CONSENT'

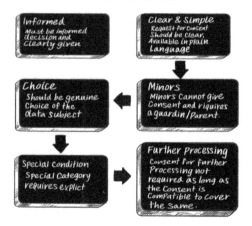

GDPR Recital 42 states that for consent to qualify as "informed," the data subject "should be aware at least of the identity of the controller and the purposes of the processing for which the personal data are intended."[151] In all privacy laws, the onus is on the data controller or collector to ensure transparency, specificity, lack of ambiguity, and clarity of the terms under which the data processing occurs.

Additionally, Article 13 discusses the information that must be provided when personal data are collected, regardless of the legal ground for lawful processing.[152] When giving consent, one should consider the following:

---

151 "[GDPR III] Obtaining Informed Consent," Form Assembly, https://www.formassembly.com/blog/gdpr-obtaining-informed-consent/.

152 "Consent under the GDPR: Valid, Freely Given, Specific, Informed and Active Consent," i-scoop, https://www.i-scoop.eu/gdpr/consent-gdpr/#Freely_given_consent_and_detriment.

YOUR RIGHT – YOU CAN WITHDRAW YOUR 'INFORMED CONSENT' ANYTIME

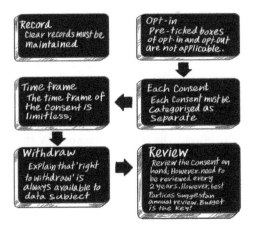

Regarding the practice of obtaining lawful consent, the International Commissioner's Office, which is the United Kingdom's independent authority set up to uphold information rights in the public interest, promoting openness by public bodies and data privacy for individuals, has released a checklist of recommended steps[153]:

a. We have checked that consent is the most appropriate lawful basis for processing.

b. We have requested consent prominently and separately from our terms and conditions.

c. We ask people to opt in positively.

d. We do not use pre-ticked boxes or any other type of default consent.

---

153 "Guide to the General Data Protection Regulation (GDPR) – Section on Consent," Information Commissioner's Office (ICO), 22 May 2019, https://ico.org.uk/for-organisations/guide-to-data-protection/guide-to-the-general-data-protection-regulation-gdpr/lawful-basis-for-processing/consent/.

e.   We use clear, plain language that is easy to understand.

f.   We specify why we want the data and what we are going to do with them.

g.   We give separate, distinct ("granular") options so that respondents can provide consent separately to different purposes and types of processing.

h.   We name our organisation and any third-party controllers who will be relying on the consent.

i.   We tell individuals they can withdraw their consent at any time.

j.   We ensure that individuals can refuse to consent without detriment.

k.   We avoid making consent a precondition for receiving a service.

l.   If we offer online services directly to children, we seek consent only if we have age-verification measures (and parental-consent measures for younger children) in place.

The following two items on recording consent are included in the checklist[154]:

a.   We keep a record of when and how we got consent from the individual.

b.   We keep a record of precisely what individuals were told at the time.

---

154 "Guide to the General Data Protection Regulation (GDPR) – Section on Consent," Information Commissioner's Office (ICO), 22 May 2019, https://ico.org.uk/for-organisations/guide-to-data-protection/guide-to-the-general-data-protection-regulation-gdpr/lawful-basis-for-processing/consent/.

Finally, these are the checklist items for managing consent[155]:

a. We regularly review consents to check that the relationship, the processing, and the purposes have not changed.

b. We have processes in place to refresh consent at appropriate intervals, including any parental consent.

c. We consider using privacy dashboards or other preference-management tools as a matter of good practice.

d. We make it easy for individuals to withdraw their consent at any time, and we publicise how to do so.

e. We act on withdrawals of consent as soon as we can.

a. We do not penalise individuals who wish to withdraw consent.[156,157,158]

This checklist is an example of efforts by leading bodies to preserve the privacy of end users and consumers. However, if you are unaware of the rights that this checklist seeks to preserve, it would be virtually impossible for you to protect your privacy and exercise your rights.

155 "Guide to the General Data Protection Regulation (GDPR) – Section on Consent," Information Commissioner's Office (ICO), 22 May 2019, https://ico.org.uk/for-organisations/guide-to-data-protection/guide-to-the-general-data-protection-regulation-gdpr/lawful-basis-for-processing/consent/.

156 "Consent Lawful Basis," Sovy, https://www.sovy.com/kb/consent/.

157 "QUICK GUIDE Consent and General Data Protection Regulation (GDPR)," Isle of Whight, https://www.iowsab.org.uk/wp-content/uploads/2020/07/Quick-Guide-Consent-and-General-Data-Protection-Regulation-GDPR.pdf.

158 "Best Practices for GDPR Consent," Clarip, https://www.clarip.com/data-privacy/gdpr-consent-best-practices/.

CHAPTER 9

PRIVACY-RELATED LEGAL AND ETHICAL CHALLENGES WITH MANAGING DATA

A. DATA AND LEGAL CHALLENGES

Data management has inherent legal risks for businesses that collect, use, or store the personal information of living individuals. Privacy laws apply to companies if the data they store or process contain personal information, such as names, health records, addresses, bank details, credit card details, or other identifiers.

Complying with the data privacy protection laws constitutes the most significant legal challenge for businesses. For regulators, the legal challenges related to determining which rules and regulations apply, given the unstructured and cross-jurisdictional nature of data, can be pretty confusing.

Major privacy laws, especially those adopted in Europe and the United States, have increased the compliance burden for companies that use, collect, or store big data while increasing accountability obligations.

Privacy: Businesses handling personal data must have adequate security and privacy compliance processes in place while ensuring transparency as to how they will collect and process information. The legal risks of data management start with consumer privacy—many laws worldwide focus on the security and confidentiality of personal information. Websites, mobile apps, and online services have their privacy policy and terms of use/service. While it is a good business practice to include a privacy policy, it is now mandated by GDPR, CCPA, and other international laws. It is essential to review privacy policies periodically to ensure that they reflect the best business practices are in line with current regulations.

In the United States, several state and federal laws apply to personal information of dissimilar categories, such as financial or health information. Apart from these, there are consumer protection laws that are designed to prevent unfair/deceptive practices.

In healthcare, HIPAA regulates the collection, processing, and disclosure of protected health information (PHI). The Federal Trade Commission Act prohibits deceptive trade practices and applies to online and offline data security and privacy. The COPPA (Children's Online Privacy Protection Act) regulates the collecting of personal information of children below thirteen years of age. The Gramm-Leach-Bliley Act (GLBA) establishes the guidelines for financial institutions concerning handling personal data.

The California Online Privacy Protection Act (CalOPPA) of 2003 applies to any company whose online service, website, or app collects or stores personal information about California's consumers. The geographic impact of this law is massive, given the widely accessible nature of Internet-based businesses. The law requires commercial websites to have a conspicuous privacy policy, which includes the following details:

a. Categories of personal information collected
b. List of third parties that the information is shared with
c. Process by which users can review or request the modification of personally identifiable information
d. Process of notification to consumers regarding policy changes
e. Whether "do not track" is honoured

CalOPPA enforces a "do not track" (DNT) policy. The objective is if you are browsing with DNT enabled, these are features available as add-ins on your browsers, such as Google Chrome, Firefox, Safari, and the like; you can read/see the content in the logged-out state; and generally, the analytics will not receive information about any person. Furthermore, if enabled, YouTube videos will not load without anyone actively clicking through a DNT overlay. It is about choice at the end of the day. Doing this provides the subject (human being) with an option to send or not send data to a third party. Parties/web do at a very minimum scale as allowed under the W3C.[159]

Unfortunately, as an alternative argument, this tracking is needed to make the medium work; else, you might not be able to use that medium at all. Additionally, as we all are aware, during the pandemic, while working from home, we need a good user

---

159 Wikipedia.com, https://en.wikipedia.org/wiki/World_Wide_Web_Consortium, 3 March 2021, defines W3C as "*The World Wide Web Consortium is the main international standards organization for the World Wide Web. Founded in 1994 and currently led by Tim Berners-Lee, the consortium is made up of member organizations that maintain full-time staff working together in the development of standards for the World Wide Web.*"

experience. How can a service provider of the medium (may it be any!) in question be able to provide you with a tailored experience if they cannot learn anything about you? It is a catch-22 situation! The burden of responsibility falls on the shoulders of the person using the service and the importance of privacy of them. Remember, #myprivacy #myright!

"DO YOU WANT PRIVACY OR CONVENIENCE?"

So the "choice" will protect the person's data, but the 'convenience by the nature of choice will always be inversely proportional to protection. If anyone wanted zero online tracking, the person would need to give up comfort to some extent. The picture that I am trying to paint here is that there are no 100 per cent privacy-focused and fully-compliant enabled systems; exceedingly rare if they will ever exist.[160]

---

160 "Costs of Non-Compliance with Privacy Laws," Elizabeth C., Privacy policies, 18 February 2020, https://www.privacypolicies.com/blog/costs-non-compliance-privacy-laws/.

Security: From HIPAA to GDPR, many regulations establish security standards to protect personal information. These laws mandate appropriate administrative, technical, and physical safeguards to protect data integrity, confidentiality, and security. Although California was the first in the United States to enact a law concerning security breach notification, other federal and state laws have also established the same. Businesses that use or store personal data are required under these laws to disclose the security breach to not only consumers but also to the supervisory authority within a defined time frame.

I also wish to highlight the European Union's cookies directive. A cookie is a small computer file that is downloaded to a user's browser when they access websites. A cookie is a helpful piece of information that can provide a better browsing experience for users, such as ads of interest to the user—basically a customised experience. While cookies are relatively harmless and extremely useful for almost all companies, since they collect information, there are still a few risks associated with using them. The penalties for violating the EU cookies directive are monetary fines that can reach a total maximum amount of £500,000, approximately $665,000, at the time of writing, and more.

One of the most massive fines that have been handed down was to NPO, a Dutch public broadcaster, when in 2014, it was given a fine of €25,000 because NPO failed to implement an adequate consent mechanism regarding the use of cookies.[161]

---

161 "Costs of Non-Compliance with Privacy Laws," Elizabeth C., Privacy policies, 18 February 2020, https://www.privacypolicies.com/blog/costs-non-compliance-privacy-laws/.

B. Ethics – A Challenge for Managing and Storing Data[162]

The multidirectional demand and complexities involved in managing data in the digital age give rise to an urgent need for data privacy protection. Information protection is a crucial security function that ensures appropriate compliance with data privacy policies, processes, and standards. The standards or policies must be logically sound, legally justifiable, technically efficient, and ethically consistent while being socially acceptable.

The challenges of technology abuse led to the complexity of data privacy protection. For instance, if employees take the USB device home, this may breach the company's regulations, which may state that no property of the company leaves the premises without permission.

The risk also translates into data risk if the device contains other employees' or consumers' personal information. Using technology in contradiction to ethical principles also constitutes an ethical risk. In the above example, while not every employee takes the USB device home, those who choose to exploit the risk do so based on their understanding of ethics and sense of morality. Thus, in most circumstances, corporate policies are designed to constitute a clear violation and result in such circumstances.

The ethical risk in such instances is partially related to technology and partly to people, making data privacy protection a challenging affair. Ethical issues that involve data are more complex than other advanced technologies that do not include

---

162 "An Ethical Approach to Data Privacy Protection," Wanbil W. Lee, Wolfgang Zankl, and Henry Chang, ISACA, 24 December 2016, https://www.isaca.org/resources/isaca-journal/issues/2016/volume-6/an-ethical-approach-to-data-privacy-protection.

data, as data are complex, ubiquitous, and can impact every aspect of life.

Ethical challenges in managing data arise because of the many facets of data, including[163]

> *a.* the pervasiveness of data technology which makes it a component of societal infrastructure;
> *b.* the interconnectedness of data;
> *c.* data's dynamic and evolving nature, which enables future discoveries;
> *d.* real-time decision-making and analysis as data arrive;
> *e.* absence of limitation on time, space, and social context—data can be used irrespective of location, purpose, and time;
> *f.* data analysis can reveal unexpected information;
> *g.* potential risks for misuse and privacy breach; and
> *h.* ownership issues.

C. Ethical Responsibilities

Companies collect and use huge volumes of data related to customers. There are wide-ranging ethical issues concerning the collection, processing, and storage of such data. These ethical issues can be evaluated from three perspectives:

> *a.* Ethical responsibilities that a company has towards its customers
> *b.* Ethical responsibilities that employees have towards the company and customers
> *c.* Ethical responsibilities that customers have to the company

---

163 "Aspects of Data Ethics in a Changing World: Where Are We Now?" David J. Hand, Mary Ann Libert, Inc. Publishers, 17 September 2018, https://www.liebertpub.com/doi/full/10.1089/big.2018.0083.

For companies, ethical responsibilities are related to collecting only the necessary data, protecting data, correcting errors, ensuring the accuracy of data, and informing customers about the purpose of collection. Employees have the ethical responsibility not to access customer records or company data unless necessary, not to sell such data to third parties, and not to disclose the personal data of customers to related parties. Customers have the responsibility of providing accurate data when necessary and not using or disclosing data related to the company that has access.

With technology occupying an essential aspect of people's lives, data ethics is taking centre stage. It is critical for data regulators to translate data ethics into sound business practices to balance internal and external stakeholder interests. The starting point in this process is the consideration of the human impact. Privacy leaders can expect to include ethics assessments into the process of data collection or handling while asking what is fair and what is right.

Ethical considerations concerning data privacy protection play a key role in validating existing data protection laws.

A case in point relates to the "electronic wallet" called the Octopus Card that Hong Kong residents use for purchases and daily transportation. In 2010, the fact that the electronic wallet owner, Octopus Cards Limited, was selling the membership of card owners to insurance companies came to light. Following a public outcry, investigators concluded that although customer records sales were not legally prohibited, the card company had not made meaningful efforts to obtain customers' consent[164]

---

164 "Octopus Sold Personal Data of Customers for HK$44m," SCMP Reporter, *South China Morning Post*, 27 July 2010, https://www.scmp.com/article/720620/octopus-sold-personal-data-customers-hk44m.

The incident highlights the criticality of ethical considerations in the absence of a legal framework. People no longer accept businesses doing the bare minimum as required by law; they also need to act ethically. In other words, for businesses and agencies, it is not only essential to do what is legal but also what is right.

D. Digital Assistant – A Blessing or Curse in Disguise?

Speaking of ethical responsibilities, we as humans are embarking on a journey that was neither heard of nor thought of by the common man. It is the world of digital assistants: Siri, Alexa, Cortana, and Google assistant.

Alexa has been known for its notoriousness in the past. In one instance covered by NPR in December 2018, a German national requested to see his data under the European Data Protection Law and found the list of websites that he had browsed, and in addition to his data, he found 1,700[165] audio files of a stranger curtsey Alexa as a part of his data. In the beginning, he tried making sense of the audio file, thinking it was his, only to later release that none of the files belong to him. Some of the recordings had intimate conversations too. Through the NPR and with the help of Twitter and Facebook, they could identify the couple who had no clue that their conversation were being recorded without their knowledge. Was it an abrupt command, or was the artificial intelligence kicking in? This case is a testament to the fact that once a conversation leaves a person's mouth, it becomes public. Not even the spousal

---

165 "Amazon Customer Receives 1,700 Audio Files of a Stranger Who Used Alexa," Sasha Ingber, NPR, 20 December 2018, https://www.npr.org/2018/12/20/678631013/amazon-customer-receives-1-700-audio-files-of-a-stranger-who-used-alexa.

privilege can come in handy in such cases. As noted in recent case laws that with limited adequate justifications, the courts may allow the spouse's testimony to be admissible. This is not the first time, and there has been another case where a conversation was recorded and sent to one of their friends. At least there were no strangers in this case.

Alexa is not alone; Siri has been known for her naughtiness too. So you might have read the statement, which generally says, "We would need to collect your data for quality improvements." Most users click the "I agree" without reading these statements. The engineers listened to some of the commands and heard private personal details. Moreover, according to the *Bangkok Post*,[166] in August 2019, Apple faced a class-action lawsuit because of privacy issues. The buck does not stop there; Google Assistant is also meddling in the same invasion. A journalist bought a review unit and placed it in his bathroom.[167] The Google Home Mini was recording surrounding conversations and uploading the data to Google's server. We now know what Google contractors have; however, Google claims that it has now improved that device.

Even with such fiascos, all these companies rule our lives, and we have no choice but to grant them access to conduct our daily routine. The irony is that individuals who are sensitive to issues limit the usage of their digital tools, while other users who are less prone to defend their privacy extensively incorporate personal assistants into their digital lives. Let us not forget the business side of the coin that all these companies have significant market share when it comes to smart home equipment (Ahem!).

---

166 "Apple Apologizes over Siri Privacy Mishaps," *Bangkok Post*, 30 August 2019, https://www.bangkokpost.com/business/1739307/apple-apologises-over-siri-privacy-mishaps.

167 "10 Times We Forgave Voice Assistants for Messing Up," Alistair Charlton, Gear Brain, 5 November 2019, https://www.gearbrain.com/smart-speaker-voice-assistant-mistakes-2641226265.html.

These items are supposed to make lives more manageable, and they are best defined as work-in-progress because with such programs and technologies, there is always a person whom you are unaware of, standing behind the mirror spying on you. The more tech-savvy we get, the more we are surrounded by the risk of invasion of privacy. No wonder, with most of these cases taking place in Europe, the European government has levied fines, which are nothing but a slap on the wrist to them.

E. Initiatives on Data Ethics in the United Kingdom

GDPR and other international data privacy regulations have been designed to empower data subjects. GDPR has also opened debates on "ethics-driven compliance," a value added to the data protection laws.

In a proactive stance, the European Data Protection Supervisor encouraged data controllers to monitor, design, and implement data processing in a manner that is ethics-responsive. This suggests the need for data controllers to engage with the data subjects and develop policies concerning accountability and transparency in the data processing. While doing so, data controllers need to consider what impact information-based applications have on the data subjects' rights.

Likewise, there is an ongoing debate in the United Kingdom on data ethics and on clarifying what this practically includes. Two recent initiatives aim at providing clarity on the application of ethics and its practical impact under the GDPR.

The first of the two initiatives are

    a.   the setting up of the Centre for Data Ethics, and

b. Innovation (CDEI) in January 2019.[168]

This centre aims to work with the public to build their trust in data processing and to build a data protection ecosystem to "maximise benefits of data and AI" to society. CDEI additionally seeks to balance objectives to ensure the ethical use of artificial intelligence and data.

Second, the government has invited stakeholders in healthcare and digital market industries to actively develop a code of conduct concerning data-driven technology.

Data ethics application is slowly but surely gaining recognition as not only an asset but also as a safeguard for companies and institutions. It encourages corporate social responsibility, innovation, and most importantly, GDPR compliance.

One of the critical roles that CDEI will play is to investigate data in shaping people's online experiences and associated biases in decisions made using algorithms.[169]

F. What Happens When You Violate Privacy Law?[170]

I. Fines under GDPR

Monetary penalties under GDPR for more minor non-compliance offences can be €10 million or 2 per cent of a company's turnover, whichever is higher. In comparison, more

---

168 "The Centre for Data Ethics and Innovation (CDEI) 2019/20 Work Programme" From: Department for Digital, Culture, Media & Sport, Gov. UK, 20 March 2019, https://www.gov.uk/government/publications/the-centre-for-data-ethics-and-innovation-cdei-2019-20-work-programme.

169 According to the *Shorter Oxford Dictionary*, the word "algorithm" means a procedure or set of rules for calculation or problem-solving, now especially with a computer.

170 "What Happens after a Data Breach?" Sara Kassabian, True Vault, 17 January 2019, https://www.truevault.com/blog/what-happens-after-a-data-breach.

severe violations fines as high as €20 million or 4 per cent of an agency's turnover.[171]

Many factors come into play in determining the number of fines. These factors are listed in Article 83 of GDPR and include

    a. the duration, gravity, and nature of privacy violation;
    b. the number of people (data subjects) affected;
    c. negligence or intentional infringement, if any;
    d. whether actions have been taken to minimise the damage caused by the breach incurred by data subjects
    e. previous infringements, if any;
    f. categories of data affected;
    g. whether the agency notified appropriate authorities of the breach; and
    h. compliance measures taken for past breaches, if any.

The most urgent responsibilities under GDPR in the event of a data breach are to

    a. notify supervisory authority and
    b. notify data subjects.

Under Article 33 of GDPR, notification of the breach to the supervisory authority should be within seventy-two hours from becoming aware of the information breach. The report must incorporate the details on

    a. the nature of data breach;
    b. the categories of data subjects, personal data, number of data subjects, and records affected;
    c. the data protection officer's contact details;

---

171 "GDPR Penalties and Fines," IT Governance, https://www.itgovernance.co.uk/dpa-and-gdpr-penalties.

d. the consequences of the breach; and

e. the measures taken to minimise the impact of the breach.

II. CCPA Penalties

Violations under CCPA have potentially massive civil penalties apart from statutory damages. Consumers can sue for up to $750 per violation, while intentional violations can face fines of $7,500 each. Violations without intent have a maximum penalty of $2,500 per violation.[172]

III. Penalties under HIPAA

Non-compliance with HIPAA may have civil and/or criminal penalties. If there is a violation of HIPAA's criminal provisions, the Office for Civil Rights (OCR) refers the same to the US Department of Justice (DOJ).

The DOJ considers the severity of criminal violations under HIPAA in imposing penalties. Individuals or entities that wilfully obtain and/or disclose identifiable personal health information face imprisonment of up to one year and fines amounting to $50,000.

Penalties can go up to $100,000, along with imprisonment for up to five years.

Violations committed with the sole intention of obtaining a commercial advantage, malicious harm, or personal gain by selling, using, or transferring identifiable health information

---

172 "Top 5 Operational Impacts of CCPA: Part 5 - Penalties and Enforcement Mechanisms," Nicholas Schmid, IAPP, 21 August 2018, https://iapp. org/news/a/top-5-operational-impacts-of-cacpa-part-5-penalties-and-enforcement-mechanisms/.

imposes a fine of $250,000, apart from an imprisonment of up to ten years.

For civil violations committed "unknowingly," the fines per violation can range between $100 and $50,000, while repeat violations enforces $25,000 penalty. When there is a "reasonable cause," each violation lays a fine between $1,000 and $50,000, while the maximum fine is $100,000 per annum for repeat violations. If "wilful neglect" is established, the annual maximum goes up to $250,000 in case of repeat violations, while each offence fines between $10,000 and $50,000.[173]

Failure to comply with the ePrivacy Regulation can be penalised as high as €20 million or 4 per cent of global annual turnover.

IV. Violations of Other Acts

Violation of ECPA slaps penalties up to $250,000 and a five-year jail term. Victims can also file civil suits to recover actual damages, along with attorney's fees and punitive damages.

COPPA violations are considered deceptive or unfair trade practices at the federal level under the Federal Trade Commission Act. The FTC can impose civil penalties for the offence. In the original provision, violators were liable for as much as $11,000 per violation. However, in 2016, the FTC increased the penalties for breach of COPPA to $40,000. The FTC authorises the state attorney general to bring actions against violators to enforce compliance and obtain compensation.

As technology advancement becomes increasingly prominent in our daily lives, the question of ethics would also be intertwined with the same wavelength and intensity. And thus,

---

173 "HIPAA Violations & Enforcement," AMA, https://www.ama-assn.org/practice-management/hipaa/hipaa-violations-enforcement.

the question is, should there not be a mechanism whereby the proceeds (in addition to the regulator) find their way to those violated? An answer to this subject is in the way lawmakers like to craft out the system.

In 2016, InMobi, a mobile advertising network, faced a penalty of US$950,000 for violation of COPPA, where it tracked the geolocation of users under thirteen years without parental consent. The advertising software tracked user location continuously despite privacy preferences opted for on the mobile device.[174]

Because of COPPA, many famous sites, such as MySpace.com, Facebook.com, Friendster.com, Xanga.com, and other social networking sites, have come under severe scrutiny by the FTC.

V. Other Consequences of a Data Breach

Not all infringements under GDPR enact monetary penalties. The Information Commissioner's Office (ICO)[175] can also take many other actions, such as

a. issuing warnings;
b. reprimanding;

---

174 "Children's Online Privacy Protection Act," Admin of yourparentingwiki.blogspost.com, 26 July 2018, http://yourparentingwiki.blogspot.com/2018/07/childrens-online-privacy-protection-act.html.

175 According to Wikipedia.com, 7 October 2020, https://en.wikipedia.org/wiki/Information_Commissioner's_Office, "The Information Commissioner's Office (ICO) is a non-departmental public body which reports directly to the United Kingdom Parliament and is sponsored by the Department for Digital, Culture, Media and Sport (DCMS). It is the independent regulatory office (national data protection authority) dealing with the Data Protection Act 2018 and the General Data Protection Regulation, the Privacy and Electronic Communications (EC Directive) Regulations 2003 across the UK; and the Freedom of Information Act 2000 and the Environmental Information Regulations 2004 in England, Wales and Northern Ireland and, to a limited extent, in Scotland."

c. imposing a ban that could be temporary or permanent on data processing;

d. ordering restriction, rectification, or deletion of data; and

e. suspending transfers of data to third countries.

Apart from the actions of the supervisory authorities and monetary penalties, organisation's face other consequences of a data breach which can include

a. **Loss of data and trade secrets:** Loss of customers' data, as in the Equifax data breach of 2017, where hackers accessed data related to eight hundred thousand UK consumers, which hugely impact businesses.[176] The trade secrets or intellectual property of companies/ entities are at risk of being stolen.

b. **Downtime:** Businesses spend a considerable amount of money and time to ensure they remain visible and responsive to customers. Data breaches and ensuing investigations can lead to significant downtime that affects the bottom line.

c. **Reputation at risk:** A Radware survey revealed that 43 per cent[177] of businesses that participated in the study said they faced reputation loss and negative customer experiences because of a breach. As highlighted by previous studies, one third of consumers want to avoid doing business with a particular company that has faced a data breach. In a Gemalto study that questioned ten

---

176 "Cybersecurity Incident - Information for UK Consumers," Equifax.Co.Uk https://www.equifax.co.uk/incident.html.

177 "Cyberattacks Now Cost Businesses an Average of $1.1M," Radware, 15 January 2019, https://www.radware.com/newsevents/mediacoverage/2019/cyberattacks-cost-businesses-average-of-1-1m.

thousand people,[178] 70 per cent said they would not do business with any company that has encountered a data breach.

As an example, a cyberattack took place on a major telecom company called TalkTalk in 2015. It cost the firm an estimated £77 million, but there was such severe rage amongst the customers that it ruined the company's reputation. The firm claimed it lost around 101,000 customers because of the incident. It is no surprise that the Marsh and Microsoft Global Cyber Risk Perception Survey in 2018 found that reputation loss after a cyberattack was the biggest concern of companies, and fifty-nine of respondents rated it as a significant concern.[179]

G. GDPR VIOLATIONS: BRITISH AIRWAYS AND MARRIOTT CASE ANALYSIS

GDPR has been designed to improve data security and privacy for EU citizens. Under the regulation, businesses and agencies are held to a higher standard concerning how personal data are collected and managed.

The penalties for non-compliance with GDPR have dramatically increased in comparison to previous legislation.

On 8 July 2019, the regulator of GDPR in the United Kingdom, the Information Commissioner's Office (ICO),

---

178 "Majority of Consumers Would Stop Doing Business with Companies Following a Data Breach, Finds Gemalto," Thales Group, 28 November 2017, https://www.thalesgroup.com/en/markets/digital-identity-and-security/press-release/majority-of-consumers-would-stop-doing-business-with-companies-following-a-data-breach-finds-gemalto.

179 "New Research Reveals Extent of Reputation Loss after a Cyberattack," Titan HQ Web Titan, 25 January 2019, https://www.spamtitan.com/web-filtering/new-research-reveals-extent-of-reputation-loss-after-a-cyberattack/.

announced hefty penalties for British Airways[180] and Marriott International for violation of privacy laws. While the penalties are notable for the sheer magnitude, the cases are the best examples of how organisations are liable for "unintentional" non-compliance. In the first year of enforcement of GDPR, most penalties levied were small and applied only to agencies that deliberately ignored the regulations. Marriott and British Airways inherited an existing security breach during merger and acquisition (M&A).[181]

I. What Were GDPR Breaches?

Information Commissioner's Office (ICO) is the United Kingdom's independent authority set up to uphold information rights in the public interest, promoting openness by public bodies and data privacy for individuals. Commissioner Elizabeth Denham came out with the following statements, which is clearly what privacy is meant and how important it is becoming day by day: "The GDPR makes it clear that organisations must be accountable for the personal data they hold. This can include carrying out proper due diligence when making a corporate acquisition and putting in place proper accountability measures to assess not only what personal data has been acquired, but also how it is protected,"[182] also "Personal data has real value. Hence,

---

180 "UK's ICO Fines British Airways a Record £183M over GDPR Breach That Leaked Data from 500,000 Users," Ingrid Lunden, Tech Crunch, 8 July 2019, https://techcrunch.com/2019/07/08/uks-ico-fines-british-airways-a-record-183m-over-gdpr-breach-that-leaked-data-from-500000-users/.

181 "UK Information Commissioner Confirms Intention to Fine British Airways and Marriott International, Inc under GDPR," Rohan Massey and Clare Sellars, Ropes Gray, 16 July 2019, https://www.ropesgray.com/en/newsroom/alerts/2019/07/UK-Information-Commissioner-Confirms-Intention-Fine-British-Airways-Marriott-International-Inc-GDPR.

182 "GDPR Fines vs Marriott, British Air Are a Warning For . . .," Kate Fazzini, 10 July 2019, CNBC, https://www.cnbc.com/2019/07/10/

organisations have a legal duty to ensure their security, just like they would do with any other asset. If that does not happen, we will not hesitate to take strong action when necessary to protect the rights of the public . . ."

The quote mentioned above sums up why the penalty levied on the following organisation is so high and the purpose and importance of safeguarding individuals' privacy. Thus, people need to speak up and report their concerns through an appropriate whistle-blowing website.[183]

British Airways (BA) got the ICO's attention in September 2018, a cyberattack that is believed to have begun in June 2018. The breach was caused by a web application that was poorly secured. Attackers modified the website's JavaScript code to include Magecart, a malware that steals credit card information. The attack compromised the personal information of five hundred thousand customers of BA. The airline issued a statement in which it said, "personal and financial details" of passengers who booked using BA's app or website in the time frame of 21 August to 5 September 2018 were compromised. BA also said that although passport or travel information was not taken, 380,000 card payments had been compromised. The airline later confirmed data of 185,000 people booked between April and July and might have been compromised.

Attackers diverted the traffic to a fraudulent website from the BA website to obtain customer details. The data compromised included addresses, names, historical logs, payment card information, and travel booking details. After the investigation, the ICO concluded that BA's website security arrangements were inadequate.

gdpr-fines-vs-marriott-british-air-are-a-warning-for-google-facebook.html.

183 "Statement on Data Protection and Brexit Implementation," ICO.Org.UK, 29 January 2020, https://ico.org.uk/about-the-ico/news-and-events/news-and-blogs/2020/01/statement-on-data-protection-and-brexit-implementation-what-you-need-to-do/.

The ICO issued a statement on 8 July 2019, confirming its intention to levy a record penalty of approximately £183 million on British Airways for breaches of GDPR. The proposed fine is 1.5 per cent of BA's global turnover for 2017. ICO's investigation revealed "that a variety of information was compromised by poor security arrangements including login, payment card, and travel booking details as well name and address information." The penalty was the highest ever levied by the ICO for a data breach since the introduction of GDPR.[184]

The very next day another statement was issued by the ICO approximately £99 million penalty against Marriott International for GDPR breaches[185]:

Marriott International's case is similar as it brought to the ICO's attention a cyberattack on the guest reservation database in November 2018. The attack compromised 339 million global guest records, out of which, 30 million records belonged to thirty-one European Economic Area (EEA) countries' residents, and 7 million records belonged to UK residents. The data breach impacted the personal and financial information of millions of people who made bookings at Marriott International's global network of hotels.

The affected Starwood guest reservation database stored combinations of names, mailing addresses, phone numbers, e-mail addresses, passport numbers, Starwood Preferred Guest (SPG) account numbers, dates of birth, and gender.

Marriott disclosed in November 2018 that since 2014, hackers had been accessing its guest reservation database.

---

184 "Intention to Fine British Airways £183.39m under GDPR for Data Breach," Information Commissioner's Office, 8 July 2019, https://ico.org.uk/about-the-ico/news-and-events/news-and-blogs/2019/07/ico-announces-intention-to-fine-british-airways/.

185 "Marriott Faces $123 Million GDPR Fine in the UK for Last Year's Data Breach," Catalin Cimpanu for Zero Day, ZD Net, 9 July 2019, https://www.zdnet.com/article/marriott-faces-123-million-gdpr-fine-in-the-uk-for-last-years-data-breach/.

Although initially, the company said 500 million guests' data were compromised, after a thorough investigation, the number was modified to 383 million.[186]

Though Marriott acquired Starwood Hotels in 2016, the breach was exposed only in 2018. An extensive investigation by the ICO into the incident identified that in 2014, passport numbers, names, contact details, and in some cases, information related to payment cards in the database of Starwood Hotel group were compromised.

According to the ICO's statement, Marriott "failed to undertake sufficient due diligence when it bought Starwood and should have done more to secure its systems." Under GDPR, organisations must carry out appropriate due diligence before the acquisition and put in accountability measures to evaluate what personal information has been acquired and the steps taken to protect the same.[187]

These cases also show that data breaches are not only a public relations liability that destroys the customer's trust but also a financial liability. Apart from the hefty penalty under GDPR, IAG (International Airlines Group), the parent company of BA, experienced volatile trading, with shares going down by 1.5 per cent at the time. In BA's case, the GDPR principle violated relates to lack of "appropriate technical and organisational measures" to protect the confidentiality and integrity of personal data.[188] Marriott had not carried out due diligence during its acquisition

---

186 "Marriott International Fined Almost £100m by ICO for 2018 Data Breach," Jay Jay, Teiss, 10 July 2019, https://www.teiss.co.uk/marriott-international-fined-ico/.

187 "ICO Issues First Intentions to Fine under the GDPR," Kelly McMullon on 25 July 2019, Privacy law Blog, https://privacylaw.proskauer.com/2019/07/articles/data-privacy-laws/ico-issues-first-intentions-to-fine-under-the-gdpr/.

188 "Legal Notice & Privacy Policy – ARMIPRO: Mina Providencia," Antonio Reyes, Mina Providencia SARL (ARMIPRO), http://www.minaprovidencia.com/legal-notice-and-privacy-policy/.

of Starwood and failed to take adequate measures to enhance its IT systems' security.

The hefty penalties levied in the above cases serve as a warning for other tech giants, including Facebook and Google. Both companies are under investigation, with Google's potential penalty being $5 billion while Facebook may be fined more than $2 billion based on its global annual revenue in 2018.[189]

The ICO stated its intention to investigate Google for leaking personal information about customers on its advertising platform. Brave, Google Chrome's rival, submitted a report to the Data Protection Commission of Ireland after alleging Google was leaking personal data to advertisers in violation of GDPR.

Facebook faced a modest penalty of $644,000 for the Cambridge Analytica[190] scandal, where it had not notified its users regarding a survey that was used for advertising and political research. The social media platform has been investigated for a data breach on Instagram and Facebook platforms that compromised passwords and usernames.

These penalties highlight the critical importance of putting in place appropriate web and data security protections at all levels in an organisation, particularly during mergers and acquisitions. Neither of the two breaches resulted from

---

189 "France Fines Google Nearly $57 Million for First Major Violation of New European Privacy Regime," Tony Room, *Washington Post*, 21 January 2019, https://www.washingtonpost.com/world/europe/france-fines-google-nearly-57-million-for-first-major-violation-of-new-european-privacy-regime/2019/01/21/89e7ee08-1d8f-11e9-a759-2b8541bbbe20_story.html?noredirect=on.

190 "Facebook Fined $644,000 over Data Breach in Cambridge Analytica Scandal," Associated Press, Financial Express, 25 October 2018, https://www.financialexpress.com/industry/technology/facebook-fined-644000-over-data-breach-in-cambridge-analytica-scandal/1361025/.

deliberate non-compliance, and it was possible to prevent them by implementing data monitoring and protection solutions.

Marriott's case also is indicative of the overarching scope of GDPR principles. Apart from European firms, any company that collects and processes the personal data of EU residents is liable for violations of the data privacy regulation.

CHAPTER 10

WHAT DO JUDGES LOOK AT WHEN A PRIVACY CASE GOES TO COURT?

A. AN OVERVIEW AND SCARCITY OF CASE LAW

This chapter looks at various nuances associated with filing a privacy lawsuit. As depicted in previous chapters, some form of privacy law is intertwined with a country's court mechanism and closely related to whether you are perceived as a victim or an unsympathetic party. When a privacy case goes to court, judges always consider what harm the party bringing the lawsuit has suffered. Under Article 3 of the US Constitution, plaintiffs can bring a case to court only if the damage was suffered, and they are the actual party that sustained an injury (called having "standing" to sue).

Thus, concerning the ruling in Spokeo v Robins *in 2016,[191] which found that a plaintiff must affirmatively suffer an injury.*

---

191 "The Year Ahead in Cybersecurity Law," Tara Swaminatha, 9 January 2018, https://www.csoonline.com/article/3245743/the-year-ahead-in-

The court system in the United States, which is considered to be one of the most advanced legal systems, is divided on potential future harm which could have been caused by cyberattacks.

The second critical point that courts tend to look at with a magnifying glass is jurisdiction. That is, the cyber/online criminal might belong to a location or jurisdiction different from the party that has suffered any sort of harm such as loss of data, incorrect transaction because of a hacker, identity theft, and the like. Then comes the question of prosecution and extradition and ties that the country has with the other country.

In the 2018 case of Carpenter v United States, the Supreme Court ruled that the protection against "unreasonable searches and seizures" granted in the Fourth Amendment applied to location data in mobile phones. This means police need to obtain a warrant to trace the activities of the smartphone owner in a criminal investigation. The chief justice and justices stated that "declined to grant the state unrestricted access to a wireless carrier's database of physical location information," while noting the "deeply revealing nature of the location information, its depth, breadth, and comprehensive reach, and the inescapable and automatic nature of its collection."[192]

This ruling is an extension of the US courts' stance on the privacy rights of Americans. Over the past six years, judges in the US courts have ruled that the police need the court's permission to access an individual's mobile phone in an arrest or carry out GPS tracking of suspects' cars.

Instead of seeking a search warrant to obtain Carpenter's data, federal investigators used a provision in the federal Stored Communications Act - 2703(d) order. The distinction is a

cybersecurity-law.html.
192 "The Supreme Court Cares about Your Digital Privacy | The . . .," Matt Ford, The New Republic, 22 June 2018, https://newrepublic.com/article/149328/supreme-court-cares-digital-privacy.

crucial one. A warrant requires investigators to show they have
"probable cause" to believe the search will uncover evidence of a
crime, while 2703(d) orders have a lower threshold under federal
law: Police need only offer "specific and articulable facts" that
the records sought will be "relevant and material to an ongoing
criminal investigation." The investigators obtained 127 days of
cell-site data from two different mobile providers, which yielded
12,898 location points that revealed Carpenter's movements.
Finally, it was proven that those points placed him near four of
the robberies in question. A jury found him guilty, sentenced
him to more than one hundred years of imprisonment.[193]

Carpenter did ask the lower courts to throw out the
evidence on Fourth Amendment grounds. But they declined,
citing two Supreme Court precedents dating back to the 1976
case, which was the *United States v Miller*; the court upheld a
whiskey bootlegger's conviction after prosecutors obtained his
bank records without a warrant. Three years later, in *Smith v
Maryland*, the court signed off on the warrantless use of a pen
register, a device that recorded which phone numbers were
dialled on a particular telephone line.[194]

Thus, to me, it seems like a complete shift in the thought
process of the courts coming from the decision of *Smith v
Maryland* in 1979, where the Supreme Court ruled that a robbery
suspects' right to privacy does not extend to the numbers he
dialled from a landline phone. In essence, it means that the
courts (or the attorneys persuaded the court) interpreted that

---

193 "Former Mayoral Candidate Convicted for Exposing Himself At . . .," Whitney
     Miller, KBTX-TV, 23 June 2016, https://www.kbtx.com/content/news/
     Former-mayoral-candidate-convicted-for-exposing-himself-at-Brenham-
     office-384216411.html.
194 "The Supreme Court Cares about Your Digital Privacy," Matt Ford, TNR,
     22 June 2018, https://newrepublic.com/article/149328/supreme-court-cares-
     digital-privacy.

dialling numbers from a third-party telephone was equivalent to voluntarily handing over your details to a third party; while in the case of Carpenter, sided with Carpenter in the light of the legitimate expectation of privacy.[195]

The problem is compounded with complexities for the law and layers when the phone or the medium belongs to someone legitimate and the service is illegitimate. Will the courts consider the greater good of the public instead of using illegitimate service? That is yet to be decided as the facts would be remarkably close to Edward Snowden's case.

In 2012 as well, in the case of the United States v Jones, *Justice Sonia Sotomayor ruled that by attaching a GPS device without a warrant to a car, federal agents violated the privacy rights under the Fourth Amendment. The third-party doctrine[196,197] is the reasonable expectation of privacy used by the Supreme Court to determine whether a warrant is needed for "search." Per the doctrine, citizens lose reasonable expectation of privacy if a third-party stores their personal information.[198]*

Challenging the third-party doctrine instead of advancements in digital technologies, Justice Sotomayor held

195 "US Supreme Court Expands Digital Privacy Rights in Carpenter v. United States," Jeewon Kim Serrato (US), Anna Rudawski (US), and Alexis Wilpon (US), 27 June 2018, https://www.dataprotectionreport.com/2018/06/scotus-expands-digital-privacy-rights-carpenter/.

196 In an article by wired.com – "New Ruling Shows the NSA Can't Legally Justify Its Phone Spying Anymore," Jennifer Granick, 13 June 2014, https://www.wired.com/2014/06/davis-undermines-metadata/, it mentions, "Third-party doctrine, which says that you have no Fourth Amendment interest in a third party's business records because you have voluntarily disclosed information to the business and assumed the risk of that information being further disclosed to the government."

197 Key cases that formulate the "third-party doctrine" were *Smith v Maryland*, 1979, and *United States v Miller*, 1976.

198 *United States v Jones*, Wikipedia.org, last updated 6 February 2021, https://en.wikipedia.org/wiki/United_States_v._Jones.

that the approach was ill-suited to the digital age where people reveal to third parties, vast amounts of information about themselves such as phone numbers dialled, website URLs visited, e-mail addresses used to correspond and the things they purchase online.

This trend continued in the 2014 Riley v California *case, where the court drew a line for searching for suspects in an arrest when it came to mobile phone searches. Chief Justice John Roberts wrote that while technology made it possible to store massive volumes of personal data in the mobile phone, it does not mean that the information is any less worthy of protection.*[199]

When it comes to privacy, no crime is too small. Can privacy charges pressure lead to the pressure of suicide?

In the United States v Aaron Swartz, *under the weight of the prosecution and potential prison sentence, Swartz committed suicide in January 2013. What happened here was that Aaron Swartz, who was a computer programmer, entrepreneur, and activist, was charged for CFAA violations, which included unlawfully obtaining information from a protected computer and recklessly damaging a protected computer. For what reason? He allegedly downloaded approximately 4.8 million articles from JSTOR, a not-for-profit digital library, using the MIT network by spoofing his computer's address to trick the JSTOR servers (all allegedly). JSTOR's policy limited the number of downloads.*

Swartz's criminal exposure could have been up to fifty years of imprisonment and $1 million in criminal fines, leading to his tragic end. After his death, federal prosecutors dropped the charges—too late, sadly.[200]

---

199 Riley v California, epic.org, https://epic.org/amicus/cell-phone/riley/.

200 "CFAA Cases," NACDL, 10 March 2020, https://www.nacdl.org/Content/CFAACases.

European courts have taken a consistent view of upholding individuals' right to privacy. A large number of data privacy cases were adjudicated during 2018 across England and elsewhere in Europe, as we have seen with the judgements passed by the European Court of Human Rights.

In the high-profile case of Sir Cliff Richard v BBC (British Broadcasting Corporation), the High Court awarded damages to the tune of £210,000 to the claimant. Sir Cliff Richard filed a privacy claim against the broadcasting corporation for its coverage of the 2014 South Yorkshire Police raid at his home. While the raid was part of the investigation into child-sex allegations, the singer claimed this to be a "serious invasion" of his privacy. While the BBC must pay 65 per cent of the claim amount, South Yorkshire Police will have to pay 35 per cent.[201]

In hindsight, people could argue as to know why this was even a question, the data around a suspect, as details are not generally released until the charge has been made. So my assumption would be to note that an actual charge was made pursuant to another crime; at the same time, the concerned officials might not have had enough evidence, but the official decided to use the raid to bring the claimed allegations to light.

In *ABC v Telegraph Media Group Ltd*, the publication of a high-profile executive's alleged "discreditable conduct" was prevented by the Court of Appeal.

On 22 February 2018, the High Court directed Channel 5 to pay Shakir Ali and Shahida Aslam £20,000 in damages.[202] *The TV production company had filmed in 2015 the couple's eviction*

---

201 "Cliff Richard: Singer Wins BBC Privacy Case at High Court," BBC.Com, 18 July 2018, https://www.bbc.com/news/uk-44871799.

202 "Case Law: Ali v Channel 5, Can't Pay? We'll Take It Away (Then You Can Make Us Pay) – Zoe McCallum," Inforrm.org, 25 February 2018, https://inforrm.org/2018/02/25/case-law-ali-v-channel-5-cant-pay-well-take-it-away-then-you-can-make-us-pay-zoe-mccallum/.

from their Essex home as a result of rent arrears. The film that was broadcast on the show Can't Pay? We'll Take It Away *showed the couple being evicted with no prior warning and in their shock and distress; following which, they filed a case of "misuse of private information."*

In my opinion, this should have been a hammering for the reporters as the people are not really criminals, and the public does not have a right to know their names and emotions without consent.

Asian Court: In India, there have been several cases throughout history where the courts have upheld the right to privacy as a fundamental right.

In the 2014 case of Unique Identification Authority of India (UIDAI) v Central Bureau of Investigation (CBI), *the latter sought access to the UIDAI database to investigate a criminal offence. The Supreme Court ruled that UIDAI cannot transfer personal data without first obtaining consent.*[203]

In 2017, Supreme Court's nine-judge bench[204] declared privacy right as a fundamental right in the legal case of *Puttuswamy v Union of India*. The landmark judgement is likely to result in formulating a comprehensive law on privacy while addressing previous inconsistencies in judgements that had different interpretations with regard to the right to privacy being a fundamental right.

---

203 "State of Privacy India," Privacy International, 26 January 2019, https://privacyinternational.org/state-privacy/1002/state-privacy-india.

204 As defined by wikipedia.org, 3 October 2019, https://en.wikipedia.org/wiki/Division bench#:~:text=From%20Wikipedia%2C%20the%20free%20encyclopedia,referred%20to%20a%20larger%20bench, "a Division Bench is a term in judicial system in India in which a case is heard and judged by at least 2 judges. However, if the bench during the hearing of any matter feels that the matter needs to be considered by a larger bench, such a matter is referred to a larger bench."

Another famous case in time was a connection with the legal challenge to India's national identity project called the Aadhaar Card on whether it should be made available. The advocate argued based on (a) MP Sharma v Satish Chandra, *decided 1954, and (b)* Kharak Singh v State of Uttar Pradesh, *1962. Both cases had held that the Constitution of India does not explicitly protect the right to privacy. However, post fifty-five years, it is not the same scenario, and keeping the bureaucracy in mind, Kharak Singh passed a confusing judgement that held, on the one hand, that any intrusion into a person's home is a violation of liberty but went on to say that there was no right to privacy contained in our Constitution. Since these were eight- and six-judge benches of the Supreme Court, every subsequent court had to deal with this confusion as best they could.*[205]

However, in the subsequent case of *Gobind v State of Madhya Pradesh*, a three-judge bench, mindful of its inability to overturn a judgement of a larger bench, skirted around the inconsistency by "assuming" that the right to privacy was protected under the Constitution, relying on the first part of the Kharak Singh judgement without explicitly calling out its inconsistency with the second.

Many smaller benches followed suit, building on these principles to articulate a fundamental right of privacy in multiple contexts, such as medical privacy, matrimonial privacy, reputational privacy, the privacy of sexual orientation, and many more. However, given that this jurisprudence had been on uncertain foundations, it was always susceptible to challenge.

---

205 "India: Supreme Court Declares Right to Privacy a Fundamental Right," by trilegal, Mondaq, 31 August 2017, https://www.mondaq.com/india/privacy-protection/625192/supreme-court-declares-right-to-privacy-a-fundamental-right.

The task before the nine-judge bench in the present case in India was to settle the law once and for all. They did so emphatically, overruling MP Singh and Kharak Singh to the extent that those decisions had held that there was no fundamental right to privacy. They also overruled the ADM Jabalpur case—a decision that had allowed for fundamental rights to be suspended during a state declared an emergency—and called into question the judicial reasoning in the Naz Foundation case, which had suggested that the "minuscule minority" LGBTQ community was not entitled to a right to privacy. This decision has connected privacy jurisprudence over the years with international commitments and established our conformity with comparable laws around the world.

The Indian courts have given a robust and insightful outline or at least attempted to contribute to the resolution of future cases, establishing these points[206]:

(a) The right to privacy is a fundamental right.

(b) The right to privacy is not an absolute right[207]; it is subject to reasonable restrictions.

(c) Other incidental implications on such matters may change from time to time.

---

206 "India: Supreme Court Declares Right to Privacy a Fundamental Right," trilegal, Mondaq, 31 August 2017, https://www.mondaq.com/india/privacy-protection/625192/supreme-court-declares-right-to-privacy-a-fundamental-right.

207 As defined by Merriam-Webster, https://www.merriam-webster.com/legal/absolute%20right, an absolute right is "an unqualified right: a legally enforceable right to take some action or to refrain from acting at the sole discretion of the person having the right."

B. Specificity of Cases: A Blindfolded Judicial System

When I look at the prevailing case system, I feel they are all subjective. However, in most cases and the way rules of laws go, courts generally apply an objective rule of law to iron out subjectivity within the legal cases. I believe this depends on the seat you have when you are looking at the legal case. I see it divided into two major categories when it comes to invasion of privacy, for (I) known people and (II) unknown people (or not so known).

I. Known People

This category belongs to the people who gain popularity that can span from a well-known activist to a celebrity to a sportsperson. In my opinion, it all boils down to:

a. what is privacy from a reasonable man's point of view versus
b. what one believes is someone's privacy.

When answering these two questions, there are so many other factors that lawyers try to battle over to sway the judgement of the court with factors such as, but not limited to,

a. the location being public or private;
b. whether the act committed by the person was inviting enough for the person invading the privacy or not; this also contains the knowledge of the person whose privacy is invaded; is he/she/they a minor or capable person or an adult;

c.   how is the matter portrayed by the person invading the privacy – is it secretive and demonstrating a negative light of the person whose privacy is invaded; and

d.   the freedom of expression of a person invading that moment to the expectation of privacy of the individual and the alike.

If it falls under the category of reasonable expectations, then the act committed by the person invading the privacy is wrong. However, if it falls under the other category of self-assumption and from the viewpoint of the person whose privacy has been invaded is caught up in the wrong time and wrong place, there is a strong possibility that courts might rule it in favour of the person. You will ponder what happens to the people related to the person who can be considered a known or famous person. I mean, his/her spouse, children, friends, do they also forgo the right to privacy?

The below circles explain the expectation of privacy when it comes to a known or a famous person.

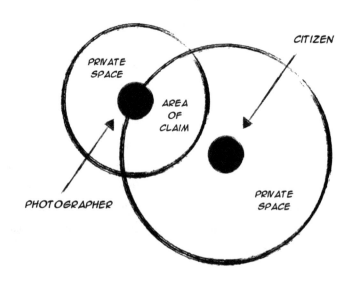

In *Murray v Express Newspapers Plc*,[208] where the plaintiff were the not only the parents of a child whose privacy was infringed but also the author of the famous book titled *Harry Potter, in turn, they were known and famous.* The case commenced; where the parents were pushing the buggy with the child in it, a picture of their child was published in the newspaper. The court held that the parents could retrain the defendants from publishing the photographs taken of him on the public street. So basically, his privacy was invaded as it was viewed that the child had a reasonable expectation of privacy. This implies that a reasonable person in their position would feel that the photograph should not be published. While in a similar sound case of *AAA v Associated Newspaper Ltd*,[209] the same court held that since the mother of the child was "willing" to reveal to strangers the identity of the child's father, who was a well-known person himself, through various media, and allowed unknown people to speculate about their relationship and never came forward to stop them, displayed knowledge and attitude that the person was not private in her nature. Thus, because the claimant was a conscious adult with own behaviour, the case was weakened, and therefore, the "freedom of expression" of the person invading the privacy outweighed the "right to privacy" of the claimant's parent.

It is clear from the above figure that though the ripple effect of people surrounding the famous or the known person is lesser than the focal point, it does deplete the expectation of privacy of people around.

---

208 "England and Wales Court of Appeal (Civil Division) Decisions," bailii.org, March 2008, https://www.bailii.org/ew/cases/EWCA/Civ/2008/446.html.

209 "Case Law: AAA v Associated Newspapers Ltd – 'Mother Knows Best . . .' – Kirsten Sjøvoll," inform.org, 2 July 2013, https://inforrm.org/2013/07/02/case-comment-aaa-v-associated-newspapers-ltd-mother-knows-best-kirsten-sjovoll/.

II. Unknown People

This category speaks about people who might not be a public figure, though may be rich or not. One of the most common forms of argument between the defence and plaintiff claimants is around the invasion of privacy under Article 8 of the European Convention on Human Rights (ECHR)[210] of one party over the freedom of expression of the other party, which falls under Article 10 of ECHR.[211] When you look at a person or his associated members, whether it may be focal points from the diagram below, their children, his/her spouse, or friends, the critical matter under discussion becomes who is on the right side of the law. Though law equally enshrines all rights, I believe that in the eyes of the court of law, the "right to privacy" takes a higher presence than freedom of expression in such or similar cases.

---

210 According to Wikipedia.org article, last edited on 16 September 2020, https://en.wikipedia.org/wiki/Article_10_of_the_European_Convention_on_Human_Rights#:~:text=Article%2010%20of%20the%20European%20Convention%20on%20Human%20Rights%20provides,and%20impart%20information%20and%20ideas, Article 10 of the European Convention on Human Rights provides the right to freedom of expression and information, subject to certain restrictions that are "in accordance with law" and "necessary in a democratic society." This right includes the freedom to hold opinions and to receive and impart information and ideas.

211 According to Wikipedia.org article, last edited on 16 September 2020, https://en.wikipedia.org/wiki/Article_10_of_the_European_Convention_on_Human_Rights#:~:text=Article%2010%20of%20the%20European%20Convention%20on%20Human%20Rights%20provides,and%20impart%20information%20and%20ideas, Article 10 of the European Convention on Human Rights provides the right to freedom of expression and information, subject to certain restrictions that are "in accordance with law" and "necessary in a democratic society." This right includes the freedom to hold opinions and to receive and impart information and ideas.

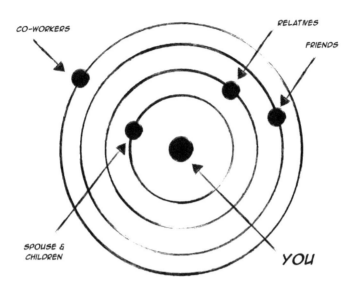

So it all boils down to one additional factor: the sympathetic party. If the party at the time of the court proceedings can show a mindset of innocence, being aware and exercising privacy in a fundamental sense, then that would stand a better chance of winning than the party claiming freedom of expression.

III. What Should People Do to Protect Themselves and Their Close Ones?

The answer has long been iterated through various concepts in this book, and it would boil down to the type of choices one would make. This topic is further dealt with in chapter 11 under the heading "What Can Individuals Do to Protect Their Privacy?"

CHAPTER 11

PRIVACY SOLUTIONS FOR ORGANISATIONS AND INDIVIDUALS

A. WHAT CAN ORGANISATIONS DO TO MAINTAIN PRIVACY?

Privacy, for organisations, is a business-critical discipline enforced by a myriad of regulations. Privacy requirements significantly impact the strategy, objectives, and methods used for data processing in organisations. Business leaders in data and risk management need to focus on privacy emphases, such as those highlighted in a 2019 Gartner report,[212] to ensure transparency and data privacy.

According to Gartner, for 70 per cent of organisations, the most significant privacy risk area as of 2020 concerns the archiving and backing up of personal data. Currently,

---

212 In an article by Gartner (Smarter with Gartner), by Gloria Omale, 14 January 2019, https://www.gartner.com/smarterwithgartner/gartner-predicts-2019-for-the-future-of-privacy/, it mentions, "Security and risk management leaders, including CISOs and privacy professionals, must recognize maturing privacy regulations to ensure a privacy-friendly operation."

organisations hold vast volumes of personal data in backups that are vulnerable and sensitive, without clear intentions to make use of all these data. The massive volume of potentially sensitive data heightens the risk, and the stiff penalties for privacy violations are making it expensive to hold unused data.

Over the next two years, organisations that fail to revise their data retention policies will face an elevated risk of sanctions related to data breaches and non-compliance. Data retention is a problematic area for all corporations. It is not only complex and sector-dependent, but it is also dependent on the cross-jurisdictional laws playing their role, its cultural impact with local policy dependencies as well and other considerations. For instance, non-compliance could lead to a fine of 4 per cent of a business's global annual turnover or a whopping €20 million under GDPR.

Blockchain technology is gaining popularity, with many businesses looking to implement it. According to predictions, 25 per cent or more of data consent implementations under GDPR will relate to blockchain technology by 2023 compared to less than 2 per cent in 2018.[213] Businesses intending to implement promising blockchain technology must conduct due diligence concerning compliance with privacy laws.

Whereas public blockchains have an immutable data structure in which data cannot be modified or deleted once recorded, privacy laws grant the "right to be forgotten" to citizens. The principal concern with blockchain technology is that personal data cannot be structurally deleted, anonymised, or replaced. Organisations that use blockchain systems without

---

213 In an article by Gartner (Smarter with Gartner), by Gloria Omale, 14 January 2019, https://www.gartner.com/smarterwithgartner/gartner-predicts-2019-for-the-future-of-privacy/, it mentions, "Security and risk management leaders, including CISOs and privacy professionals, must recognize maturing privacy regulations to ensure a privacy-friendly operation."

managing the accompanying privacy issues will face the risk of compromising privacy laws.

In 2019, cybercrimes resulted in losses as high as $2 trillion, according to a Juniper study, and global spending on security is expected to reach $10 billion by 2027. Many organisations are investing heavily in training and upgrading cybersecurity. Still, small business owners who are frequently the targets of cyberattacks do not pay the necessary amount of attention to this concern. According to the Gartner study, at least 50 per cent of cyberattacks involve small businesses. Hackers access consumer information and other personal data, such as credit card numbers, personal information, and Social Security numbers. Small businesses account for 13 per cent of the cybersecurity market, but the average amount they invest in security is less than $500. According to Cabinet, 60 per cent of companies have been the targets of cyberattacks, such as phishing, distributed denial of service (DDoS) attacks,[214] and social engineering attacks.[215]

---

214 In an article by Norton.com by Steve Weisman for NortonLifeLock, 23 July 2020, (https://us.norton.com/internetsecurity-emerging-threats-what-is-a-ddos-attack-30sectech-by-norton.html), it defines distributed denial-of-service attacks as "a type of attack on targeted websites and online services that seeks to overwhelm them with more traffic than the server or network can accommodate. The goal is to render the website or service inoperable. The gaming industry has been a frequent target of DDoS attacks, along with software and media companies. In one famous DDoS case, a 15-year-old boy with the screen name of 'MalfiBoy' hacked into the computer networks of a number of universities. He then used their servers to carry out a DDoS attack that crashed several major websites, including CNN, E-Trade, eBay, and Yahoo. The boy was convicted of crimes in the Montreal Youth Court. As an adult, he became a 'white-hat hacker,' identifying vulnerabilities in the computer systems of major companies."

215 "11 Eye Opening Cyber Security Statistics for 2019," Matt Powell, *CPO Magazine*, 25 June 2019, https://www.cpomagazine.com/tech/11-eye-opening-cyber-security-statistics-for-2019/.

Some of the most significant data breaches involving high-profile organisations have resulted in millions of accounts being hacked. For instance, in 2013, a cyberattack on Yahoo! led to 3 billion accounts being compromised, and 500 million Marriott guest accounts were hacked between 2014 and 2018.

The 2019 ISTR (Internet Security Threat Report) from Symantec indicates that organisations get one malicious e-mail for every 302 e-mails received.[216]

I. The Impact of Breaches

Data breaches have immediate and wide-ranging impacts on small businesses. The average costs of a data breach have been rising rapidly; in addition, victimised companies may face a prolonged recovery period. Short-term effects include the following:

a. Monetary loss because of imposed fines, account hacking, and compensation payments

b. Cancellation of contracts by suppliers, clients, or customers

c. Broader impact on customer loyalty

d. Time-consuming and expensive repetition of work in case of data loss

e. Redundancy of staff members and downsizing to cope with monetary loss

The longer-term implications include loss of credibility, increased customer acquisition costs, loss of competitive

---

216 "80 Eye-Opening Cyber Security Statistics for 2019," Casey Crane, The SSL Store, 10 April 2019, https://www.thesslstore.com/blog/80-eye-opening-cyber-security-statistics-for-2019/.

advantage, difficulties in hiring, and challenges in preventing future data breaches.

II. Why a Forward-Looking Data Privacy Policy Is a Must for Organisations?

Data privacy, which was initially a problem mainly for the healthcare and finance sectors, has rapidly evolved to become a priority for almost all organisations across various industries, particularly those that collect personal information to conduct marketing analysis. A growing number of companies are gradually realising that not anticipating the demands of privacy legislation may make them vulnerable to lawsuits and considerable financial losses. An organisation's compliance with a privacy policy can depend on the industry to which it belongs, its target audience, its location, and the nature and amount of data it collects. Staying current with standards and regulations is ideal for keeping pace with changing demands and regulations concerning data privacy.

Although it may be difficult for organisations to draft a privacy policy that anticipates regulatory authorities' future demands, it is advisable to focus on the actions and trends that are driving privacy policy revisions. These actions and patterns can include worldwide enforcement actions or new data categories. Joining privacy groups like the International Association of Privacy Professionals (IAPP)[217] can also help organisations stay abreast of regulatory changes.

Although privacy laws are evolving and emerging rapidly, an organisation's privacy policy needs to incorporate some

217 "Why You Should Create a Forward-Looking Privacy Policy," John Edward, InformationWeek, 6 August 2019, https://www.informationweek.com/strategic-cio/security-and-risk-strategy/why-you-should-create-a-forward-looking-privacy-policy/a/d-id/1335440.

fundamental considerations. These include policies concerning asset management, data retention, data disposal procedures, and asset classification. Privacy policies also need to address the purpose of data collection, types of data collected, access and security details, data transfers, and data-sharing partnerships with affiliates and others.

Before a company drafts a forward-looking data security policy, conducting a data inventory to understand the types of data being collected, where they are stored, and how they are processed is crucial. It is essential to carry out frequent audits of existing IT practices and assets. Businesses should carry out reviews about whether employees are vulnerable in terms of protecting confidential information. Regular IT audit reports on business partners and vendors are also needed to ensure that privacy policies remain in line with future demands on security made by regulatory authorities and governments.

An organisation's privacy policy must reflect its actual practices. An inaccurate policy or one that is not adequately followed can increase the risk of liability. One key aspect of drafting a forward-looking data privacy policy is to have a designated person for policy. Someone who makes the policy is an integral aspect of everyday business decisions.

Rapid technological changes make it difficult for laws to keep pace, so predicting future regulatory requirements is challenging. Although regulations alone do not ensure data privacy, according to Dawn Rogers, counsel for applications security provider Veracode, they are "aimed at making collectors and processors of data better custodians of collected data, and more accountable for what they do with the data."[218]

---

218 "Why You Should Create a Forward-Looking Privacy Policy," John Edwards, Information Week, 6 August 2019, https://www. informationweek.com/strategic-cio/security-and-risk-strategy/ why-you-should-create-a-forward-looking-privacy-policy/a/d-id/1335440.

III. Pain Points for Data Breaches

One of the most common pain points in data privacy involves consumer transparency, though, in concept, easy to achieve but practically exceedingly challenging to implement. As witnessed in the following cases, such as in a case of a sports association in Poland accidentally leaked personal data of referees,[219] or when the fines were imposed on a Bulgarian bank for contacting clients who had opted for the "right to be forgotten," even though the bank called the customer to enquire about their unpaid bills.[220] On the other hand, in both cases, however, transparency was used as a defence by the Polish sports association; they wanted to be transparent. The same was with the bank that circulated the list of defaulters amongst the bank, and the customer service reached out to their client.

However, the most prominent issues arise from improper data handling and storage and insider threats. Additionally, low employee awareness or lack of training, resulting to mishandling or misuse of data, can be hugely costly to employers.

Employees servicing customers often may not know where data are stored or about customers' right to be forgotten. Most data breaches under GDPR are related to Article 12, which deals with transparency and data subject rights, and Article 5, which defines personal data and data processing principles. Other commonly-violated articles include Article 32, data processing security, and Article 33, concerning notification of the supervisory authority on the subject of a breach. Articles 6 and 13 also stand out as key pain points, dealing with the

---

219 "Poland: GDPR Penalty for Sports," easygdpr.eu, 25 April 2019, https://easygdpr.eu/gdpr-incident/poland-gdpr-penalty-for-sports-association/.

220 "Fine against Bulgarian Bank," easygdpr.eu, 4 December 2018, https://easygdpr.eu/gdpr-incident/fine-against-bulgarian-bank/.

lawfulness of processing and the collection of personal data, respectively.

The same applies to the concept of the "right to be forgotten." This is a very tricky concept because the "right" will be at odds with the business "transaction" at times. For the sake of argument from the viewpoint of businesses offering services, the question to dwell upon is to seek the extent to which the "right to be forgotten" can be exercised, say for instance, in case of backups, traditional legacy systems, disaster recovery, and the like. Again, though an easy concept to conceptualise, it is difficult to implement in practicality.

IV. How Can Businesses Maintain Data Security?

Here are some essential steps to help businesses ensure data security[221]:

Create a data policy: This is the first essential step. Organisations should segregate sensitive data from non-sensitive data to develop an efficient process to protect critical data. By classifying corporate data into private, public, and restricted categories, data controllers can deploy appropriate security measures accordingly. Whereas minimum security is required for public data, confidential data must be handled with the utmost caution. To protect sensitive data, access can be given to employees only on a need-to-know basis, a principle by which most governmental bodies operate.

As GDPR and other data privacy laws mandate, it is also essential for a company's data policy to establish data collection

---

221 "To Regain Consumers' Trust, Marketers Need Transparent Data Practices," Kevin Cochrane, *Harvard Business Review*, 13 June 2018, https://hbr.org/2018/06/to-regain-consumers-trust-marketers-need-transparent-data-practices.

limits. Collecting only the necessary information makes it easier to protect sensitive information.

Dedicated servers: Small businesses are likely to use a shared server for data storage. A dedicated server can cost more money upfront; protecting sensitive data in your business's server considerably enhances data security.

Data encryption[222]: Data encryption has the core objective of securing and protecting confidential digital data stored or transmitted across business networks. Modern encryption algorithms have replaced older encryption methods and are vital to protecting an organisation's communications and IT systems.

These algorithms ensure data confidentiality and security initiatives, such as integrity, authentication, and non-repudiation. Authentication enables the verification of the integrity and origin of the message. Data encryption is not only a business necessity but is also mandated by privacy laws across the world. Under CCPA, for instance, companies that do not employ data encryption technology can be sued by consumers if their data are compromised. Overall, the encryption will be out of the box and is easy to deploy, so there should be no reason that a business cannot achieve the same while relying on its processes and procedures.

GDPR applies to all organisations that process or use data of European Union citizens. Under the law, companies that do not employ "appropriate safeguards" to protect citizens' data are non-compliant and can face fines and penalties.

Password policies: Evaluate whether your business has a formal and robust password policy. If not, private data belonging to the business could be exposed to unnecessary risk. Most hacking happens because hackers can easily guess the company's login details. Implementing a complex password policy, along

---

222 "GDPR Encryption," GDPR-info, https://gdpr-info.eu/issues/encryption/.

with two-factor authentication (2FA),[223] is desirable. Even when a password and username are compromised, two-factor authentication makes it impossible to use the username or password without access to an individual's e-mail, biometrics, or physical device.

Experts note that it is equally essential to ensure account lockdown after a specified number of unsuccessful login attempts.

Training employees: Because violations of data privacy laws can trigger monumental criminal and civil penalties, businesses must train employees concerning online data security threats and their role in keeping the company's and their data safe. The training program should also make the staff aware of their rights and responsibilities related to computer use and network access. Employees must know what online practices are acceptable when using e-mails, computers, or other devices. Employees must be trained to use strong passwords, identify fraudulent e-mails, avoid opening suspicious attachments, and report any malicious online activity. They must be vigilant regarding the proper use of file-sharing applications, such as Dropbox, Jungle Disk, and OwnCloud.

Phishing scams are often used by hackers, particularly in tax season. According to one estimate, these phishing swindles compromise the identity of 120,000 individuals each year in the United States. Cybercriminals seek W-2 (wage and tax statement) information from US employees to collect tax

---

223 According to an article in Investopedia by Will Kenton, updated 28 September 2020, https://www.investopedia.com/terms/t/twofactor-authentication-2fa. asp#:~:text=Key%20Takeaways-,Two%2Dfactor%20authentication%20 (2FA)%20is%20a%20security%20system%20that,fingerprint%2C%20 face%2C%20or%20retina, "Two-factor authentication (2FA) is a security system that requires two separate, distinct forms of identification in order to access something."

returns and target vulnerable businesses. By creating fake
e-mail accounts that can seem very realistic or hacking into
corporate accounts, cybercriminals can send e-mails posing as
human resource professionals or senior officials to ask for W-2
information.[224]

Some businesses send phishing e-mails to their teams to
demonstrate how easily an individual can fall for such scams.
Giving employees tools to prevent such attacks is essential,
and ongoing training can ensure that data security remains a
priority.

Test vulnerabilities: One of the most critical steps in data
protection is to test for vulnerabilities. Regularly testing security
measures after generating passwords, installing and updating
software, or securing the private network is crucial. Apart
from running daily malware and virus scans on the network
machines, consider hiring cybersecurity experts or ethical
hackers to identify critical security issues. This will help fix
problems before they result in a disastrous data breach. As the
case of Marriott indicates, testing vulnerabilities during and
after a merger or acquisition is critical.

Back up your data: It is critical to implement a secure
backup solution for all essential data of the organisation.
Encrypting backed-up files on the cloud is an efficient way to
restore data and recover previous versions of files in case of a
breach or data theft.

Disaster plan: Although no business wishes for a data
breach, the likelihood of a cyberattack eventually is high. While
developing security and protection plans, companies must also
plan how they will respond in case of a cyberattack. The US
Federal Trade Commission (FTC) suggests that businesses

---

224 "What Is CEO Fraud?" KnowBe4, 2020 Edition, https://www.knowbe4.com/
ceo-fraud.

have a dedicated disaster response team that includes legal, human resources, information technology, forensics, security, communications, management, and operations experts. The FTC also suggests hiring independent forensic investigators to help in determining the breach's source and scope.

Consult legal counsel: In the event of a breach, the FTC also recommends consulting legal counsel with data security and privacy expertise. This helps businesses understand which state or federal laws have been implicated by a data breach and the steps to mitigate consequences.

B. My Theory with Case Law Example and Analysis

I will now return to the forces test I presented earlier to see how the following real-life cases fit or do not fit into the prongs mentioned. In our first case, the Federal Trade Commission, one of the most aggressive and primary regulators of data security in the United States was the prosecutor.

KEY FORCES REQUIRED TO MAINTAIN PRIVACY

In January 2018, the FTC pursued and later settled a case where a toy manufacturing company had violated the COPPA or the Children's Online Privacy Protection Act by obtaining personal information without parental consent as required under the act. Per the FTC, the company also had failed to take "reasonable steps"

for securing data while falsely stating in its privacy policy regarding data encryption. FTC fined the company $650,000.[225]

The forces test analysis: I believe this is simple to see in the light of the three forces mentioned. The company failed to exert the proper force on the first force and second force. Though they did not comprehend the law well enough, the root cause was the cultural imbalance. Good policies impact the culture of an organisation with adequate training. Robust policy without sufficient training or policies not in line with the practices would result in employees finding more ways to escape the policy than to accept it. This results in self-driven practices and the non-adherence culture of an organisation.

In another case in 2018, FTC settled with a mobile phone company[226] *over allegations that the latter collected personal information of consumers, such as location data and text message content, without consent while making promises that it would ensure privacy and security of consumer data.*

FTC alleged that the mobile manufacturer falsely claimed it would collect only the necessary data and implemented controls to safeguard consumer information.

The settlement mandates that the company establish and maintain a security program while prohibiting it from making false statements on data privacy and security measures.

The forces test analysis: In this case, follow the word very carefully, "falsely" justifies the action of individuals who are looking to make a quick buck and while making sure they are

225 "IoT Kids' Toys Privacy Breach Case Settles," George Khoury, Esq., FindLaw, 10 January 2018, https://blogs.findlaw.com/technologist/2018/01/iot-kids-toys-privacy-breach-case-settles.html.

226 "Mobile Phone Maker BLU Reaches Settlement with FTC over Deceptive Privacy and Data Security Claims," Federal Trade commission, 30 April 2018, https://www.ftc.gov/news-events/press-releases/2018/04/mobile-phone-maker-blu-reaches-settlement-ftc-over-deceptive.

compliant with the minimum level of requirement of law. In some areas, the law is not going to be adequate, and thus, the burden would fall upon the organisation's culture, which is the second force in effect.

In a HIPAA-related judgement, a top health insurance company agreed to pay $16 million Office for Civil Rights (OCR) in 2018. The insurer also agreed to take "substantial corrective action" for the alleged HIPAA violations, where a string of cyberattacks in 2015 led to hackers obtaining the PHI of 79 million individuals.

OCR stated that the insurance company had "failed to implement appropriate measures for detecting hackers who had gained access to their system to harvest passwords and steal people's private information."[227]

The insurer had not conducted a risk analysis, had insufficient procedures concerning information system activity, and failed to implement minimum access controls to protect sensitive PHI from cyberattacks.

The forces test analysis: As an insurer, it is incumbent for them to access their internal corporate environment, and by its very nature, this amounts to a risk assessment.

Therefore, it is inferred that the risk assessment conducted was inadequate in ensuring the proper scope and value assigned to the data assets. Although this is not a legal requirement, it is a reasonable expectation for the public to have a company that, when engaged in the vital insurance sector, the safeguards being enabled are technologically sound. This failure of technology deployment is not only careless but also amounts to incompetence. In short, companies should not be practising trade in that particular sector with some form of baseline understanding, such as a certificate.

---

227 "Biggest Healthcare Data Breaches (And What You Can Learn)," Medicus IT, https://knowledge.medicusit.com/healthcare-data-breaches.

Perhaps a proactive measure by the company could have done the trick. That is not a legal requirement, but the values and culture you carry shape the organisation's future. So they did not fail in the second force, by not implementing the suitable measures, they were also unable to exert adequate third force to attain adequate technology to prevent hacking.

C. WHAT CAN INDIVIDUALS DO TO PROTECT THEIR PRIVACY?

In the digital age, almost every transaction made offline or online involves providing some type of personal data.[228] Whether the context is an in-store purchase, providing e-mail identification for a promotion code, or using a rideshare service such as Uber, you are exposing your data to privacy risks day after day.

As the Cambridge Analytica scandal (in which the company gained access to personal data of millions of Facebook users) or the Google bug that allowed third-party access to Google users' personal data has shown, data privacy threats are ubiquitous.

Even your beloved social media site needs to be looked at with an eye of scrutiny. The Electronic Frontier Foundation (EFF), a non-profit organisation that focuses on championing privacy and civil rights, examined twenty-six tech giants concerning how they were protecting user privacy. Of the twenty-six companies, only nine received a five-star rating.[229]

Each company was rated on five components:

---

228 "How to Keep Your Personal Information Secure," Federal Trade Commission – Consumer Information, July 2012, https://www.consumer.ftc.gov/articles/0272-how-keep-your-personal-information-secure.

229 "This Scorecard Shows Which Tech Companies Protect User Data from the Government (And Which Don't)," Taylor Hatmarker, Tech Crunch, 11 July 2017, https://techcrunch.com/2017/07/11/eff-2017-government-privacy-scorecard/.

a. Following data privacy best practices
b. Informing users if the government requests their data
c. A promise not to sell data
d. Representing a united front against acts or laws not in the best interest of the societies
e. Supporting reform of the US National Security Agency's surveillance program under Section 702, in which the agency can collect individuals' information from Internet and phone companies without a warrant.

Interestingly, Twitter, Snapchat, Tumblr, and Airbnb got favourable reviews in three areas, while WhatsApp and Amazon checked off only two boxes. The one-star rankings awarded to all major phone carriers on the list were not surprising, given their history.[230] It seems that these tech giants are so good with their balance sheet and stock prices that even a poor security rating does not hurt them as much as it pains the common man.

According to a McAfee survey, more than 40 per cent of people worldwide feel they do not have control over their data.[231] The survey also found that 52 per cent of participants across the world do not know how they can secure apps and connected devices, while 40 per cent do not change default passwords immediately.

Moreover, nearly 33 per cent of respondents said they were not aware of the risks well enough to explain them to their children. This is perfectly understandable, but would we give

230 "How Do Tech Giants Compare at Protecting Privacy?" Mondo, https://www.mondo.com/blog-tech-giants-rank-protecting-privacy/.
231 "Key Findings from Our Survey on Identity Theft, Family Safety and Home Network Security," Gary Davis, McAfree, 2 January 2018, https://www.mcafee.com/blogs/consumer/key-findings-from-our-survey-on-identity-theft-family-safety-and-home-network-security/.

our children medication without knowing the medicinal drug's purpose? Then why should online risks be any different?[232]

Although identity theft is a common concern, it is not the only risk your personal data faces:

- a. Hackers sell your personal data to the dark web or black market, where it fetches a considerable price.
- b. Hackers can overwhelm you with e-mails or robocalls to get additional information.
- c. They can also attempt to hack into social media accounts and obtain information about their friends and family.
- d. They can obtain privileged information on your business or company.
- e. And they can access your utility or bank accounts.

I. Opt Out or Request for Deletion

Always read the company's privacy policy. The link for their privacy policy is generally embedded in the footer of the website. By law, they must publish a policy, such as a privacy policy, which would explain what they plan to do with the consumer's/client's personal data.

Do not shy away from requesting the company to opt out from sales of your data. All prominent laws across the globe, such as, but not limited to, GDPR, CCPA, and like, permit and allow for the companies to stop the sale of their data and erase data. The erasure can be denied by the company if they cannot identify you as a legitimate owner of the data or are unable to confirm your identity. Thus, the only thing business

---

232 "Top 5 Concerns to Focus on for Data Privacy Day," Tony Bradley, *Forbes*, 2018, https://www.forbes.com/sites/tonybradley/2018/01/27/top-5-concerns-to-focus-on-for-data-privacy-day/#6f6e44d94f3c.

can do is grant the request for deletion but archive a copy of the information if the requestor was not the actual consumer.

II. Know Your Rights against Discrimination

Many privacy laws grant consumers or business clients specific privacy rights over their personal data held or processed by businesses. The companies sometimes do charge a small fee to push individuals away from their goals to safeguard their privacy. The reason for their action is that they would go out of existence if they are not able to get a hold of your data; otherwise, how would a company send you targeted marketing ads, campaigns, and the like? But as individuals, one should not give up on your privacy because the service costs an amount. These include the rights to

(a) be apprised whether their personal information is sold or disclosed and to whom and
(b) equal service and price, even if they exercise their privacy rights.

Again, a few laws that are referred to in this book allow individuals the right to sue if any of these privacy guidelines are violated, even if there is no breach, and businesses have specified days, thirty, such as under CCPA, to cure alleged violations.

III. Install Security Software!

Use anti-spyware and antivirus software apart from a firewall. Update these security protections often and install security patches for software programs and your computer's operating system. Malware (i.e., malicious software) is a vital issue that plagues computer users, and installing anti-malware software adds another layer of security. Malware includes viruses, spyware, worms, trojan horses, and much more—all designed to enter your computer without your consent.

There are many paid and free versions of security software. It is essential to install antivirus software from trusted companies and be aware of fake antivirus programs that generate pop-ups stating that your computer is infected. Look at the current ratings on the available antivirus and malware products in the market and choose the ones with the highest ratings.

IV. Manage Your Account's Privacy Activity

All good e-mail providers have settings associated with privacy. As a sample, I will use a Google/Gmail account as an example. Make sure you carry out the following when you go to your Google account[233] and sign in with your username and password.

Google Account	Location History	Auto Delete Location History	You Tube history	Aauto Delete You Tube	Web & App activity	Auto Delete Web & App Activity
Email Account	Paused*	3 months**	Paused*	3 months**	Paused*	3 months**

Legend
* These activities can only be paused BUT NOT stopped (as of March 2021)
** Minimum period allowed by Google before they can delete data (as of March 2021)

Similarly, in Google, you can customise your ad preferences; this is a crucial step. Though this might take away the comfort of personalised advertisements, it will preserve your privacy by not disclosing your critical attributes on which personalisation of advertising is based. Simply go to your Google Account, and on the left navigation panel, click "Data & Personalization." This is where you would find the "Ad Personalization" panel. Choose "Ad Settings" and turn off "Ad Personalization."

---

233 https://myaccount.google.com

Last, you can go to optout.aboutads.info to opt out of offered services, which are considered unnecessary. You might find it strange, but if you try to opt out of all the services, no matter how many times you try, you will never be able to opt out of all of the services. Try it and see!

Suppose at any stage you feel you have precious data on your Google account. In that case, you can go to https://takeout. google.com. This service allows you to download any and all types of data that is associated with your Google account, may it be e-mail, Chrome-related data, Google photos, and the like.[234]

I have taken Google as an example because Google provides the most data collection points, and thus, such services can be managed; the only problem is not many Google account holders are aware of this.

V. Back Up All Data

Backing up data is an essential but often overlooked step. It ensures that there is a duplicate copy in case your device is stolen, lost, or hacked. Ideally, you should create a backup on an external hard drive, which helps you recover your personal information quickly in case of a data breach.

VI. Encrypt or Tokenise Your Data

Search the Internet for reasonably-priced encryption and tokenisation methods or keys, key to an offline system that you do not connect to the Internet all the time. Even if your data are compromised, the hacker will not be able to do much as it will take him or her multiple years to decrypt your data.

---

234 This service was available during the time the book was published - March 2021.

VII.   Use Two-Factor Authentications (2FAs)

Two-factor authentications are no longer only available for banks. This technology is now available for everything: Your bank account, e-mail accounts, and social media accounts allow for two-factor authentication. This method typically uses either a one-time code sent by text message or a one-time code generated by a dedicated mobile app.[235] Yes, you might need to give your mobile number to these sites so that they can send you a computer-generated code as a second-factor authentication before you or anyone can log on to that website. Suppose you are worried about sharing your mobile number. In that case, some apps can also carry out the second-factor authentication, such as Google authentication or the Authenticator app available at iOS and Android Play Stores.

VIII. Using a VPN Might Help If Your Country's Laws Allow It

A virtual private network generally enhances privacy and anonymity online by masking who you are and where you are connecting. Most VPNs, such as Hotspot Shield, Tor, and many more, are compatible with various browsers, such as Chrome, Firefox, Safari, and others. Using VPN/proxy servers is a fashionable way to conceal your identity and spoof geolocations. Masking your IP address is a good start since you essentially create an intermediary that does not exist.[236]

---

235 "Surveillance Self-Defense," SSD.EFF.ORG, 29 October 2019, https://ssd.eff. org/en/module/how-enable-two-factor-authentication.

236 "What Is Metadata, And How Do You Maintain Your Privacy?" Hotspot Shield, https://www.hotspotshield.com/blog/metadata-maintain-privacy/.

IX. Do Not Open Phishing E-Mails

Malware can be present in e-mails or hidden in photos, downloadable files, freeware, videos, or shareware. Do not click on links or open or download programs from suspicious e-mails sent by strangers. This could expose your system to malware or spyware that captures personal data or passwords.

File-sharing platforms are rife with malware, besides being illegal. Avoid downloading files from untrustworthy websites. A 2014 research study conducted by Intelligent Content Protection[237] indicated that 90 per cent of the top thirty pirate sites contained malware and potentially-unwanted programs designed to defraud or deceive unwitting viewers. These sites are also teeming with credit card scams.[238]

Many pirate sites link to malware and other questionable products. Still, the sites themselves do not host any of the material, as reflected by the fact that the top pirate sites, https://torrentfreak.com/ and https://thepiratebay.org/, were not flagged by Google's safe browsing tool.[239]

X. Use Secure Wi-Fi

With Wi-Fi freely available in hotels, libraries, coffee shops, airports, and other public places, it is essential to check whether the wireless network is secure.

237 "Pirate Sites Are Rife with Malware and Scams, Report Claims," Ernesto van der Sar, Torrent Freak, 30 April 2014, https://torrentfreak.com/pirate-sites-rife-malware-credit-card-fraud-report-claims-140430/.

238 "Internet Security Threat Report," Symantec, 2014, https://www.itu.int/en/ITU-D/Cybersecurity/Documents/Symantec_annual_internet_threat_report_ITU2014.pdf.

239 "Safe Browsing Site Status," Google Transparency Report, 20 November 2020, https://transparencyreport.google.com/safe-browsing/search?url=thepiratebay.se.

XI. Lock Your Laptop and Protect Your Devices

Use a login feature that requires a password and username and avoid automatic login. Avoid storing financial information on your laptop, and always log off. Use a strong password for all devices, including mobile phones and tablets. Change the passwords frequently and avoid using the same password twice. Avoid using sensitive information, such as your bank account number or Social Security number, as combinations or numbers in passwords, PINs (personal identification numbers), or user IDs.

XII.   Understand Privacy Policies

Although they are complicated and lengthy, privacy policies inform you about how a website collects and processes personal information and whether the information is provided to third parties. If the site does not have a privacy policy or the policy wording is not clear, consider another website with a better-worded policy. Furthermore, check the privacy settings on websites and social media accounts. Websites such as social networking platforms offer various privacy options. For instance, you can make videos viewable only by specified users on YouTube and make your status visible only to selected contacts on WhatsApp. Privacy controls are typically offered in the sign-up process for a new online service or account. To protect your data privacy, you should know about the privacy controls available on any platform before deciding to share personal information.

XIII. Review Your Granted Permissions

Mobile apps ask for permissions to access the device's camera, geolocation, microphone, and files. Some apps cannot function without these permissions, such as shared ride apps like Uber and Lyft, but some apps use the information for marketing or hacking. By reviewing what kinds of permission each of the apps has, it is possible to control such access. Browser extensions also have spying capabilities, and it is important not to install any browser extensions that are not needed.

XIV. Limit Your Social Media Accounts

Limit the information you provide on social media platforms. Check sharing and privacy settings on all the social media accounts you use and review them regularly. Know the risks of using ridesharing apps and digital personal assistants such as Alexa. On publicly accessible sites, avoid posting your full name, address, Social Security number, phone number, or other sensitive data.

XV. Secure Your National ID Number/ Social Security Number

All countries leading regulatory bodies urge their citizens to keep their national ID safe and secure. The Federal Trade Commission (FTC) advocates always guarding your Social Security number and asking questions before you agree to share it. If anyone requests your Social Security number for a transaction, always ask if a different identification can be provided.

XVI.   Learn to Examine Your Digital Footprint

Taking stock of your digital footprint includes evaluating your online presence and finding old accounts that are no longer in use. It is essential to think about what kind of personal information is found on different sites. For instance, consider across how many websites your card information is stored and where your most critical files, photos, or documents are stored on the web. Start by listing the number of sites and types of sensitive information associated with each of them. Delete your profiles in accounts you no longer use.

In the digital age, data are a valuable asset for individuals, governments, and businesses. Protecting and safeguarding information is the responsibility of governments and must be a priority for everyone in society. Although legislation helps to provide a framework for adopting best practices of data collection, processing, and storage, with petabytes of data being generated every day at breakneck speed, individual vigilance is necessary to support legislative intent with a keen sense of ethical and moral principles and personal ownership of data.

XVII.   Understand the Use of Cookiebot

Cookiebot is a consent management solution that you can integrate on your website directly from the cloud with a few simple codes within JavaScript. Once Cookiebot is up and running on your website, it automatically scans the depths of your domain to find all cookies and trackers present.

Then Cookiebot automatically blocks the cookies until your users have given their consent to the cookies' activation and the collection of their personal data. You can test whether a website is GDPR-compliant at https://www.cookiebot.com/

en/. Cookebot also comes in various plug-in formats such as WordPress and includes a compliance check with the CCPA.[240]

XVIII. Prevent Video Teleconference Hijacks

Like the early days of chatrooms, a good deal of video teleconferencing (VTC) tools, such as Zoom, Microsoft Teams, and many others, can attract trollers determined to disrupt private conversations. These attempts are not technically hacking, as they result from improper settings. The term for crashing a Zoom meeting uninvited is "Zoom bombing." Zoom responded to this problem by adding security measures promptly.

The FBI and other entities have recommended some ways to keep your video teleconferencing secure:[241]

a. No social media: Do not post your meeting links on social media.

b. Manage screening options: Ensure that your meetings are private by requiring a password or code; prevent people who have been banned from entering.

c. Updates: Make sure your meeting software is updated and patched. All VTC providers release regular updates, so ensure that your VTC tool is up-to-date.

---

240 "Cookie Consent | How Do I Comply with the GDPR Cookie Consent Requirements?" Cookiebot, 27 October 2020, https://www.cookiebot.com/en/cookie-consent/.

241 "FBI Warns of Teleconferencing and Online Classroom Hijacking During COVID-19 Pandemic," Kristen Setera, FBI Boston, 30 March 2020, https://www.fbi.gov/contact-us/field-offices/boston/news/press-releases/fbi-warns-of-teleconferencing-and-online-classroom-hijacking-during-covid-19-pandemic.

XIX.   Use Google's Safe Browsing Tool

Google's safe browsing technology, available at https://transparencyreport.google.com/safe-browsing/search, examines billions of URLs per day looking for unsafe websites. Thousands of new hazardous sites come up, many of which are legitimate websites that have been compromised. When we detect unsafe websites, we show warnings on Google Search and in web browsers. You can search to see whether a website[242] is currently dangerous to visit.

XX.   Remove Old Credit Cards from Shopping Websites

All credit cards carry vital information for a sophisticated hacker, even your expired ones. So make sure to remove your unused or expired cards from the saved payment method mode.

XXI.   Have a Basic Sense of the Laws and Your Rights

One of the objectives of this book is to make readers aware of existing laws. No one is expected to know the laws by heart, but you need to know that these laws exist so that you can respond effectively in case of an invasion or breach.

Additionally, Article 13 of GDPR indicates what companies collecting data are obliged to tell you (or at least they must make you aware that such information exists). At the time of collecting their data, people must be informed clearly about at least the following[243]:

---

242 "Google Malware Checker," HackersOnlineClub, https://seo.
      hackersonlineclub.com/google-malware-checker.
243 "What Information Must Be Given to Individuals Whose Data Is Collected?"
      European Commission, https://ec.europa.eu/info/law/law-topic/data-
      protection/reform/rules-business-and-organisations/principles-gdpr/what-
      information-must-be-given-individuals-whose-data-collected_en.

a. Who/What is the company/organisation? (contact details and those of the data protection officer (DPO), if any)

b. Why will the company/organisation use personal data? (purposes)

c. What are the categories of personal data concerned?

d. Does it have a/What is the legal justification for processing the data?

e. How long will the data be kept?

f. Who else might receive it?

g. Will the personal data be transferred to a recipient outside the European Union?

h. That they have the right to a copy of the data (right to access personal data) and other fundamental rights in the field of data protection.

i. That they have the right to complain to a data protection authority (DPA).

j. That they have the right to withdraw consent at any time.

k. Where applicable, that they the right to know the existence and scope of automated decision-making and the logic involved, including the consequences thereof.

You can find the complete list here: https://eur-lex.europa.eu/legal-content/EN/TXT/?uri=CELEX:32016R0679#d1e2254-1-1

XXII. Concluding Thoughts

CONSTANTLY
CHECK PRIVACY
SETTINGS

STORE YOUR
CARDS WITHOUT
CVV

CHANGE YOUR
PASSWORD

UNDERSTANDING
THE COOKIES

USE A SECURE VPN

"#MYPRIVACY #MYRIGHT"

Money and data can act as leverage for anyone. For smart people, data would be enough. The world is controlled by a few individuals who lobby with the politicians or control the economies, as such people have all realised the measure and power of data. What is the means and source of the power by which certain people seem to be controlling large segments of the modern world? The answer is simple and direct: control of consumer and user information. Once people in power know the information or weaknesses through the information, you virtually control people like a puppet master.

How do they gain access to the information is the crucial question. And I passionately believe the easiest way to gain access to any personal information is by understanding a person's emotions and personal life. We, as humans, are driven through sentiments in real life and over the virtual experience (the Internet). Emotional, sentimentally-absorbing hashtags like Unabomber, CEO sex scandal, or political criticisms of a particular nationality draw our attention. Behavioural scientists call this high arousal with emotion. Such arousal is instigated through something joyful or emotionally draining, which can instil fear in public. Arousal is a common feeling that ranges from excitement to relaxation. These feelings have been some of the factors that cause the information to go viral over the Internet.[244]

Any social media app is looking to attract new likes and shares, and to do so, they need to instigate these emotions and mimic the feelings of real-world actions. The best example is the US elections, which replicated that same mood and swayed the voters' emotions.

The people who want to shift the momentum post messages that play with the emotions of Internet users. To me, people who post in this way are demonstrating traits similar to that of a person suffering from a narcissist personality disorder (NPD). But others fall victim to these messages. When coupled with the algorithm that supports such movement (because a social media app survives on such activities), this snowballs as a viral message translating the effect of the Internet into the real world.

People with NPD have remarkably high intelligence quotient[245] but exceptionally low or negligent emotional quotient.[246] So we need to manage our feelings as we would do

---

244 "The Emotional Combinations That Make Stories Go Viral," Kerry Jones, Kelsey Libert, and Kristin Tynski, *Harvard Business Review*, 23 May 2016, https://hbr.org/2016/05/research-the-link-between-feeling-in-control-and-viral-content.

245 In an article by Alison Pearce Stevens in sciencenewsforstudents.org, 13 October 2016, https://www.sciencenewsforstudents.org/article/what-iq-and-how-much-does-it-matter /, IQ is defined as "a measure of a person's reasoning ability. In short, it is supposed to gauge how well someone can use information and logic to answer questions or make predictions."

246 According to HelpGuide, October 2020, https://www.helpguide.org/articles/mental-health/emotional-intelligence-eq.htm, "Emotional intelligence (otherwise known as emotional quotient or EQ) is the ability to understand,

in the real world and not hide behind a black box and let such people take over our sentiments.

I see a revolution brewing, with people like Edward Snowden, Christopher Wylie, and the like, who, started by the love of technology or as a tech enthusiast, worked closely with such technologies until they realised they had enough. It is not about "I do not have anything to hide," but it is about the whole society being aware and questioning the issue of privacy. I believe you may be doing a disservice to people around you and the next generation when you say that you do not have anything to hide, and it is okay if the big tech giants collect your data through mobile phones or laptops or other gadgets. Most tech companies rely on this same attitude, user apathy, as it is giving them the liberty to put such technologies out in the market and collect your information for marketing purposes. By now, these tech companies know that you, as an end user, never read the terms and conditions and click "I agree" blindly.

Take your attitude to the next level of not just stating what you believe or not believe, but also why you believe that way.

 a. To use your right to freedom of speech
 b. To support a healthy society and for the social well-being of people and the next generation
 c. To be the agent of change and not an agent of this dystopian regime

---

use, and manage your own emotions in positive ways to relieve stress, communicate effectively, empathize with others, overcome challenges and defuse conflict. Emotional intelligence helps you build stronger relationships, succeed at school, and work, and achieve your career and personal goals. It can also help you to connect with your feelings, turn intention into action, and make informed decisions about what matters most to you."

The future lies in your hands. Do not make your next generation's future one of inevitable disaster but one of world of possibilities, change, and hope. Once people in power know the information or weaknesses through the information, you virtually control people like a puppet master.

APPENDIX

WHAT IS THE OUTLOOK OF DATA PRIVACY IN THE UNITED STATES AND EUROPEAN UNION?

Data privacy laws have been evolving since 1890 when two lawyers in the United States wrote an article on "the right to privacy" that defined privacy as the "right to be left alone." In 1948, the right to privacy as the twelfth fundamental right was adopted by the Universal Declaration of Human Rights. The evolution continued through the 1960s when the Freedom of Information Act was passed in the United States, giving everyone the right to access documents from the state.[247] In the 1980s, the European Union adopted the Data Protection Convention as data privacy became a legal imperative.

---

247 "The Invention of the Right to Privacy," Dorothy J Glancy, Arizona Law Review, 1979, http://law.scu.edu/wp-content/uploads/Privacy.pdf.

Over the past decade, the spate of cybercrimes and data or identity theft has sparked intense debate on the scope of data privacy regulations. Highly-publicised data privacy breaches and growing concern over the way businesses collect, store, or use consumer data put the spotlight on data privacy regulations and policies. Recent cybersecurity scandals showcase improper use of data. Users have no control over how their data is used while highlighting the need for enhanced transparency and accountability in this area.

The digital age and technological disruption have changed the perception of personal data and the way information is collected, processed, or stored. These developments have led to the acceleration of the pace of evolution of data privacy laws in recent times. Lawmakers and data experts realised that protecting data is imperative to ensuring data privacy.

In the United States, data related to consumers, such as credit reports, have long been a commodity of the enterprise rather than the data subject. Until 2004, individuals had to pay a fee to obtain their own data held and collected by the credit bureau.

On the other hand, in Europe, data privacy has been linked closely with human rights. The GDPR or General Data Protection Regulation (EU) 2016/679 is a comprehensive regulation that gives the data subjects (consumers) complete control over their personal data.

A. DATA PRIVACY LAWS IN THE UNITED STATES: A GENERAL OUTLOOK

Although there is no single data protection law at the federal level in the United States, various laws regulate data privacy in different sectors at state and national levels. Respective authorities enforce many privacy laws sources at state and federal levels, and most of them empower individuals with the right to sue organisations for violation of these laws. In 2018, legislative activity at the state level signalled a shift towards a consumer privacy legislation that is broader with a wider and more encompassing scope and rights for the individual.

California was the first state to enact privacy legislation with the California Consumer Privacy Act (CCPA), partly inspired by the General Data Protection Regulation (GDPR) of the European Union. CCPA aims to protect individuals' personal information across industries. Since then, many states have also proposed similar privacy legislation, and several comprehensive privacy bills were introduced in the US Congress at the federal level.[248]

Additionally, there is no single regulatory authority in the United State that oversees data protection law. The authority responsible at the federal level depends on the regulation or statute in question. For instance, in the financial sector, the Consumer Financial Protection Bureau and various other financial services and state insurance regulators oversee the Gramm-Leach-Bliley Act (GLB), which controls how firms use, disclose, or process personal information. In the healthcare sector, the Department of Health and Human Services (HHS) enforces the Health Insurance Portability and Accountability Act (HIPAA) of 1996. Apart from these sector-specific regulators, the FTC (Federal Trade Commission) is the primary privacy regulator at the federal level in the United States. Section 5 under the FTC Act, a consumer protection law prohibiting

---

248 "DATA PRIVACY DAY," Mississippi Department of Information Technology Services, 28 January 2020, https://www.its.ms.gov/Services/Pages/January-28th-is-National-Data-Privacy-Day.aspx.

"unfair or deceptive acts or practices in or affecting commerce," is the primary enforcement tool for FTC.

Under section 5, the commission has exercised its authority for enforcement actions on a wide range of privacy violations and "deceptive" or "unfair" information policies. Although FTC does not have the authority to a fine under section 5, enforcement actions, such as consent decrees, prohibit the entity from future misconduct and twice a year audit for as long as twenty years.

At the state level, the attorney general has the authority to bring enforcement actions in case of deceptive/unfair trade practices or state privacy law. For instance, CCPA violations can be enforced by the California attorney general.

There are no structures or regulations that require the cooperation of state and federal data protection authorities with one another. However, many attorneys general at state levels establish a multistate task force in the event of a data breach to investigate a privacy breach or collectively litigate.

Here are some of the prominent laws related to data privacy and protection in the United States.

B. Federal Laws In The Usa That Safeguard Privacy[249]

Sector-specific data privacy laws include the Gramm Leach Bliley Act (GLBA) that is aimed at protecting personal information in possession of financial institutions, banks, and insurance companies. The FCRA,[250] or the Fair Credit

---

249 "U.S. Cybersecurity and Data Privacy Outlook and Review – 2019," Gibson Dunn, 28 January 2019, https://www.gibsondunn.com/us-cybersecurity-and-data-privacy-outlook-and-review- 2019/#_Toc536360195.

250 "Fair Credit Reporting Act (FCRA)," Julia Kagan, reviewed by Thomas Brock, Investopedia, 2 May 2020, https://www.investopedia.com/terms/f/

Reporting Act, restricts how data related to an individual's credit standing or creditworthiness is used. The HIPAA (Health Information Portability and Accountability Act) is designed to protect the personal information of individuals against unauthorised disclosure or collection.

Electronic Communications Privacy Act of 1986[251]: The ECPA is a federal law that regulates the interception of communications and revises and expands the provisions under the Wiretap Act, Pen Register Act, and Stored Communications Act. ECPA is concerned with restrictions on wiretaps on phones from the government, electronic transmissions of data, and prohibition of access to electronically-stored communications.

The Wiretap Act was enacted in 1968 at the federal level and designed to protect individuals' data privacy in wire and electronic communication. The law regulates the interception of wire and electronic communications that include any "aural transfer" conducted with the aid of communication facilities, such as cable, wire, or other similar connections. Oral communication refers to communication uttered by an individual with an expectation that there is no interception by a third party. The act made it illegal to intentionally intercept, use, or disclose oral, electronic, or wire communication that was facilitated by a "device." While the Wiretap Act addressed communication interception using "hard" devices, such as telephone lines, it did not include digital and computer-based communications. The amendments brought in the ECPA address digital communication as well.

The law aims to protect communications through electronic and oral routes while they are being created, in transit, and

---

fair-credit-reporting-act-fcra.asp.

251 "Privacy & Civil Liberties," Justice Information Sharing (US DOJ, Office of Justice program, Bureau of Justice Assistance), https://it.ojp.gov/PrivacyLiberty/authorities/statutes/1285.

when they are stored in computers. The legislation applies to telephone conversations, e-mails, and electronically-stored data. Title II of the act, also known as the Stored Communications Act of 1986 (SCA), relates to protecting the privacy of file contents and subscriber records maintained or stored by service providers that include personal data, such as billing records, subscriber name, or IP addresses.

Title III of the act addresses the use of trap-and-trace and pen register devices, where the pen register is a device that captures the outgoing call details of a subject. In contrast, the trap-and-trace device captures details of incoming calls. The amendment requires that law enforcement and government entities obtain a court order for installing and using these devices.

While the Wiretap Act relates to the interception of communications, the SCA, or Stored Communications Act, deals with stored communications that are not in transit. In the current context, the law pertains to e-mails that are not in transit. The SCA makes it illegal to intentionally access electronic communication services and obtain access, alter, or disclose electronically-stored communication. An employer, under ECPA, is forbidden from gaining access to employees' private e-mails unless explicit consent regarding the same is obtained from the employee in the employment contract.

To keep pace with the technological advancements, the ECPA was updated and amended significantly by a host of subsequent legislation, including the CALEA (Communications Assistance to Law Enforcement Act of 1994), the USA PATRIOT Act of 2001, and the 2008 FISA (Foreign Intelligence Surveillance Act) Amendments Act.

Computer Fraud and Abuse Act: The federal CFAA prohibits surveillance activities and is focused on addressing hacking and computer trespass. While the act came into effect in 1986, it amended the computer fraud law, which was the first of its kind in the United States. Over the years, the law has been amended many times with the result that it now covers a broad range of provisions beyond the original intent.

The CFAA makes it illegal to access a computer intentionally without authorisation, although it does not clearly define what "without authorisation" means. Critics of CFAA have pointed out that the broad interpretation of the law can lead to criminal charges against employees for violating terms of use or the company's acceptable use policy. An amendment was introduced in September 2011 to the CFAA, where the focus was brought back to illegal intrusion as part of the 2011 Personal Data Privacy and Security Act.

A case in point for CFAA violation is the 2013 case of United States v Matthew Keys.[252] *Former social media editor Matthew Keys allegedly supplied passwords and usernames for Tribune Company websites to hackers. Per the government, Keys made this disclosure after he was fired from the company, conspired to damage and make unauthorised changes to Tribune Company's websites. The government brought three criminal indictment charges for CFAA violations that included conspiracy to damage the computer and an attempt to transmit malicious code. In 2016, Keys was sentenced to two years of imprisonment and a restitution amount of approximately $250,000.*

Controlling the Assault of Non-Solicited Pornography and Marketing Act of 2003: A handful of regulations target electronic marketing specifically. At the federal level, commercial e-mail is regulated by the CAN-SPAM.

The Telemarketing and Consumer Fraud and Abuse Prevention Act of 1994 and the Telephone Consumer Protection

---

252 "CFAA Cases," 10 March 2020, https://www.nacdl.org/Content/CFAACases.

Act of 1991 are two federal laws that regulate telemarketing, text message marketing, and fax marketing, while there are also state laws that pertain to telemarketing. Many other regulations address data privacy, including:

Fair Credit Reporting Act of 1970: The FCRA aims to protect information related to consumers' creditworthiness. The act restricts permissible purposes for the dissemination of credit information. Credit reporting agencies, under the law, must also verify that there is a permissible purpose for requesting a consumer report. The Fair and Accurate Credit Transactions Act (FACTA) of 2003 was an amendment to FCRA with the primary aim being the prevention of identity theft. The act sets requirements concerning information accuracy, privacy, and disposal while limiting how consumer information is shared.

FCRA governs primarily the collection and reporting of consumers' credit information concerning how the information is obtained, how long it is stored and shared with consumers and others.

The enforcing agencies for FCRA are the Consumer Financial Protection Bureau (CFPB) and the Federal Trade Commission (FTC). Many states have formulated laws for credit reporting. The type of data that credit bureaus, such as Equifax, TransUnion, and Experian, can collect under this law includes past loans, bill payment history, current debts, employment information, earlier and current addresses, whether the person has ever filed for bankruptcy, arrest record, and child support. FCRA lays down rules as to who can access a credit report and for what purpose.

Consumers under FCRA have a right to access their credit reports. By law, they are entitled to a free credit report from all three major credit bureaus every year. The request for viewing the credit report can be made at the government-authorised website.

Consumers also have the following rights under FCRA:

(a) Verify the report's accuracy when the information is required for employment.

(b) Receive notification in case the information is used against them to deny the application for credit, employment, or insurance.

(c) Dispute and request for correction of inaccurate or incomplete information in the credit report.

(d) Request for removal of harmful or outdated information.

Children's Online Privacy Protection Act (COPPA) of 1998: COPPA is aimed to protect the privacy of children below the age of thirteen. The US Congress passed the act in 1998 and has been in effect since April 2000. The Federal Trade Commission oversees and enforces COPPA. The federal law imposes stringent obligations on businesses that collect personal information online of children below the age of thirteen. This act aims to give more control over the personal information of children to parents or guardians.

The act specifies

a. obtaining parental consent before collecting or using the personal information of children,

b. including a detailed website privacy policy with a description of the kind of information collected,

c. that website operators should seek consent from parent or guardian,

d. the responsibilities of website operators concerning online safety and privacy of children apart from restrictions on methods and types of marketing that target children under thirteen,

e. the right of parents to withdraw consent and request for deletion of information, and

f. that when children engage in online games, collection of personal data is restricted.

There is no definition in COPPA as to how parental consent needs to be obtained. However, the guidelines established by FTC can help website operators ensure they comply with COPPA. The guidelines are

a. Downloadable consent forms can be faxed or e-mailed to the operator to be clearly and visibly displayed on the website.

b. Parents to use a credit card to validate age and identity.

c. Requiring parents to call a toll-free number.

d. Accepting an e-mail with a digital signature from parents.

Website operators, under the law, must allow a parental review of information they collect of children.

Other laws designed to protect children's information privacy include Privacy Rights for California Minors in the Digital World and the California Consumer Privacy Act (CCPA) of 2018. Under the Privacy Rights for California Minors in the Digital World law, minors, defined as California residents below the age of eighteen, can ask for the removal of personal information.

Driver's Privacy Protection Act of 1994: The federal law prohibits motor vehicles' departments from sharing or disclosing personal information without the consent of the concerned individual. The act also mandates record-keeping requirements for DMV.[253]

Video Privacy Protection Act of 1988: This federal act seeks to protect consumers' privacy by prohibiting audiovisual service providers from disclosing personal information. It specifies that the audiovisual information can be disclosed only to a law enforcement agency in place of a warrant, court order, or grand jury subpoena.

Privacy Act of 1974: The act establishes a fair information practices code for the collection, use, dissemination, and maintenance of personal information of individuals maintained in the system of records federal agencies. A network of records refers to a group of documents controlled by an agency wherein the personal date of any individual can be retrieved by any unique identifier, such as name or other assigned numbers. Identifiers are critical data about individuals; once known, it helps identify the targeted individual.[254]

C. HIPAA - HEALTH INSURANCE PORTABILITY AND ACCOUNTABILITY ACT[255]

The Health Insurance Portability and Accountability Act of 1996, or HIPAA, is a federal law regulating the use and disclosure of protected health information (PHI). PHI includes

a. name, birth date, address, and Social Security number of patients;

---

253 "Driver Privacy Protection Act," Florida Highway Safety and Motor Vehicles, https://www.flhsmv.gov/privacy-statement/driver-privacy-protection-act/.

254 "Privacy Act of 1974," United States Department of Justice, https://www.justice.gov/opcl/privacy-act-1974.

255 "USA: Data Protection Laws and Regulations 2020," ICLG.Com, 7 June 2020, https://iclg.com/practice-areas/data-protection-laws-and-regulations/usa.

b. mental or physical health condition of the patient;

c. care provided to individuals; and

d. any information related to payment for the medical care identifies the patient or other information that could be used to determine the patient.

Two of the fundamental goals of HIPAA are to restrict the use of PHI to only those who have a "need to know" and to penalise entities that are non-compliant with confidentiality regulations. The act applies to

a. all people employed in a healthcare facility or a private office,

b. employees involved in activities other than patient care,

c. insurance companies,

d. students,

e. billing companies, and

f. companies that maintain electronic health records.

HIPAA is enforced by the Department of Health and Human Services (HHS). The act was expanded in 2013 to accommodate the guidelines set by the HITECH (Health Information Technology for Economic and Clinical Health Act) in 2009. In 2016, HHS issued a guidance stating cloud service providers along with other healthcare business associates are also covered under the data breach, security, and privacy rules of HIPAA.

D. HIPAA PRIVACY AND SECURITY RULES

In December 2000, the HHS published the HIPAA privacy rule, which was modified later in August 2002. The privacy rule established national standards concerning protecting identifiable health information applicable to the three covered entities of healthcare providers, health plans, and clearinghouses that conduct transactions electronically.

The HHS published the security rule in February 2003, which lays down the standards for safeguarding protected health information's integrity, confidentiality, and access. An omnibus rule was also enacted to implement many provisions of the Health Information Technology for Economic and Clinical Health (HITECH) Act to strengthen PHI's security and privacy protections. The privacy rule applies to "covered entities" who must, on request, disclose PHI within thirty days to an individual.

A court order, subpoena, warrant from law enforcement agencies, or administrative requests are the only exceptions where covered entities may make disclosures of PHI without written authorisation from patients. Covered entities may also reveal PHI to facilitate treatment, healthcare operations, or payment.

For any other PHI disclosures, prior written authorisation from the concerned patient must be obtained by covered entities. In addition, the HIPAA privacy rule also provides individuals with the right to demand the correction of inaccurate PHI. Covered entities must also notify individuals how they are using the PHI while documenting privacy policies and tracking disclosures.

Covered entities under HIPAA must provide individuals notice of privacy practice and other rights while the act also regulates entities' use of business associates or service providers. HIPAA covers extensive data security safeguards concerning electronically-stored PHI. Apart from the use and disclosure of PHI, HIPAA also requires doctors to give their patients an account as to whom their PHI is disclosed for administrative and billing purposes. Patients have a right to obtain their own PHI from healthcare providers under HIPAA.

E. Administrative Requirements Under HIPAA

The privacy rule specifies the administrative requirements which must be put in place by covered entities to safeguard PHI. These include

a. appointment of a privacy official who is responsible for the development and implementation of policies and procedures[256];
b. training of employees on privacy policies and procedures;
c. establishing appropriate physical, technical, and administrative safeguards in the covered entity to protect PHI;
d. establishing a process to lodge complaints about the policies and procedures; and
e. taking steps to mitigate any harmful effects in the event of disclosure of PHI.

F. HIPAA Penalties

Violation of HIPAA privacy rule can impose penalties as below:

a. For violating the law unknowingly, the penalty is $100 per violation, with the maximum being $25,000 per year for repeat violations.

---

256 "Data Protection and Privacy in USA," Lexology, https://www.lexology.com/library/detail.aspx?g=076d0ed2-364a-4187-9c88-14074c473e55.

b. With reasonable cause, the penalty is $1,000 per violation, while the annual cap for repeat violations is $100,000.

c. Wilful neglect of the rule fines $50,000 per violation, while the yearly cap for repeat violations is $1.5 million.

G. HITECH ACT - HEALTH INFORMATION TECHNOLOGY FOR ECONOMIC AND CLINICAL HEALTH[257]

The Health Information Technology for Economic and Clinical Health Act or the HITECH Act was signed into law in 2009. The act was created to encourage the adoption of EHRs (electronic health records). The HITECH Act is also focused on strengthening the security and privacy of electronic health records.

Under HITECH, data controllers are required to notify individuals whose protected health information is subject to any security breach. The act broadened the definition of a violation to include unauthorised use, disclosure, or access to unsecured PHI.

HIPAA-covered entities must notify affected individuals in case of any significant risk of reputational, financial, or other consequences because of the breach. Those notifications must be sent within sixty days following breach discovery. The Office for Civil Rights under the Department of Health and Human Services also should be notified within sixty days if it impacts five hundred or more people.

Cybersecurity Information Sharing Act: The federal CISA, passed in 2015, is designed to strengthen cybersecurity in the United States "through enhanced sharing of information

---

257 "What Is the HITECH Act?" *HIPAA Journal*, https://www.hipaajournal. com/what-is-the-   hitech-act/#:~:text=HITECH%20Act%20 Summary,HIPAA%20Privacy%20and%20Security%20Rules.

about cybersecurity threats, and for other purposes." Entities are authorised under this law to undertake cybersecurity monitoring, information-sharing, and defence practices to tackle cybersecurity threats. CISA grants liability protection so that businesses can conduct monitoring of information systems to ensure cybersecurity and implement defensive measures against attacks.[258]

This brings our attention to a breach reported by DOMINION NATIONAL, which caused nearly 3 million healthcare records to be compromised. Post investigation, officials said they found the unauthorised access began as early as 25 August 2010, nearly nine years before the breach was discovered in April 2019.[259,260]

Clarifying Lawful Overseas Use of Data Act: The massive data breach in 2017 at Equifax – one of the top consumer credit reporting companies – affected 147 million consumers and culminated in a $700 million settlement, fuelling more debates concerning adopting a more stringent approach to data breaches.[261]

One of the key legislations introduced is the CLOUD Act, which amends the SCA (Stored Communications Act) of 1986.

Under the CLOUD Act, the federal government can obtain a warrant to force service providers to share consumers'

258 "Cybersecurity Information Sharing Act of 2015," Thomas F. Duffy, Chair, Centre for Internet Security, May 2016, https://www.cisecurity.org/newsletter/cybersecurity-information-sharing-act-of-2015/.

259 "The 10 Biggest Healthcare Data Breaches of 2019, So Far," Jessica Davis, Health IT Security, 23 July https://healthitsecurity.com/news/the-10-biggest-healthcare-data-breaches-of-2019-so-far

260 "The 10 Biggest Healthcare Data Breaches of 2019, So Far," Health Security, 2019, https://healthitsecurity.com/news/the-10-biggest-healthcare-data-breaches-of-2019-so-far.

261 "Equifax to Pay $575 Million as Part of Settlement with FTC, CFPB, and States Related to 2017 Data Breach," Federal Trade Commission, 22 July 2019, https://www.ftc.gov/news-events/press-releases/2019/07/equifax-pay-575-million-part-settlement-ftc-cfpb-states-related.

personal information outside of the United States and to forge data-sharing agreements for law enforcement with foreign governments.

Another development in 2018 was the extension of the Foreign Intelligence Surveillance Act (FISA) of 1978. FISA established procedures to request judicial authorisation to conduct physical search and electronic surveillance of people engaging in international terrorism or espionage. Section 702 of FISA enables the federal government to collect cross-border communication without a warrant.

The law allows US federal agencies to gather information without a warrant from various devices from individuals who can be categorised as foreigners. The law also provides for programs such as the NSA's Prism and Upstream, which are widely considered to be some of the most intrusive surveillance programs run by the spy agency. This led to the headlines "NSA Continued Spying on Americans, Collecting over 151 Million Phone Records Despite Law Change."[262] With data breaches hitting a record high of 1,500 in 2017, according to Identity Theft Resource Centre,[263] congressional lawmakers rolled up their sleeves to tighten breach reporting requirements and enhance security measures for data protection.

Many pieces of legislation were proposed to this effect in 2017, including the Data Broker Accountability and Transparency Act and Consumer Privacy Protection Act of 2017. Democrats proposed increasing financial penalties for

---

262 "NSA Continued Spying on Americans, Collecting over 151 Million Phone Records Despite Law Change," India Ashok, *International Business Times*, 3 May 2017, https://www.ibtimes.co.uk/nsa-continued-spying-americans-collecting-over-151-million-phone-records-despite-law-change-1619697.

263 "The ITRC's Convenient, Comprehensive Source for Data Breach Information," Notified, 20 November 2020, https://www.idtheftcenter.org/2017-data-breaches/.

data breaches, strengthening FTC's enforcement authority on credit agencies, and legislation to notify data breach victims. The Republican report stressed forming public-private partnerships and ensuring enhanced transparency with consumers.

Telephone Robocall Abuse Criminal Enhancement and Deterrence Act: The TRACED Act, introduced on 15 November 2018, created authentication rules for service providers aimed at preventing "caller ID spoofing" and illegal robocalls. Telemarketers face stiff penalties for using unauthenticated automatic dialling services.

H. Privacy Laws At The State Level

Several states in the United States also tightened the noose on data breaches while strengthening data privacy protection.

California Consumer Privacy Act: The CCPA of 2018 that comes into effect on 1 July 2020 raises the bar for companies irrespective of their location for handling personal data of consumers in California. On the lines of GDPR, CCPA has emerged as an astringent and comprehensive approach to data privacy in the United States than other existing data privacy laws.

(a) Right to know what a business has collected personal information, the source of information, what the data is being used for if it is being sold or disclosed, and to whom it is sold or published.

(b) Right to "opt out" from allowing their personal information to be sold to third parties. For children below the age of sixteen, the act provides the right to protect their data from being sold without explicit "opt in" from their parents.

(c) Right to get personal information deleted.

(d) Right to get equitable pricing and service from the business despite exercising the above privacy rights.

The provisions of this act are designed to implement these rights into practice. As mandated by the CCPA, businesses must disclose to consumers through privacy policies or whenever they collect personal data.

For instance, businesses must disclose the rights of the consumers proactively under the act, the purpose of collecting categories of personal data, what types of personal data they collect, and what kind of information is being disclosed or sold over the preceding year. Companies must update their website privacy policies every year to comply with the act's provisions.

Per the act, which took effect on 1 January 2020, businesses are prohibited from selling minors' personal information unless affirmatively authorised by the parent or guardian. Companies that sell the personal data of consumers to third parties under the act must disclose the same while displaying the link "Do Not Sell My Personal Information" prominently on the home page. This link gives consumers the right to opt out of their information being disclosed or sold to third parties. The act's provisions also include the right to opt in, which is required to collect, use, or disclose information about children below the age of sixteen. For collecting children's personal information, affirmative consent of parents is mandatory under the act.[264]

Under the CCPA, consumers have the right of action to seek actual or statutory damages and other compensation if their personal information has been accessed, stolen, or disclosed because of inadequate or absence of security procedures.

---

264 "The California Consumer Privacy Act of 2018," Kristen J. Mathews and Courtney M. Bowman, Proskauer, 13 July 2018, https://privacylaw.proskauer.com/2018/07/articles/data-privacy-laws/the-california-consumer-privacy-act-of-2018/.

Statutory damages could be between $100 and $750 per incident per California resident or actual damages, whichever is more. However, the act does not clarify what is meant by "per incident" in the context, making the extent of statutory damages unclear.

I. How Does The CCPA Protect Data Privacy?

Per CCPA mandate, businesses that collect personal information about consumers in California are obliged to

a. disclose what information is collected and how that information is used;
b. delete personal information based on the consumer's request;
c. disclose details of the kind of personal information that is shared or sold to third parties;
d. honour the consumer's right to opt out; and
e. not discriminate against the data subject in terms of denial of services or goods, quality of services or products, or pricing for exercising the above rights.

A law concerning "connected devices" was also passed in 2018 in California, requiring Internet-enabled devices to have helpful security features. The legislation aims to protect information. Contained in such devices from unauthorised access, use, disclosure, or modification.

In the United States, most states, including the Virgin Islands, Guam, Puerto Rico, and the District of Columbia, have enacted data privacy laws that require controllers to notify affected individuals when unauthorised access or acquisition of personal information happens. In nearly twenty-three states, data privacy laws also require that notice of the breach be sent to a state regulatory authority.

South Dakota and Alabama enacted legislation concerning data breach notification in 2018, joining the other forty-eight states with such laws in place. These laws require agencies to notify data subjects in the event of a breach that involves sensitive personally-identifying information electronically stored within forty-five to sixty days after the violation comes to light.

Ten states enacted legislation to enable consumers to request security freezes on credit reports while credit reporting agencies are obliged to honour such requests without charging fees.[265]

J. Data Privacy Laws In Europe

The General Data Protection Regulation (GDPR) was agreed upon in April 2016 by the European Parliament and Council and, in 2018, replaced the Data Protection Directive as the primary privacy law. Companies that already complied with the directive must ensure compliance with GDPR's new requirements.

I. GDPR Overview[266]

Since 25 May 2018, GDPR changes the way businesses and government agencies handle consumers' personal information. More importantly, the law gives individuals control over how their personal data is collected, used, or processed.

---

265 "U.S. Cybersecurity and Data Privacy Outlook and Review – 2019," by Gibson Dunn, 28 January 2019, https://www.gibsondunn.com/us-cybersecurity-and-data-privacy-outlook-and-review-2019/#_Toc536360195.

266 "What Is GDPR? The Summary Guide to GDPR Compliance in the UK," Matt Burgess, Wired, 24 March 2020, https://www.wired.co.uk/article/what-is-gdpr-uk-eu-legislation-compliance-summary-fines-2018.

GDPR applies to all European Union members and aims to bring in consistent and uniform protection of consumers' data privacy across EU nations. Some of the essential GDPR requirements include

a. obtaining data subjects' consent for data processing,

b. anonymising collected data for privacy protection,

c. issuing data breach notifications,

d. safe handling and transferring of data, and

e. appointing data protection officer for GDPR compliance.

GDPR bounds businesses that handle EU citizens' data irrespective of their physical location to safeguard personal data processing better.

Before we deep dive into the law, it is crucial to know the history of GDPR. All laws play an essential role in how societies are shaped. The following pictorial representation will give a brief idea of the societal changes that led to the creation of GDPR. The following image has been sourced from https://sourcing-international.org/

II. Articles and Chapters

GDPR comprises of ninety-one articles and eleven chapters. The following articles and chapters have the most significant impact on data processing and security[267]:

---

267 "A Definition of GDPR (General Data Protection Regulation)," Juliana De Groot, Digital Guardian, 30 September 2020, https://digitalguardian.com/blog/what-gdpr-general-data-protection-regulation-understanding-and-complying-gdpr-data-protection.

a. **Articles 17 and 18:** These articles give more control to data subjects over their personal data, which is processed automatically. This ensures the "right to portability" of personal data, making it easier for data subjects to transfer data. Data subjects can also direct the data controllers to erase personal data under the "right to erasure.

b. **Articles 23 and 30:** Businesses, under these articles, must implement reasonable measures for data protection to protect the personal data of consumers against exposure or loss.

c. **Articles 31 and 32:** These articles lay down data breach notification requirements, which play a significant role in GDPR. Per Article 31, data controllers must notify any personal data breach to the supervisory authority within seventy-two hours of becoming aware of the data breach. They must provide specific details of the data breach, such as the nature of the violation and the number of subjects impacted. Article 32 specifies that data subjects be notified of an offence as quickly as possible.

d. **Articles 33 and 33a:** These articles mandate that companies perform impact assessments to identify potential risks to consumers' personal data while conducting a compliance review to address such risks.

e. **Article 35:** This article requires the appointment of data protection officers. Businesses that process data about an individual's health, genetic data, religious beliefs, ethnic or racial origin, in particular, are required to appoint a data protection officer. The officer serves as the single point of contact for supervisory authority while advising companies on compliance with GDPR.

Some companies that collect their employees' personal information are also subject to this regulation.

f. **Articles 36 and 37:** The data protection officer's position and responsibilities are outlined in these articles.

g. **Article 45:** This article extends data requirements to international companies that process or collect the personal data of European Union citizens. These businesses have the same penalties and compliance requirements as EU-based companies.

h. **Article 79:** The penalties for non-compliance that can be as much as 4 per cent of a company's global annual revenue are outlined in this article.

Under GDPR, agencies must provide a clear picture to the users of the data collected along with the specific tool. Personal data refers to any information about an identifiable living individual. Fragmented data or islands of data are also considered personal data if they identify a living individual when collected. Encrypted, pseudonymised, or de-identified personal data, which can be used to identify a person, also fall under GDPR's purview.

If the personal data has been made anonymous and irreversible in a manner where the individual is no longer identifiable, it does not constitute personal data.

The law protects personal data irrespective of the processing technology used. It applies to manual and automated data processing as long as the data is organised with pre-defined criteria such as in a alphabetical order. The rules apply regardless of how the information is stored, whether on paper, video, or IT system. Examples of personal data include

a. name and surname,

b. identification card number,

c. home address,

d. e-mail address,

e. location data,

f. IP or Internet protocol address,

g. cookie ID, and

h. healthcare data can be used to identify a person.

III. Data Processing under GDPR

Processing includes many operations undertaken on personal data using manual or automated modes. These activities include recording, collection, structuring, organisation, storage, modification, retrieval, use, disclosure, restriction, destruction, or disposal of personal data. Examples of data processing activities include

i. staff management,

j. payroll administration,

k. sending promotional e-mails,

l. shredding documents that contain personal data,

m. posting a person's photo on a website,

n. storing IP addresses, and

o. Video recording.

The amount and type of personal data businesses may process is dependent on the legal reason for doing so. Entities must respect the following principles of GDPR:

p. Data must be processed in a transparent, lawful, and fair way.

q. Have a specific purpose for data processing.

r. Collect and process only the information that is necessary for the specific purpose.

s. Ensure data is up-to-date and accurate.

t. Avoid using the data for any other purpose than stated.

u. Ensure the data is stored only for the period necessary for the stated purpose.

v. Install organisational and technical safeguards to ensure personal data is secure from unauthorised access, misuse, damage, or destruction.

w. Review internal policies, including training, awareness-raising programs, audits, reviews, and the like.

x. Implement data security measures, such as encryption[268] and pseudonymisation, along with regular evaluation and testing of the adequacy of these measures.

y. Designate a data protection officer.

z. Implement or review the disaster management plan in case of personal data breaches; prepare a system that enables erasure of personal data or restriction of data processing.

Entities must inform data subjects at the time of data collection:

---

268 In an article by *The Guardian* authored by Samuel Gibbs, 15 December 2016, https://www.theguardian.com/technology/2016/dec/15/passwords-hacking-hashing-salting-sha-2#:~:text=When%20a%20password%20has%20been,key,%20using%20a%20set%20algorithm, it states, "Encryption, like hashing, is a function of cryptography, but the main difference is that encryption is something you can undo, while hashing is not. If you need to access the source text to change it or read it, encryption allows you to secure it but still read it after decrypting it. Hashing cannot be reversed, which means you can only know what the hash represents by matching it with another hash of what you think is the same information. If a site such as a bank asks you to verify particular characters of your password, rather than enter the whole thing, it is encrypting your password as it must decrypt it and verify individual characters rather than simply match the whole password to a stored hash. Encrypted passwords are typically used for second-factor verification, rather than as the primary login factor."

a. Company or organisation name and contact details.

b. Purpose of data collection.

c. Categories of data collected.

d. Legal basis for collecting personal data.

e. The time frame for data storage.

f. Whether a third party will receive the data.

g. The right of data subjects to access the data.

h. The right to complain to the authority and power to withdraw consent.

This information can be given orally, in writing, or by electronic means as appropriate. Organisations must ensure that the information provided is easily accessible, transparent, concise, intelligible, and free of charge.

K. EPRIVACY REGULATION

The ePrivacy Regulation[269] (Regulation of the European Parliament and the Council concerning the respect for private life and the protection of personal data in electronic communications of 2019)[270] is a new proposal that replaces the e-Privacy Directive (Privacy and Electronic Communications Directive of 2002) and aims for enhanced electronic communications regulation within the European Union to strengthen privacy. Its lexical analysis is on GDPR and complements the letter for electronic communication. These regulations apply to any business providing any type of online communication service, engaging in electronic marketing, and using online tracking technologies.[271]

---

269 "The New EU ePrivacy Regulation: What You Need to Know," i-scoop, https://www.i-scoop.eu/gdpr/eu-eprivacy-regulation/#:~:text=The%20ePrivacy%20Regulation%20AIMS%20to,cookie%20consent%20pop%2Dups%20anymore.

270 "Personal Data Protection," Fact Sheets on the European, https://www.europarl.europa.eu/factsheets/en/sheet/157/personal-data-protection.

271 "IoT Update: The E-Privacy Regulation – Impact on the IoT Market,"

It mainly comes into play for the Internet of Things (IoT) manufacturers. The service provided by IoT manufacturers would be considered under electronic communications services within the respective application, which in turn would require the end user's consent in transmitting the data from their connected device to another connected device. This also implies that such manufactures who need to comply would be overly focused on the data subject's consent, i.e., how can a data subject declare or revoke their consent to cover relevant grounds.

The law gets very technical, as it describes in their Recital 12[272] of demarcation between the application layer of M2M communication and the underlying transmission layer, so on and so forth. This is just to give readers a bird's-eye view of the new tomorrow, which will be coming in. If you thought legal terminology was tricky, then think again as the future of legal affairs will be symbiotically attached to the technology – inseparable.

L. DATA PRIVACY LAWS IN ASIA: HOW DO THEY COMPARE WITH THE UNITED STATES AND EUROPEAN LAWS?

Asian countries, in recent times, have been making concerted efforts to strengthen data privacy protection. Growing concerns on data breaches across South Korea, India, China, Malaysia, Indonesia, and Thailand have led to the introduction

---

Liza Herberger, Inside Tech Media, 27 September 2018, https://www. insidetechmedia.com/2018/09/27/iot-update-the-e-privacy-regulation-impact-on-the-iot-market/.

272 "IoT Update: The E-Privacy Regulation – Impact on the IoT Market," Liza Herberger, Inside Tech Media, 27 September 2018, https://www. insidetechmedia.com/2018/09/27/iot-update-the-e-privacy-regulation-impact-on-the-iot-market/.

or enhancement of existing data protection and cybersecurity legislation. While the GDPR has inspired many Asian and Middle Eastern laws, some Asian countries have expanded the scope of data privacy laws beyond European legislation. Here are some of the vital legislations concerning data privacy in the following Asian countries:

>**Malaysia**[273]**:** The first comprehensive data protection legislation was the Personal Data Protection Act of 2010. In effect since 2013, PDPA regulates the collection, processing, and use of personal data of customers, employees, and suppliers. While the law governs inappropriate use of data for marketing or commercial purposes, a massive data breach in 2017 affected 46 million subscribers of an online community forum.
>
>PDPA specifically does not address online privacy that includes data related to cookies and geolocation. Also, the law is not applicable if data processing happens outside Malaysia. Malaysia announced updating of data protection laws in October 2018 to bring it on par with GDPR to curb data breaches.
>
>**Thailand:** PDPA was published in 2019 in the official gazette, and businesses have a deadline of 27 May 2020 to become compliant. Personal data has been broadly defined under PDPA and

---

273 "PERSONAL DATA PROTECTION ACT 2010 - Laws of Malaysia," by agc.gov.my, 15 June 2016, http://www.agc.gov.my/agcportal/uploads/files/Publications/LOM/EN/Act%20709%2014%206%202016.pdf.

includes any information that can be used to identify an individual directly or indirectly. The privacy law also limits the concepts of "processor" and "controller" in line with the GDPR.

The PDPA mandates

a. a legal basis for organisations to collect, use, or process personal information;
b. enhanced focus on sensitive personal data;
c. implementation of adequate security measures; and
d. notification of data breaches.

Singapore[274]**: Data protection in Singapore is set out in the Personal Data Protection Act (PDPA) of 2012, establishing the principal data protection authority to be the Personal Data Protection Commission (PDPC). Apart from maintaining the "Do Not Call" registry, the PDPC enforces the data protection act. Organisations under PDPA have the following obligations related to**

a. Consent: Organisations must obtain the individual's consent to collect, use or disclose personal data.
b. Purpose Limitation: Personal data needs to be collected only for specific purposes that are considered "appropriate" by the concerned individual.
c. Accuracy: Organisations must make reasonable efforts to ensure that the collected personal data is complete

---

274 "PDPA Overview," Personal Data Protection Commission Published by PDPC.gov.sg, https://www.pdpc.gov.sg/Overview-of-PDPA/The-Legislation/Personal-Data-Protection-Act#:~:text=Personal%20data%20in%20Singapore%20is,and%20care%20of%20personal%20data.

and accurate if the information is utilised to make decisions that impact the individual.

d. Notification: The act specifies notification obligations for organisations where individuals must be informed of the purpose of collection, use, or disclosure of personal data.

e. Access and Correction: An organisation must provide access to personal data to an individual on request and correct errors or omissions in such data.

f. Transfer: The act prohibits the transfer of personal data of individuals to any country outside Singapore.

g. Protection: An organisation must make reasonable security arrangements to protect personal data to prevent unauthorised disclosure, use, access, copying, disposal, modification, and other similar risks.

h. Openness: An organisation must implement necessary policies to ensure the obligations laid down by the PDPA are met.

i. Retention: An organisation should not retain documents that contain personal data when its retention no longer serves the stated purpose of data collection or retaining such data is no longer required for business or legal purposes.

PDPA is similar to GDPR because it exerts extraterritorial reach and applies to entities that do not have a presence in Singapore and those that are not recognised under Singapore law. The other similarity is the definition in PDPA of personal data, which like GDPR, is technology-neutral. However, unlike GDPR, the scope of PDPA is limited and does not apply to the public sector or organisations that are agents of a public sector agency. The act also excludes business contact information and data intermediaries. A key factor missing in PDPA was the breach notification obligations.

In March 2019, the PDPC issued a statement stating its intent to amend PDPA to include data portability and breach notifications. If the amendment is made, businesses must notify the PDPC and affected individuals in case of a data breach.

Future amendments would also address data portability which gives individuals more control over their personal data.

Japan[275]: The APPI (Protection of Personal Information Act) was established in 2003 and was amongst the first in Asia concerning data protection regulations. After a string of data breaches in 2015, the act was overhauled in the same year. The modified regulations came into effect in May 2017. The Personal Information Protection Commission was formed under this amendment, which focuses on protecting individuals' rights concerning data privacy. APPI defines two categories of personal data – personally, identifiable information (PII) such as name, e-mail address, date of birth, numeric references, and "special care-required" information that includes marital status, medical history, criminal records, and religious beliefs, amongst others that may cause prejudice or discrimination. Prior consent is mandatory to process particular care required information.

China: Cybersecurity laws in China have expanded the personal information definition and introduced sensitive personal information, along with mandatory consent obligations. Since 2011, five significant pieces of legislation about data privacy have been enacted, indicating that China is moving away from a "sectoral" approach to a coherent structure, much like GDPR concerning data privacy.

---

275 "Japan: Data Protection Laws and Regulation 2020," ICLG, 7 June 2020, https://iclg.com/practice-areas/data-protection-laws-and-regulations/japan.

South Korea[276]: The relevant data privacy law in South Korea is the Personal Information Protection Act (PIPA) of 2011. Deemed to be one of the most stringent privacy laws, the PIPA confers many rights to its citizens regarding personal data protection. Much like the GDPR, citizens can opt out to provide personal information and retain the right to get their data deleted. In addition to PIPA, South Korea also has the "Network Act," pertaining to information collected through the Internet. Interestingly, like all the other laws on our list, they look to safeguards the same way the other laws are. Like all the laws, it also has the disclosure requirement, opt-out requirement, and more importantly, the condition to explain. When a company intends to share personal information with a third party, it must obtain separate consent and critically need to explain to the subjects how the company plans on using the data they have collected. Remarkably interesting, they have modelled their structure on GDPR, which also covers international transfers, which requires consent to having their personal information even if the data is related to employment.

India[277]: There is no specific law yet to address the data privacy of individuals in India. The Information Technology Act or the IT Act of 2000 has some provisions against computer systems' data breaches. These provisions are aimed at preventing unauthorised access and use of computer systems and the data contained therein. While it imposes personal liability for unauthorised use, the act does not address the responsibility of network service providers or data controllers. Vendors or

276 "Data Protection in South Korea: Why You Need to Pay Attention," Paul Sutton, Vistra, 15 August 2018, https://ieglobal.vistra.com/blog/2018/8/data-protection-south-korea-why-you-need-pay-attention.

277 "India Gears Up for Historic Data Protection Law," Saikat Datta, *Asia Times*, 24 June 2019, https://www.asiatimes.com/2019/06/article/india-gears-up-for-historic-data-protection-law/.

outsourcing service entities who distribute and process data are not within the purview of the IT act.

Section 79 of the act further dilutes the liabilities by adding "best efforts" and "knowledge" before the quantum of penalties is determined. This means a service provider or vendor would not be held liable for a data breach if it is proven that the contravention or offence was committed without the vendor's knowledge or due diligence was exercised to prevent the crime. Key employees, such as directors or managers, are typically personally liable for negligent or intentional violations of the act. Concerning penalties for the data breach, the maximum fine under this act is $222,000.

Another law that caters to the requirement of privacy is the Indian intellectual property law. The law prescribes punishment for piracy concerning the copyrighted violation. Section 63B of the Indian Copyright Act provides that any person who knowingly makes use of a computer to infringing shall be punishable for a minimum period of six months and a maximum of three years in prison, and the fines range approximately from $1,250, up to a maximum of approximately $5,000.[278]

The other law that pertains to data privacy is the CICRA or Credit Information Companies Regulation Act of 2005. The act mandates that credit information of Indians be collected according to the enunciated privacy norms in the regulation. Entities that collect and maintain personal data are liable for any possible data breach. Similar to the GLBA and FCRA (Fair Credit Reporting Act), CICRA has a rigid framework for credit information and finances of companies and individuals.

---

278 "Overview of Data Protection Laws in India," Manjula Chawla, Ehcca.Com, http://www.ehcca.com/presentations/privacysymposium1/steinhoff_2b_h1.pdf.

The Modi government in India is set to take up the new data privacy bill to regulate how data is collected, stored, and shared. In 2018, an expert committee submitted the recommendations and assessment on data privacy. The committee proposes the establishment of an independent regulatory authority, outlining jurisdiction for data processing and hefty penalties for non-compliance and many other provisions. The bill, if passed, is expected to apply to data collected and processed by government and private entities in India.

The committee also proposes that while critical data of Indians should be stored mandatorily in India, sensitive information of individuals should also be processed and stored in the country but maybe transmitted out of the country. "Sensitive personal data" is defined in the original proposal as data related to passwords, health, financial data, genetic data, sexual orientation, biometric data,[279] caste or tribe, political or religious affiliations. The original draft had also proposed that all personal data of Indians be stored mandatorily in India.[280]

In the wake of the fiasco of the Cambridge Analytica scandal, a draft bill that builds on the Supreme Court judgement advocated privacy as a fundamental right and creates a framework for all stakeholders to be more responsible while dealing with personal data.[281]

---

279 The UK GDPR defines "biometric data" in Article 4(14), www.legislation.gov. uk, as *"personal data resulting from specific technical processing relating to the physical, physiological or behavioural characteristics of a natural person, which allow or confirm the unique identification of that natural person, such as facial images or dactyloscopic data."*

280 "Changes Likely in Proposed Data Privacy Rules: Only Critical Data May Need to Be Housed in India," Anandita Singh Mankotia, *Economic Times*, 24 July 2019, https://economictimes.indiatimes.com/tech/internet/changes-likely-in-proposed-data-privacy-rules-only-critical-data-may-need-to-be-housed-in-india/articleshow/70355298.cms.

281 "New Data Protection Law to Impact 50 Existing Acts," *The Hindu Business Line*, 27 July 2018, https://www.thehindubusinessline.com/info-tech/

GDPR was a wake-up call and sent shockwaves across the globe. Apart from the immediate implications in terms of compliance for companies that use or store the personal data of Europeans, the EU law has far-reaching consequences. Data protection authorities and lawmakers across Asia study GDPR intending to reform their laws and upgrade to a comprehensive data privacy regulation that is on par with the digital disruptions.

The laws in Asian countries are evolving at a rapid pace, given the fact that there is an increased demand for data privacy protection even as citizens are becoming immersed in the emerging digital reality. Per a report from A T Kearney titled "Cybersecurity in ASEAN: An Urgent Call to Action," cybercriminals use Southeast Asian countries as launch pads for attacks.

From a health data breach[282] in Singapore that affected the medical information of 2,400 people in Singapore to the data breach that compromised 3.1 billion client accounts on Toyota Motor's servers in Japan,[283] Asian countries have continued to face privacy challenges.

The spate of data breaches has resulted in governments moving concertedly to adopt a comprehensive and invasive approach to electronic surveillance. To this end, some countries have cherry-picked some of the GDPR concepts. For instance, data breach notifications have been mandatory in the Philippines. In India, "White Paper of the Committee of Experts on a Data

new-data-protection-law-to-impact-50-existing-acts/article24534699.ece.

282 "Parliament: 2,400 Singaporeans Affected by HIV Data Leak Contacted by MOH," Rei Kurohi, *Straits Times*, 13 February 2019, https://www.straitstimes.com/singapore/2400-singaporeans-affected-by-data-leak-contacted-by-moh.

283 "New Toyota Data Breach Exposes Personal Information of 3.1 Million Customers," Scott Ikeda, *CPO Magazine*, 9 April 2019, https://www.cpomagazine.com/cyber-security/new-toyota-data-breach-exposes-personal-information-of-3-1-million-customers/.

Protection Framework for India" was published along with expert committee recommendations in 2018.[284]

White Paper conducts an in-depth analysis of concepts in GDPR, including breach notification obligations, accountability models, privacy impact assessments, the right to be forgotten, and extraterritorial application. India's privacy bill will be a significant step towards comprehensive data protection laws in Southeast Asia.

Canada: Canada released a bill called Bill C-59. Although the bill was heavily criticised for being vague, it still does a couple of things right, that is (1) increasing the intelligence community's internal and external accountability; and (2) granting intelligence agencies new tools while simultaneously articulating standards for the use of those tools. Bill C-59 is but one example of the government's campaign to publicly define the country's intelligence community's objectives and capabilities. Something that I read and found to be interesting was the type of language used in the bill, especially in their section 32, which mentions something like that these operations must not cause, "intentionally or by criminal negligence, death or bodily harm to an individual" or "wilfully attempt . . . to obstruct, pervert or defeat the course of justice or democracy."[285] Though it has been criticised for not putting in explicit limits, it is going to be hard for the law to do so; instead, the privacy activist and lawyers will have to interpret the laws to work in their favour rather than hoping for it works in their favour.

---

284 "White Paper of the Committee of Experts on Data Protection Framework for India+," My Gov, https://innovate.mygov.in/data-protection-in-india/#:~:text=.-,White%20Paper%20of%20the%20Committee%20of%20Experts%20on%20Data%20Protection,and%20draft%20such%20a%20bill.

285 "Canada Considers Most Far-Reaching Intel Reforms in Decades," Preston Lim, Just Security, 13 May 2019, https://www.justsecurity.org/64030/canada-considers-most-far-reaching-intell-reforms-in-decades/.

M. Personal Data and Its Importance[286]

According to GDPR, personal data are defined as "any information relating to an identified or identifiable natural person." Personal data are any information that enables a living person's direct or indirect identification.

Some forms of information called identifiers listed by GDPR include names, location data, e-mail, and postal address, driving licence, telephone, credit card, bank account, Social Security number, an online identifier, such as IP address, passport. It also includes biometric data, mobile device identification, web cookies, and other factors related to "physical, physiological, genetic, mental, economic, cultural, or social identity." Publicly available data, such as government records, are also covered under GDPR.

GDPR prohibits special categories of data from being processed that includes "personal data revealing racial or ethnic origin, political opinions, religious or philosophical beliefs, or trade union membership, and the processing of genetic data, biometric data to uniquely identify a natural person, data concerning health or data concerning a natural person's sex life or sexual orientation."[287]

CCPA defines personal information as one "that identifies, relates to, describes, is capable of being associated with, or may reasonably be linked, directly or indirectly, with a particular consumer or household."

---

286 "What Is 'Personal Data' and Why Is It So Important to Keep It Safe?" Redscan team, RedScan, 25 March 2020, https://www.redscan.com/news/personal-data-important-keep-safe/.

287 "GDPR Fines Hit These Companies Hard. Here's How to Avoid Them," Jenny O'Brien, Auth0, 30 December 2019, https://auth0.com/blog/gdpr-fines-hit-these-companies-hard-heres-how-to-avoid-them/.

The definition of "personal data" in CCPA is similar to that adopted in GDPR, but CCPA also includes data linked at the household or device level. Publicly-available government records and personal information covered under other specific legislation are excluded from the scope of CCPA. However, information related to individuals who are employees, sole traders, company directors, or partners constitutes personal data. CCPA lists specific categories of personal information not limited to

a. identifiers, including real names and aliases, postal address, online identifiers like IP address, unique personal identifier, e-mail address, Social Security number, account name, passport number, driver's licence number, and similar identifiers;

b. commercial information that includes private property records purchased, obtained, or considered products or services and other consuming tendencies or history;

c. biometric information;

d. Internet/network activity information, which includes search and browsing history, and information according to consumer's interaction with a website, advertisement, or application;

e. geolocation data;

f. audio, visual, olfactory, thermal, electronic, or similar information;

g. employment or professional knowledge;

h. education information that is not publicly available; and

i. inferences are drawn from the above to create a consumer profile reflecting individual preferences, psychological trends, characteristics, behaviour, predispositions, attitudes, intelligence, aptitudes, and abilities.

While GDPR defines biometric and genetic data separately, CCPA combines both under "biometric data." According to GDPR definition, biometric data is "personal data resulting from specific technical processes related to the physical, physiological or behavioural characteristics of a natural person, which allow or confirm the unique identification of that natural person, such as facial images or dactyloscopy data."[288] Genetic data is defined as "personal data relating to the inherited or acquired genetic characteristics of a natural person which give unique information about the physiology or the health of that natural person and which result, in particular, from an analysis of a biological sample from the natural person in question."[289]

Biometric data, per CCPA, is defined as "an individual's physiological, biological, or behavioural characteristics, including an individual's deoxyribonucleic acid (DNA), that can be used, singly or in combination with each other or with other identifying data, to establish individual identity. Biometric information includes, but is not limited to, the imagery of the iris, retina, fingerprint, face, hand, palm, vein patterns, and voice recordings, from which an identifier template, such as a face print, a minutiae template, or a voiceprint, can be extracted, and keystroke patterns or rhythms, gait patterns or rhythms, and sleep, health, or exercise data that contain identifying information."[290]

---

288 "GDPR Article 4," Dataguise, https://www.dataguise.com/gdpr-knowledge-center/gdpr-article-4/.

289 "What Is Personal Data under the GDPR?" Tess Blair and Patrik J Campbell Jr, Morgan Lewis, 9 July 2018, https://www.morganlewis.com/pubs/2018/07/the-edata-guide-to-gdpr-what-is-personal-data-under-the-gdpr.

290 "California Civil Code § 1798.140 (2018): 2018 California," Justia, https://law.justia.com/codes/california/2018/code-civ/division-3/part-4/title-1.81.5/section-1798.140/.

N. Pseudonymous and De-identified Data[291]

While GDPR considers pseudonymous data as personal data, the CCPA statute does not exclude or categorise pseudonymous data. If any data can be associated with a specific consumer or household, it may qualify under CCPA as personal data.

There is no restriction under CCPA on the collection, use, or retention of aggregated or de-identified data, while the regulation sets a high bar for establishing that the data is genuinely de-identified. Businesses are not obliged to apply CCPA rules for "aggregate consumer information," which is defined as "information that relates to a group or category of consumers, from which individual consumer identities have been removed, that is not linked or reasonably linkable to any consumer or household, including via a device." CCPA rules also do not apply for "de-identified" information, which includes data that "does not reasonably identify, relate to, describe, be capable of being associated with, or be linked, directly or indirectly, to a particular consumer," provided a business employs organisational and technical measures to prevent its re-identification.

While under GDPR, pseudonymised data is also considered personal data, it does not apply to genuinely anonymous personal data. This is up to great professionals in the field of Regulatory Affairs and Legal Affairs to interpret what the word "genuinely" means. Personal data can also encompass special categories of criminal conviction data. These are considered sensitive data and have limited scope in terms of processing.

---

291 "What Is 'Personal Data' and Why Is It So Important to Keep It Safe?" Redscan team, RedScan, 25 March 2020, https://www.redscan.com/news/personal-data-important-keep-safe/.

O. What Data Are Not Considered Personal?

According to the European Commission, anonymised data, company registration number, and a company e-mail ID like info@company.com are not considered personal data.

Information related to the deceased person, public authorities, and companies is also not considered personal data.

The following categories of personal data are expressly excluded from the scope of the CCPA, while GDPR does not exclude any specific individual information categories:

a. Protected health information (PHI) and medical information are covered under the Health Insurance Portability and Accountability Act (HIPAA) and Confidentiality of Medical Information Act
b. Data collected in clinical trials
c. Information sale between or from consumer-reporting agencies
d. Personal information is covered under the Gramm-Leach-Bliley Act and Driver's Privacy Protection Act
e. Publicly-available government records

P. Why Businesses Need to Understand Personal Data

With increasing touchpoints across different online and offline channels with consumers, businesses gather megabytes of data at breakneck speed. As massive volumes of data are residing in structured and unstructured data stores, it is difficult for companies to obtain an accurate picture of where the data resides, what data they have of whom, and how it is being used.

Businesses worldwide use online marketing tools, such as e-mail, website, e-commerce, and social media, to reach out to their target audience. While 50 per cent or more small businesses in the world invest in websites to reach a broader audience, 22 per cent of retail sales globally will be through e-commerce by 2023.[292] With more than a billion people buying goods online globally, businesses must focus on data privacy and protection. According to a Global Privacy Enforcement Network (GPEN) survey, 85 per cent of the 1,200 mobile apps studies failed to explain how personal data is collected, handled, or stored.[293]

A vast number of data breaches have hit the headlines in the past decade. The Yahoo data breach in 2014 compromised the personal information of more than a billion,[294] while the eBay incident impacted 400 million accounts.[295] Businesses including Equifax, Uber, JP Morgan Chase, Marriott, Google, Facebook, and many other corporations with an online presence have been the targets of data theft that have compromised millions of personal user data.

It is essential for businesses, government entities, and digital agencies to fully understand the meaning of personal data and why protecting it is critical. Even when a company has taken the required steps to protect personal information, it is still

292 "E-Commerce Share of Total Global Retail Sales from 2015 to 2023," Statista Research Department, Statista, 27 August 2020, https://www.statista.com/statistics/534123/e-commerce-share-of-retail-sales-worldwide/.

293 "Mobile Apps Fail to Provide Basic Privacy Information According to GPEN's Mobile Apps Sweep Results," Lexology, 11 September 2014, https://www.lexology.com/library/detail.aspx?g=674acc90-6728-44ca-87bd-59d830e4d3f3.

294 "Yahoo Says Hackers Stole Data from 500 million Accounts in 2014," Dustin Volz, Reuters, 22 September 2016, https://www.reuters.com/article/us-yahoo-cyber/yahoo-says-hackers-stole-data-from-500-million-accounts-in-2014-idUSKCN11S16P.

295 "eBay Asks 145 Million Users to Change Passwords after Data Breach," Andrea Peterson, *Washington Post*, 21 May 2014, https://www.washingtonpost.com/news/the-switch/wp/2014/05/21/ebay-asks-145-million-users-to-change-passwords-after-data-breach/#:~:text=The%20data%20breach%20occurred%20between,network%2C%22%20the%20company%20said.

vulnerable to significant sanctions in the event of a failure in detecting and reporting data breaches.

Many businesses are taking necessary action to revise their data handling and collection practices to comply with GDPR. However, a recent TrustArc survey found only 20 per cent of companies in the United Kingdom and the United States were compliant. Here are some ways online businesses can ensure compliance with state, Federal, or GDPR:

> **Get unambiguous consent:** One of the most critical aspects that online businesses should focus on is obtaining unambiguous consent. Silence, inaction, or pre-ticked boxes on the website are not regarded as the user's consent under GDPR. The user must take "clear affirmative action," such as ticking or checking the box to indicate they have understood the explanation on data collection the business gives.[296]

> If your online business had already collected many types of data before GDPR came into effect, such data would become obsolete unless fresh consent is obtained from users. A W8 Data survey found that 75 per cent of data collected by US businesses online would become obsolete.

> According to GDPR, a data breach means loss, destruction, unauthorised access, or personal data disclosure. Failure to report breaches of

---

296 "State-Specific Data Privacy Laws for Online Businesses," Robin Singh, Ms. (Law), CFE, CCEP-I, 19 April 2019, Navex Global, https://www.navexglobal. com/blog/article/state-specific-data-privacy-laws-for-online-businesses/.

personal data translates to a violation of the rights of individuals.[297]

Beyond notification of a data breach, organisations need to share details of the data breach's nature, the type and amount of data that has been compromised, and measures the company is taking to address the breach. Failure to comply imposes penalties of €20 million or 4 per cent of global annual turnover, whichever is higher.[298]

The key takeaway in the CCPA refers to personal data that is "capable of being associated with, or could be reasonably linked, directly or indirectly, with a consumer or a household." This creates an expansive legal interpretation of what is considered personal information. This definition goes well beyond traditional data concepts associated with a name or other simple identifiers such as an address, Social Security number, or birthdate. The challenge for businesses is related to indirect information in the form of geolocation data, product preference, or IP address that can be used to identify a person.

---

297 "What You Need to Know about International Privacy Laws When Running an Online Business," Robin Singh, The Compliance and Ethics Blog, 11 January 2019, http://complianceandethics.org/what-you-need-to-know-about-international-privacy-laws-when-running-an-online-business/.

298 "Costs of Non-Compliance with Privacy Laws," Elizabeth C., Privacy Policies, 18 February 2020, https://www.privacypolicies.com/blog/costs-non-compliance-privacy-laws/.

CCPA and GDPR definitions of personal data mandate a different approach for businesses in identifying and correlating data compared to what has traditionally been done.

Q. IS YOUR BUSINESS PROCESSING PERSONAL DATA?

Understanding if your business is processing personal data is critical to know if you are compliant with GDPR or CCPA. The following guidelines can help enterprises to identify if they are processing personal data:

a. Personal data is any information that relates to an identifiable or identified individual.

b. If any data you are processing can be used to directly identify an individual, then the information is considered personal data.

c. When it is not possible to directly identify an individual from the data you collect, you should consider if the individual is identifiable indirectly.

d. It is essential to consider the purpose of data collection, the content of personal information, and the possible impact on the individual.

e. The same information could be personal data for one data controller but may not be for another controller.

f. Pseudonymous data is also considered personal data under GDPR.

g. GDPR does not apply to genuinely anonymous data.

h. Factually-incorrect information is also personal data as long as it relates to an individual.

Baringa Partners, a research firm, surveyed in 2017 to evaluate consumers' attitudes towards data protection. Results showed that companies could lose 55 per cent of their customers if there is a significant data breach. When a breach occurs, the survey found 30 per cent switch providers immediately while 25 per cent wait for media and other responses before switching their loyalties.[299] A Ponemon study found that 65 per cent of consumers who had their personal data stolen lost trust in the business that experienced the breach.[300]

299 "GDPR: The New Frontline in Corporate Reputation," Daniel Golding, Baringa.com, September 2017, https://www.baringa.com/getmedia/ f94f0671-ba12-41bd-b664-dc4f54ebf4ac/GDPR-Report-WEB-FINAL/.
300 "2018 Cost of Data Breach Study: Impact of Business Continuity Management," Ponemon Institute LLC, IBM.Com, October 2018, https:// www.ibm.com/downloads/cas/AEJYBPWA.

ADDITIONAL REFERENCES

www.wikipedia.com

https://www.lexology.com/gtdt/workareas/data-protection-and-privacy

https://www.washingtonpost.com/

https://searchhealthit.techtarget.com/

https://www.hipaajournal.com/

https://www.gibsondunn.com/us-cybersecurity-and-data-privacy-outlook-and-review-2019/

https://www.ftc.gov/tips-advice/business-center/guidance/data-breach-response-guide-business

https://www.forbes.com/sites/insights-intelai/2019/03/27/rethinking-privacy-for-the-ai-era/#3d676d557f0a

https://www.faronics.com/assets/White-Paper-Small-businesses-face-failure-through-data-breaches.pdf

https://fpf.org/wp-content/uploads/2018/11/GDPR_CCPA_Comparison-Guide.pdf

https://www.jdsupra.com/legalnews/california-s-consumer-privacy-rights-66462/

https://www.workplaceprivacyreport.com/2020/11/articles/california-consumer-privacy-act/prop-24-california-privacy-rights-act-extends-ccpas-anti-discrimination-retaliation-provision-to-employees-applicants-and-independent-contractors/

https://www.cookiebot.com/en/cpra/#:~:text=In%20short%2C%20the%20California%20Privacy,enforcement%20called%20the%20California%20Privacy

https://www.manatt.com/insights/newsletters/client-alert/the-california-privacy-rights-act-has-passed

https://www.law.com/legaltechnews/2020/11/05/with-the-passage-of-cpra-california-privacy-law-is-leaps-and-bounds-closer-to-gdpr/?slreturn=20201103010915

DISCLAIMER

The views and opinions expressed in this book named #MyPrivacy #MyRight and any related discussion(s) are solely those of Robin M Singh (the Author) and DO NOT represent the views and opinions of the Author's organization (current or past) or its entities or its affiliates. Nothing herein constitutes legal advice, nor should it be construed as the same or similar. The Author has made good faith efforts to refer to all possible public information sources used in this book. To streamline, the Author has not repeated the source everywhere. In case a reference is not appropriate, incomplete, or absent, it is not the Author's intention to cause any harm to the sourcing entity, website, or digital outfit, except for a human error. The Author understands there could be multiple sources for the same information; however, he has tried his best efforts to place one source that is practically possible to guide the readers to more information on that subject. The Author would leave it to the readers' sound judgement to identify similar or relevant sources to material liked by them. Furthermore, all cases and examples used in this book are interpretations of the author for reference. High-level guidance is needed, and the reader should not construe information herein as full and final.

Furthermore, all the surveys carry the Author's interpretation and understanding. Thus, the readers should carry out in-depth research of the court opinions before imbibing them. It is essential to note that the web environment is very dynamic and changes every microsecond. Any recommendation that I have made is based on good-faith judgement and should not be blindly followed. The Author strongly suggests his readers carry out due diligence and ensure the readers' safety through vigorous research and White Papers prior to implementing recommendations or suggestions.

www.ingramcontent.com/pod-product-compliance
Lightning Source LLC
LaVergne TN
LVHW042134040326
832903LV00001B/2